THE INVISIBLE CONTINENT

Books by
KENICHI OHMAE

The Mind of the Strategist

Triad Power

The Borderless World

The End of the Nation-State

THE INVISIBLE CONTINENT

Four Strategic Imperatives
of the New Economy

KENICHI OHMAE

HarperBusiness
An Imprint of HarperCollins*Publishers*

Excerpt on pages 219–20 appears by permission of Dr. Mahathir Mohamad, "Case study for a country under economic stress," August 2, 1999, *Mainichi Daily News,* © 1999 by Mainichi Newspapers Company, Japan.

HarperCollins books may be purchased for educational, business, or sales promotional use. For information please write: Special Markets Department, Harper-Collins Publishers Inc., 10 East 53rd Street, New York, NY 10022.

FIRST EDITION

Designed by Iva Hacker-Delany

Printed on acid-free paper

Library of Congress Cataloging-in-Publication Data

Ohmae, Kenichi, 1943–
    The invisible continent: four strategic imperatives of the new economy / Kenichi Ohmae—1st ed.
      p. cm.
    ISBN 0-06-019753-6
    1. Information technology. 2. Free trade. 3. Internet (Computer network)
    4. Competion, International. I. Title

    HC79.I55 O45 2000
    382'.71—dc21   00-02613

00 01 02 03 04 RRD/❖ 10 9 8 7 6 5 4 3 2 1

CONTENTS

CHAPTER 1: THE AGE OF EXPLORATION   **1**

The Four Dimensions of the Invisible Continent   3

Modeling the New Continent? No Dice.   8

Staking Out a Claim in Four Dimensions   9

Japan: The Contradictions of a Crisis   12

A Strategic Approach to the Invisible Continent   15

Year 15 "After Gates"   21

The New Cold War   24

Learning to Embrace the Old and New   26

CHAPTER 2: THE GOLDEN PLATFORMS   **29**

The Platforms of American Success   32

Principles of Platforms   41

Seeing the CEO as a CIO   58

CHAPTER 3: ARBITRAGE AND THE NEW ECONOMY   **61**

The Essential Nature of Arbitrage   63

A Field Guide to the New Arbitrage   65

A Priceability-Based Economy   78

The Greatest Economic Strength   82

A Portal Revolution   84

The Invisible-Continent Dog and the Old-World Tail   85

CHAPTER 4: WAKE-UP CALL FOR CORPORATE STRATEGISTS   89

Traditional Companies in a Land of Godzillas   92

A Strategy for the New Continent   96

Becoming a Godzilla Company   103

Making the Transition   117

The People of a Godzilla Company   118

CHAPTER 5: REGIONAL WINNERS AND NATIONAL LOSERS   119

Setting the Stage for New Relationships Between Corporations and Government   122

The American Zebra   124

The Rise of the Region-State   128

Deer Hunters   131

Prescriptions for a National Leader   133

The Role of Regional Government   136

CHAPTER 6: THE LONG TUNNEL   141

Following the American Example   149

Dark Miles Ahead   154

Understanding the Asian "Crash of '97"   158

The Japanese Choice: Borrowing from Our Grandchildren . . . or Ourselves   162

The Crisis Throughout Asia   173

Beyond the Asian Crash   184

CHAPTER 7: THE NEW COLD WAR   187

Anatomy of a New Cold War   189

The Impact of a New Cold War   198

Sharing a Vision of Wealth in the New Economy   200

Don't Speak, for Fear It May Happen   207

Chapter 8: Taming the New Wild West   211

Rethinking the Value of Work   212

Governing the New Frontier   215

An Evolving Design for Democracy   223

Educating the New Citizen   227

The Revolution Against Ourselves   231

A Declaration of Interdependence   233

Epilogue   235

Endnotes   241

Index   247

ACKNOWLEDGMENTS

A number of people deserve thanks for contributing to or abetting this book. I would like to thank, in particular, Art Kleiner, the contributing editor who helped develop, shape, expand, and refine this material; Kiyoko Koshimizu, whose assistance was invaluable; literary agent Wes Neff; New York–based assistant Magdalen Piper; HarperCollins editor Zach Schisgal; and others involved with the literary development process. I owe a special debt of gratitude to the senior executives and CEOs at companies that have opened bridges to the invisible continent—bridges that other leaders of countries and nations will be glad to know about. Finally, I wish to offer my friends and family my continued gratitude for all of their love and support. Some of them are traveling on the invisible continent already, and I have been privileged to be connected to their remarkable journeys.

1

THE AGE OF EXPLORATION

Throughout human history, sudden sweeping changes can often be traced to the discovery of new lands—the opening up of contact with a new geographic region with a different way of life. As explorers and settlers have come to new continents, they have shifted their ways of life—not just for themselves, but also for the old worlds they left behind. Exploration routes in the Americas, from Columbus to the Oregon Trail pioneers, carried information and people in both directions; so too did the "road to Yam" that the Egyptians of 2300 BC followed in their treks up the Nile to Nubia. And so did the mountain and desert pathways, known as the Silk Road, that Buddhist monks and Arabian merchants trod in their wanderings from Afghanistan and India to China, then to Korea, and ultimately to Japan. All of these travels, and many more, took place because people with courage and curiosity (and, of course, greed) cannot be held back from exploration. Motivated nearly always, at least in part, by the attraction of business and trade, these travels have arguably provided the creative spark that keeps civilization from growing stagnant.

In our time, it seems as if no remaining new continents are left to be discovered. The entire habitable world is known; there are no new places to settle. Yet, during the past fifteen years, civilization has changed at a planetary scale more quickly and continuously than ever before. It's as if some kind of new continent has been discovered—a continent without land.

In that context, all of the continents we live upon—including Asia, Europe, North America, South America, Africa, and Australia—are part of an established geopolitical "old-world" environment. In this old world, national economies are rooted in the ownership of land, as well as in the use of machines and capital. Each nation's economy is distinct from every other's, and economic activity is linked by the flows of tariffs and taxes. Government leaders are regarded as the directors of the economies they "run," responsible for inflation, for the money supply, and ultimately for jobs. In democracies, people judge the leaders by the degree of prosperity that they have "produced," which in turn generates taxes that fund the state's activities. Macroeconomics and microeconomics are separate endeavors. When a nation can operate effectively in the old-world milieu, we assume that its corporations, governments, labor unions, and consumers will all thrive or fail in unison.

Just as the opening up of new worlds has changed the prevailing assumptions of the old world in the past, the discovery and exploration of the "new continent" is already changing all of these attitudes and ideas about wealth creation and human endeavor.

As in the past, the impetus for exploration has come from business. Once again, people with courage and curiosity have discovered new ways of life, which are irrevocably changing the way of life on the old continents they left behind. The only difference is that this new continent has no land. It exists only in our collective minds. That is why I call it "invisible." Nonetheless, in its economic, political, and social effect, particularly on business, the invisible continent is as palpable and vital, as tangible and solid, as if you could find it on a map.

The invisible continent is new, in the sense that it has been discovered only in the past fifty years. It has only begun to be settled, arguably, since the mid-1980s. Despite its short history, its presence is well known, even obvious, to anyone who pays attention to global-scale changes. In my own career, I have continually researched and discussed the implications of the new continent: as the former head of McKinsey in Japan, as a Japanese sociopolitical reformer (with the explicit goal of realigning Japan so it can enter into the invisible continent), as an entrepreneur, and as the author of a series of a books on the subject, including *Triad Power* (1985), *The Borderless World* (1990), and *The End of the Nation-State* (1995).[1]

And I have hardly been alone in this endeavor. A growing number of theorists and writers, including Marshall McLuhan, Herman Kahn, Alvin Toffler, Nicholas Negroponte, Peter Drucker, and many more, have helped to map the primary characteristics of the new continent, and the forces that have brought it to life.[2]

While the emergence of the new continent has been widely commented upon, the linkages between the forces that created it are not well understood. People do not always see the ways in which the changes of the last twenty years strengthen each other, and they do not recognize the implications for organizations and governments. Many decision-makers, in business and in the political sphere, intellectually recognize that the world has shifted to a borderless, fluid political-economic environment.

They are aware of the new continent, and pay lip service to its importance. They even understand how their decisions helped lead to its existence. *But they still can't operate effectively in the world they have created.* They don't know how to translate their understanding into action. Sometimes, they fall prey to an "Oregon Trail" gold-rush mentality.

Businesspeople recognize that, in the early days of any new continent, there is an opportunity to make a killing—*if* you can snap up the part of the territory that might one day, for instance, be Hollywood or Miami. As they swarm after the wealth of the new continent, however, at times they overextend themselves in risky ventures. At other times they hold back, assuming that events out on the invisible continent will not affect them much. They then risk being overtaken, far more rapidly than they suspect, by a new wave of voracious competitors. Even growing companies with roots in the old world, companies like General Electric and IBM, find themselves compelled to explore the new continent if they want to grow. If they remain in the old world, they can thrive only by cutting costs and laying off people.

Politicians, similarly, recognize that they have a responsibility to master the demands of the new continent, or they will risk losing their country's assets to competitive forces from other countries. But there are even fewer clear guidelines in the political sphere. The old world may feel familiar, and still respond predictably to government and corporate policies, but there is no growth in it. And the new world is far more unpredictable.

THE FOUR DIMENSIONS OF
THE INVISIBLE CONTINENT

It often seems, however, as if each of the pundits of change is describing only a part of the emerging geopolitical economy. For example, it is tempting to conceive of the invisible continent as simply a metaphor for the accelerated evolution of computer and communications technology. Some have gone so far as to call the invisible continent "Cyberia," or to label it as a form of cyberspace. But that label is misleading. Admittedly, had there been no computers, the new continent would never have come to pass. The technologies were necessary for it to exist. *But they were not sufficient.* Even with the change in technologies, other things might have happened to prevent the new continent from emerging. Keynesian economics might have been reinforced by a long period of deflation in the 1970s. The Thatcher/Reagan revolution, and the wave of deregulation that went with it, might never have taken place. Entrepreneurialism might not have been reinforced by the global awarding of platform status to the American dollar.

In short, the new continent has four separate dimensions, and it cannot be understood without recognizing the interplay of all four. To make a stake, or to effectively regulate, the invisible continent, you must be able to see, and act, in each of these dimensions:

The Visible Dimension

Quantum physics is widely accepted and recognized for its significance. Nonetheless, we continue to expect that gravity will play a role in daily life. In a similar way, we do not discard all of the economic dimensions of the old world. Thus, on the invisible continent, there may not be a version of "Japan, Inc." and "America, Inc." as separate entities battling for dominance. That is strictly an old-world phenomenon. But there are still entities that grow in steady, predictable ways, along a linear, step-by-step evolution.

When I headed the McKinsey Japanese offices, I worked primarily in the visible dimension. My regular consulting practice included calculating how much to pay for companies in acquisitions. These estimates of potential worth were based on the mathematical projection known as "net present value" or NPV. This calculation of future costs and revenues still drives most market capitalization values—and thus the value of companies. NPV plays this role because it has proved an accurate predictor of corporate performance in the old-world economy of the past. There is a consensus among old-world economists that it will prove accurate in the future. And to some extent, its predictions will hold even on the invisible continent.

In other ways, the visible dimension will also continue. Local commerce will continue to deliver goods and services. Bakeries will continue to bake cakes; delivery trucks will continue to make the rounds of streets and highways. Paradoxically, the more growth that occurs because of the other dimensions, the more growth will occur in this dimension as well. That is the "mortar" component of the so-called clicks-and-mortar world. Throughout the book, therefore, the conventional business and political activities of the visible dimension will assume paramount importance, particularly in its interrelationships with the other dimensions.

For there are an increasing number of ways in which this economic dimension, *by itself*, does not accurately represent reality.

The Borderless Dimension

Twenty years ago, the question of free trade was far more controversial than it is today. In 1999, a few Americans picketed the November meeting of the World Trade Organization in Seattle and made headlines in the process. But compare that to the early 1980s, when there was a widespread movement to "Buy American," and when one of the most prominent businesspeople in America, Lee Iacocca, talked openly of free trade with Japan as accepting a new "yellow peril."

Today few people still think in these terms. The world has moved a long way toward a fully borderless economy—in the sense that economic borders between nations are far less important than they used to be. This has happened because of the growing sophistication and interconnection of consumers and citizens around the world, who have been acclimated to a global point of view by a century's worth of increasing cross-border communication, travel, and consumption. People today live in an international "information climate," which, even without the computer or the Internet, would have been unimaginable in the 1950s. (Arguably, most of the wars of this century would have been very different if, say, Cable News Network had existed.) Electronic commerce (e-commerce) inherently transcends national borders, tariffs, and trade restrictions. And distinctions and barriers (and the competitiveness that goes with them) are fading not just among nations and regions, but between corporations, between for-profit and nonprofit endeavors, and between government bodies and nongovernmental concerns.

In this dimension, the idea of Japan or America as economic aggressors is simply a "cartographic illusion"—a misperception derived from the false idea that national borders represent lines of true political autonomy. The U.S. "imports" prosperity from all over the world, just as Japan can import "land" by having access to Australian grain and (old) American beef. The economy of this dimension is not tied to nation-states at all. It is driven by consumers and financial investors who care not at all for national stability, who avoid taxes wherever possible, and who take the availability of jobs for granted, because they know they can work for anyone, anywhere, in the world. (Perhaps there are not many people who fit this description now, in real terms, but the number is increasing exponentially, from Ireland to Bangalore to Austin.)

Similarly, the expectations of wealth generated by the invisible continent have generated a massive cross-border migration of capital. In a 401K-type pension system, a worker in Germany or Japan can choose to buy GE and IBM in his or her portfolio. This means that the individual worker/consumer and corporations can hedge their odds against the idiosyncrasies of their own managements and governments.

I have been thinking and writing about this dimension for twenty-five years, most prominently in my 1989 book *The Borderless World*. The "borderlessness" that I (and others) saw then has continued to accelerate, to the point where politicians and executives alike can no longer find success with the same types of "competition-based" decisions that allowed them to thrive in, say, the 1970s. The invisible continent, with its easy-to-traverse links to so many entities in the old world, not only is partially defined by borderlessness; it accelerates the phenomenon.

The Cyber Dimension

So much has been written about this aspect of the changing world that it hardly seems necessary to add anything. Suffice, then, to say that computer and communications technologies have not just enhanced communication. They have changed the consumer, producer, and civic environments—the environments of commerce and civilization—in profound and irrevocable ways. Those who cannot create a presence and develop a facility in the cyber dimension of the invisible continent will find it very difficult to prosper. Although many of the current examples of invisible-continent activity involve the Internet, the Internet in itself does not represent anything like the totality of the cyber dimension. Many of the most successful businesses of the new continent, like retirement services and destination tourism, do not *need* to be "plugged in to the Web" in any conventional sense. But they thrive on the new continent because they respond to the flexibility of their customers, with an innate flexibility derived from a variety of new communications technologies. This can be accomplished, for example, through a call center with video capability. Whenever you need a counselor, he or she appears on your television screen or your mobile phone, and gives you advice. With a mobile phone as your electronic wallet, wherever you go, you no longer walk alone.

The Dimension of High Multiples

In 1998, the collapse of the hedge fund operator, Long-Term Capital Management, demonstrated not just the danger, but also the robustness, of an economy based upon the leverage of unprecedented amounts of money. For every dollar in LTCM's coffers, investors, including many major banks, were willing to spend between $45 and $250 (depending on the transaction) to bet on its success. To put this into perspective, consider the equivalent funds that existed in America during the 1920s' stock market boom—funds with a similar reputation for high-risk, high-yield, daring experimentation and uncanny savvy. Known as "brokers' funds," these were available with multiples of only 5 (borrowing five times the money held in house); they were seen later as one of the factors leading to the stock market crash of 1929 and the Great Depression. Much later, during the "go-go years" of the 1980s, the American stock market averaged multiples (defined as share price divided by earnings) of 25. Germany had multiples of 8. At the high point of the Japanese bubble, the Japanese equity market had multiples of 75. All of these multiples, at that time, were accused of being wildly out of control.

Now, even after the example of LTCM, international hedge funds have multiples two orders of magnitude higher than their 1929 counterparts, and some of the NASDAQ heroes have multiples approaching 1,000 (or, since the earnings are negative, multiples of "infinity"). The sheer magnitude of money involved in the invisible continent, and the cross-border and cross-currency nature of these large multiples and their derivatives, make the invisible continent a terrifyingly slippery entity for governments, businesses, and even speculators to deal with.

The most significant aspect of this dimension is the application of unprecedented leverage. Multiples—whether they take the form of speculators' leverage or the P/E ratios of equity markets—are a creation of mathematics based on a set of imaginative assumptions. Viewed through the visible dimension, companies are worth an amount based on net present value. But for a company claiming a presence in the invisible continent, the expectations of the territory that this company might occupy could lead to a market value anywhere from zero to close to infinity—like the value of a land claim in California in 1848. Because of the high multiples of its stock price (leading to its enormous market capitalization), an upstart profitless e-commerce company like Amazon.com can acquire other companies with an equity swap. AOL has used multiples to take over phone companies. Qwest, a company with almost no history, acquired US West, a regional Bell telephone operating company, because of the leverage that multiples gave it. The power of multiples is not fictitious. If it uses them properly, a company with large multiples can become a "real," big, influential blue chip company in a short time.

Not all of these multiples are primarily cyber-related. AgeCare, a health care company, has a market cap of 500 times earnings. Investors like George Soros and Julian Robertson use large multiples to bet on changes in national currencies. Government treasury officials must respond to aggressive speculators without such contemporary weapons— with neither the resources nor the authority to cope with the force of multiples whipsawing through their local economies.

This is what gives the new continent its "Wild West" flavor. It's not just the ability to get rich quick, but the realization that the dangers are unknown and multiplying, because a new civilization is unprotected.

MODELING THE NEW CONTINENT?
NO DICE.

For at least a century, economists have tried to use mathematics to model the real economy—the first dimension of the invisible continent. There is no good economic model for the second dimension, or the borderless economy, even today. I tried to build one in the '80s, to explain the currency exchange part of the interlinked economy, but I could not complete even the simplest model.[3] When I used nonequilibrium and nonlinear equations for the dollar-yen relationship, I could explain why the currency exchange rate remained stable at different rates depending on recent history. But I could not incorporate such a finding into the real economies of countries that still maintained partially closed economies, and that increasingly interacted with the global economy through a kind of semipermeable membrane.

Then came the third dimension. While Paul Romer and others are trying to explain the productivity gains in the new economy, no one has even attempted to develop a mathematical model of the cyber-economy and how it interacts with the real-world economy of the first two dimensions.

An even greater challenge for mathematical modelers comes from the fourth dimension, the dimension of high multiples. Many of the multiples are the result of mathematics developed by the new wave of "rocket scientist" financiers. But not all of them, and not always. Some multiples are arrived at by a bunch of voodoo speculators and greedy manipulators. Others just represent the collective wishes of good citizens and/or "401K-ites." Ironically, these purely "mathematical" multiples are the greatest factor making the mathematical modeling of the new economy impractical (if not impossible). Thus, while multiples reshape the global balance of power and redefine the real economy, it is hard to use traditional macroeconomic approaches to explain their rise and fall.

I assert, therefore, that it is time for us to leave the mathematics and modeling behind. To seriously understand what is happening in the economy of the world, we must examine the effects of each of the four independent (and simultaneously interdependent) dimensions and then the overall behavior of the interactions among them. Instead of trying to model the economy, I propose to observe the behavior of the economy. If we agree on what we are witnessing, then that is a good enough basis for us to proceed to discuss the implications for our lives in the new continent. No model will give us an any more authoritative foundation.

STAKING OUT A CLAIM IN FOUR DIMENSIONS

The invisible continent is hard to see or chart from the old world, because it is perpetually moving—like a ghost ship hovering off the coastline, vibrating in a constant blur of activity. But from inside, it has its own form of stability.

It may well be impossible for most people to operate with an affinity for more than one of its four dimensions at once. After all, they represent four different sets of governing rules for the economy, four different sets of formulae for success, and four different attitudes for winning. But the companies—and national governments—that will be most successful in the future are those that manage to operate with an affinity for all four dimensions. Indeed, having an in-depth knowledge of all four dimensions will be a prerequisite for a leader of business or government in the future. The invisible continent holds the key to understanding many seemingly contradictory aspects of geopolitical reality. In addition, understanding the role of the new continent provides the surest guide to living well during the next few decades, because living well will require being attentive to its customs and priorities.

Already most people have a direct relationship, somewhere in their lives, with all four dimensions of the new continent. You deal with the first, visible dimension, when you buy a loaf of bread or receive a delivery of a product you have ordered. When you buy a car or any complex product, you are operating in the second, borderless, dimension, simply because most complex products are at least partially manufactured, designed, or initiated outside the country where they are purchased. Third, whenever you use a credit card, you take part in the economy of the cyber dimension. Finally, if you have a 401K retirement account, or another pension fund, your money is (you hope) expanding in the dimension of high multiples. Your funds are balancing some form of derivatives and equities with high P/E ratios in their mix. Even (presumably) conservative funds like the California Teachers' Retirement Funds are building up their portfolios this way. They have no choice, if they want to grow at a better-than-average rate.

Despite this familiarity with the dimensions of the invisible continent, policy-makers in business and government are still, all too often, basing their decisions on the intuitive sensibilities that they inherited from the old world—in other words, from an earlier geopolitical environment that has already become defunct. They are unprepared for the catastrophes of the invisible continent; for example, millions of dollars might gush in or out of a local economy in nanoseconds, with the impact of a typhoon or hurricane on the population. The Asian financial crisis of the late 1990s was a manifestation of all of these reactions to the new continent, and it contained more than its share of both gold-rush optimism and head-in-the-sand pessimism. Similarly, the complacency of American managers and politicians—as they ride their surging economy without showing much concern over their future—shows that they too do not understand the new continent, even though they have helped to shape it.

The most successful companies today are making effective decisions by the standards of all four dimensions. Cisco Systems, for example, operates with the most effective production practices of the visible dimension: superb supply chain management and the outsourcing of production to its trusted partners. It is prominent for taking advantage of the borderless dimension; Cisco's products have enjoyed a global presence since the day the company was born. In the cyber dimension, it has pioneered the Web-based integration of sales, marketing, production, and customer service. And then there is the dimension of multiples. As of December 1999, Cisco had sales of $14 billion, profits of $1.9 billion, and a *$320 billion* market capitalization. This meant that the market cap was 171 times its earnings. Phenomenal multiples like this have fueled the remarkable growth of the company, allowing it to take over other companies with equity swaps.

When the press write about companies like Cisco, they tend to notice only one of the four dimensions. Some observers focus only on computer/communications technology (the cyber dimension), and its impact on business realities. Others write about low-cost, overseas production and the effects of the borderless economy. And, of course, there are many people wondering about the effects of the cyber dimension, or observing the decline of the visible economy. (Actually, it is less a decline than an evolution.)

In conventional management schools, these four subjects are taught separately, if at all; macro- and microeconomics, global marketing, electronic commerce, the finance of net present value, and the finance of derivatives all occupy very different parts of the curriculum. But they all influence each other, and they need to be considered in relationship to each other if they are to be understood.

Consider, for example, the simple case of an American traveling in Tokyo who purchases a piece of pottery with a Visa card. In which dimension has this transaction taken place? To start with, the object is tangible, and the transaction took place in a shop that may have been built centuries before the invisible continent existed. But the payment was made with a currency that obeys different rules than if the American had paid with cash. That Visa transaction is settled in the cyber dimension. The assignment of sales taxes to Japan is not done through a ledger in the shop-keeper's desk, but through software that can easily be reprogrammed. In the old world, the shopkeeper takes the risk that the customer will not be able to pay, and generally deals with that risk by insisting on cash up front—or else by offering store credit. Now, on the invisible continent, a bank based thousands of miles away has taken over the risk of the customer's ability to pay, and deferred that risk for at least thirty days. (Indeed, the chances are that its verification process would end up in CyberCash's Web server in Virginia.)

The influence of the borderless dimension is also quite strong. The Japanese government's jurisdiction over this transaction, while accepted through custom, is still relatively unclear. The currency exchange rate between dollars and yen is unknown, because it changes constantly through the day, and it will be known only when the bill is received from the credit-card-issuing bank. Indeed, most of the jurisdiction over the transaction exists not in the hands of any government agency, but in the hands of the credit card bank. Visa might have the jurisdiction, except that Visa itself is a network of banks, with no independent existence, whose only purpose is to share risk and information, and whose investments take place in the cyber and multiples dimensions.

So how do you measure this transaction? How do you tax, bill, charge, account for, and judge it as a signal of wealth and prosperity? Answers to all these questions depend on the dimension through which you observe the transaction. When Japanese people shop online from the U.S. in a "Web-mall," the situation moves to a higher level of complexity. And there are many more complex variations. Corporate transactions are increasingly conducted electronically. Cross-border transactions could be "netted," meaning that at the end of the day, or quarter, the net transaction is settled. What is a value added tax in a globally netted transaction? Some countries restrict the usage of multiples in their domestic markets, and other countries inherently support low P/E ratios. Yet, many such countries allow their citizens to purchase financial products from the Isle of Man or Grand Cayman. Unknowingly, some "conservative" investors could end up buying a mutual fund with derivatives of Brazilian government securities.

In another five to ten years, there should be more public awareness of these questions, and more effort made to develop worldwide, responsible answers for governance and rules. (I will offer suggestions throughout this book on many of these questions, but there is much debate and consideration to come.) By 2010 or so, the ethos and ethics of the invisible continent will have suffused throughout business and politics worldwide. Already the age of discovery is passing; the new, invisible continent has been discovered. It is now being settled. People are putting down stakes, raising new types of communities, establishing frontier outposts, and initiating trade back with the world they left behind. They no longer need to look ahead; they need to look at where they are. They need help in placing themselves in the world that is evolving around them. Many of the things that have already happened, such as the hedge fund phenomenon that nearly brought down one of the largest trading houses in 1998, can't be explained either through traditional economic theory or through common sense. They can be explained only in terms of the tension between the new continent theories and the old world psychology.

Thus, there is still a great deal that is unknown, or just becoming known, about the territory. The purpose of this book is to focus attention on the requisite possibilities and dangers: to look at the ways in which people who live on this invisible continent are reshaping their lives, along with the economic structures and political landscape where the rest of us live. It is my sincere hope that as a result of this book, people will understand better how to go about staking a claim on the new continent in a sustainable way. Fewer people will fall prey to the losses of a gold rush— or the devastating losses that will accrue to those whose leaders ignore the new continent altogether.

JAPAN: THE CONTRADICTIONS OF A CRISIS

Consider, as an example of the new pressures afoot today, the contradictory financial crisis that overtook Japan throughout the 1990s. All through the second half of the decade, news reports suggested that Japan was an economic basket case. American political and corporate leaders, who had once regarded Japanese corporations as unstoppable juggernauts, now presumptuously lectured their Tokyo counterparts about the need to "recover your bearings." Within Japanese boardrooms, deflation was a persistent worry. What if prices went so low that companies could not afford to maintain their long-standing policies of lifetime employment?

To make up the difference and prevent widespread unemployment, it was argued that the Japanese government needed to invest substantial amounts of money into public works. Outside agencies, particularly the American government, insisted that Japan should lower its interest rate and put through a $400 billion stimulus package, mostly in public works. Thus, Japan spent more than 1 trillion dollars beyond its ordinary budget in a series of "emergency economic stimulus" packages since 1992—all to no avail. Projects that were barely necessary, even according to charitable estimates, were pushed forward to stimulate the economy and guarantee jobs. Elected politicians in Japan, eager to help their constituents, issued massive government bonds to fund them. They built a school so remote that it had only a few students, a group of new bridges that nobody wanted to cross, and a state-of-the-art harbor in a locale where there was no demand for commercial shipping.

Somehow, even with all this investment, the statistics on economic growth did not improve. Only ten years before, Japan's financial institutions had proudly held "triple-A" ratings with the international investor's rating service, Moody's. Now even the *highest*-performing bank was classified as "D," not viable; many banks were classified as "E," which meant, in essence, "already failed," without external and artificial support. This was said to be the greatest economic crisis for Japan since the dark, lean years after World War II.

Yet, a visitor to Japan in the late 1990s might well have wondered, Where are the beggars? In a country faced with economic catastrophe, wouldn't you find nonprofit agencies handing out food in Tokyo, as they did in London and New York in the mid-1980s? Where were the double-digit unemployment rates? Such indicators of economic depression were indeed visible in other Asian nations, particularly in some of the former "tigers" like South Korea, Indonesia, and Thailand. But not in Japan.

Instead, in Japan, the consumption of red wine and imported mineral water were at the highest levels ever recorded. In the 1970s, a sudden rise in oil prices had threatened Japan's survival; now drinking water was selling by the boatload, at *four times* the price of gasoline. Also selling at the highest volumes in history (50 million sets in four years since its debut in 1995) were Sony PlayStations—a TV game machine that cost a typical household perhaps $2,000, mostly in software. In polls, a typical Japanese four-member family reported a monthly discretionary surplus of about 5,000 yen—equivalent to less than $50 in American dollars. So where did the money come from to buy so many Sony PlayStation games? No one knew; but when a Japanese family found something they truly wanted to buy, they seemed to escape rapidly from their declared poverty levels.

Meanwhile, in 1998 and 1999, more than 30 million cellular phones were sold in Japan. Most Japanese cities and towns were interlaced with phone booths, and the cost for public phone calls, 10 yen for three minutes, had not changed since World War II. Three minutes on a cellular phone cost 30 yen, or three times as much. Yet, it was commonplace to see young people talking on cellular phones directly in front of an empty phone booth! Some people even took their cell phones into the public phone booths to avoid the traffic noise.

Some 17 million Japanese people visited overseas each year for shopping and vacation, and that number was not declining. Cruise ships were so popular with elderly Japanese pensioners that they were booked eighteen months in advance, including round-the-world cruises costing $100,000 or more. Meanwhile, thousands of young Japanese women, between the ages of twenty and thirty but still living with their parents, indulged romantic fantasies by taking shopping trips to Paris, Milan, and Florence. The trips were so popular that three flights went directly from Tokyo to Milan every day. More conventional, less expensive sites for Japanese tourists—Australia, Singapore, Hong Kong, or even Hawaii—were dismissed as *"dasai"*—unfashionable. Even those who remained home still bought enough Hermés, Prada, Gucci, Louis Vuitton, and similar products to make Japan the number one purchasing nation for most luxury brands.

A nation where such things take place is not undergoing economic depression. It is a nation where people feel economically secure, and where the prospects for continued growth are, if not assured, at least reasonable. Indeed, in 1999, Japan was still the world's second-largest economy, after the United States, with $12 trillion in savings and a $35,000 per capita gross national product. It was the world's largest creditor nation, and most of its money was invested in the United States, the world's largest debtor nation. Japan thus financed the American triple deficits (trade, government budget, and balance of trade) and took part in the current Wall Street bonanza. At home, Japan was still left with plenty of buying power. Its rapidly escalating unemployment rate still remained well below 5 percent. And its strong industries, its companies such as Sony, Honda, and Toyota and their critical component suppliers, were still among the most capable innovators in the world.

That did not mean, however, that the crisis in Japan was a fake, or was overblown by the media. It was all too real. Without question, many of the linchpins of the Japanese economy—developers, general contractors, trading firms (*sogo-shashas*), financial institutions, and blue chip corporations—were in deep trouble. The news stories of an impending crash were legitimate. The desperation expressed by government officials and corporate leaders was heartfelt. But that desperation coexisted with the most widespread luxury consumption that Japan had ever seen.

In short, the Japanese economy was behaving differently in each kind of dimension. In the visible dimension, the established institutions of the economy were suffering. But in the borderless dimension, they were thriving. In the cyber dimension, Japanese people were saving as much as ever, but using international, computer-linked investment vehicles to store their savings. And in the dimension of multiples, taking advantage of the unprecedented growth of "dot.com" companies such as SoftBank and in many other venture funds, Japanese money was helping to fuel the American economy—at the expense of its own.

This paradoxical Japanese economy exists, in other words, because it is linked to forces outside Japan—specifically, to an invisible continent of dot.com companies with unprecedented multiples, and to an American stock market that acts (for the moment) as the gatekeeper to those investments. By orchestrating an "economic boom," the Clinton administration's financial leaders (Alan Greenspan, Robert Rubin, and Lawrence Summers) have drawn money from the rest of the world to the U.S. At the same time, by acting overly pessimistic about the future of Japan, the Japanese government did a good job of repelling its own people from reinvesting in Japan. The net effect has been a massive cross-border migration of capital from non-American nations to America and then to the invisible continent.

This migration of capital forms the underpinnings of "Japan's decline" and "America's resurgence." Like a seesaw, this imbalance between nations can't go on forever without reversal. America, the first settlers in the new continent, scored well during the last decade; how well they continue to score, and how well they do in the end, depends on their ability to share the terrain effectively. (We will return to the role that American 401K-ites play in the new continent's economy, and the damaging impact they may have for themselves and others, in Chapter 6.)

Luckily for Japan, the macroeconomic slump did not necessarily mean a decline of the Japanese people as investors and consumers. It has been a decline of Japan as a nation. Enlightened citizens and corporations have escaped from the damage at least partially, as they intuitively understood their mobility across the four dimensions of the new economy. But not all the Japanese benefited. By being overly pessimistic, the Japanese government effectively prevented its own people from reinvesting in Japan.

A STRATEGIC APPROACH TO THE INVISIBLE CONTINENT

It may seem fanciful to write of the new environment as a new "continent," but it turns out to be a very useful metaphor in plotting strategy. Those who are successful in business or politics seem to develop a model in their minds of the invisible continent and old world as two coexisting habitats, operating with completely different parameters. Rules and laws that seem to apply in one are irrelevant to the other. Strategies that work in one lead to frustrating failure in the other. Yet, these two environments coexist, and continually affect each other, often in ways that seem capricious and unpredictable.

In practice, many organizations and their leaders continually shift unknowingly back and forth between the two continents. The dilemma that Japan faces with its luxury-laden economic depression, and many of the dilemmas often faced by officials and decision-makers around the world, stem directly from the confusion that people feel about which environment they are operating within.

The Japanese government that builds bridges to create jobs is stuck fast to the old world, still relying on a Keynesian theory of demand creation that is already a century old. At best, the government is keeping up with the demands of the visible dimension of the new continent. But many Japanese citizens, buying bottled water and "i-mode" cell phone services (Internet service on cell phones sold over 3 million subscriptions in 1999 alone), are living by the rules of the other two new dimensions. So are the Japanese investors who shoot their money around the globe at the speed of light, investing in whichever currencies show the most promise—again, operating through another dimension. So are the Japanese pension-holders whose retirement funds are similarly rootless and opportunistic. So are the growing number of Japanese employees who work primarily in English for companies around the world, with little concern for the government of the nation where they were born, the nation that is nominally their home.

Since there are no clear signposts to tell you when you're entering the new continent, you can straddle the two only by building up your own capability to recognize which is which, and which is appropriate to what situation. Four characteristics of this new continent are particularly significant for decision-makers who are trying to play on this new terrain. These four characteristics help explain why some immigrants thrive on the new continent and others fail to gain a foothold.

First, because it is cyber-enabled, the new continent *easily moves information across all kinds of borders,* both national and corporate. Thus, without a monopoly on the news, governments can no longer fool their people as easily. On invisible channels, radio and TV signals crossed the boundaries of the Soviet Union and contributed to its demise. As we have seen in the case of the Falun Gong cult, Internet signals are contributing to the instability of the current regime in Communist China. Even in democratic countries like the U.S. and Japan, the free flow of information has enormous political effect, in ways that are often subtle and uncelebrated. The anti-WTO demonstrations in Seattle in November of 1999 grew bigger and more aggressive every day because the demonstrators were communicating with the rest of the world through the Internet. The Japanese government used to claim that foreign beef was tough to chew, and doused with chemicals; now 17 million Japanese people have direct access to the firsthand accounts of travelers and the beef producers themselves. The only country that has successfully blocked off outside communication so far is North Korea. North Koreans have been told all their lives that the South is much worse off economically than they are. Defectors are shocked when they first arrive in Seoul; they expect to find an impoverished nation. But how long will even a rigidly controlled country like North Korea be able to keep out the all-pervasive media?

The free flow of information makes the invisible continent capable of easily exchanging goods, knowledge, services, and capital across all kinds of boundaries. As we shall see, this makes it far more difficult for countries, and companies, to control their markets. On the invisible continent, consumers control the chain of supply and demand, and global producers follow the lead of their customers.

With the Internet acting as a continuously updated full-color catalog reaching everywhere in the world—a catalog not just of things, but of music, movies, journals, ideas, opportunities, trading potentials, critiques, and attitudes—everyone with access to that system has a highly sophisticated degree of commercial, cultural, and even "civilizational" reach, which gives them a level of freedom that no nation can shackle or inhibit. Instead of being restrained by national politics, the consumer economy is inhibited only by the aggregate tastes and needs of its customers. Products that sell in one part of Italy, Belgium, Russia, Brazil, South Korea, or Canada may not sell well in others. And the winning corporations must learn what to do about the varied nuances of consumer demand that stem from differences in regions, generations, and other demographic traits.

Second, as a continent without land, the new continent is *easy to enter, but only for those who are willing to give up their old ways of thinking.* European explorers coming to the New World of the Americas had to take enormous risks to get across the Atlantic—and when they reached the Pacific, they faced an even more daunting ocean before they could make their way to Asia. But crossing the threshold to today's new continent takes place in an instant. This makes it seem seductive to halfhearted approaches, or approaches grounded in old forms of thinking and behavior. Those approaches are just as doomed to failure as a sea explorer would be who set out without a clear idea of the location of the trade winds.

The new continent should be approached as one might approach an oasis in the desert: decisively, but warily, and ready to move fast in a new direction. There is little danger of being attacked. The danger is that you will invest your time and money in returns that you desperately need—and find out that your desperately desired wealth is, after all, just an illusion.

The technologies of the new continent are especially counterintuitive.

Only three years ago, some scholars were convinced that the Internet would soon crash. Two years ago, many argued that it would be good for retrieving information, but too vulnerable for reliable transactions. It was not until the Christmas shopping season of 1998, when something snapped in public awareness, that everyone started rushing to the new gold rush of online shopping. The fact that American business-to-consumer e-commerce in 1998 totaled about 3 billion U.S. dollars (and four times more for business-to-business) means that some people had been prescient enough to prepare for it and invest in it. It is now expected to reach $255 billion, or about 16 percent of retail credit card sales, in 2002; and $812 billion, or about 40 percent of retail credit card sales, in 2005.[4]

Even at that level, e-commerce still represents a very small portion of the U.S. economy, let alone the world economy. So, there will be a period of several decades when those who see the Internet as unsafe and unreliable keep proving their point of view, while those who see it as inevitably subsuming all commerce into itself will also have a chance to prove they are right. The key question for the corporate executives and policy-makers is whose side to take. Most corporations are already taking an "above-average" network literacy route, while government policy-makers realign their laws to proactively foster cyber-business, while at the same time remaining aware of the needs and desires of the people who are left behind. In other words, the political world will have to provide a paradoxical balance: developing an advanced legal framework (in the form of "cyber-laws") to foster cyber-business (including multiples and derivatives in the financial markets) on the one hand, but establishing a cautious "big brother/big sister" safety network (in the form of international "cyber-courts") on the other hand.

The new continent was discovered first by Americans, but no nation holds a monopoly on entrance to it. *Any nation, any company, any race, any ethnic group, or any individual may enter.* In this sense, it is far fairer than the old world. Entrance depends upon adopting new types of behaviors. Ironically, however, this means that the new continent is less diverse than any of the old continents. People who enter, no matter what their ethnic origin or gender, have all learned to act in particular ways and to hold particular beliefs. Otherwise, they don't get in. One of the challenges for the new continent is finding a way for its population to grow more diverse over time—or dealing with the consequences (in isolation and diminished markets, among others) if that diversity doesn't emerge.

Because entrance requires giving up some old ways of thinking, the new continent tends to reward only the people who recognize the leverage that accrues from being there. Having access to the old world's industrial base makes it more difficult to succeed on the new continent. There, wealth accrues to people with different skills and access to different networks. Jobs on the new continent follow consumption; consumers do not move in search of jobs. Marketability does not depend on training of the old, industrial variety—either in schools or on the job. Marketability accrues to those who can train themselves, again and again, and to those who are plugged in to networks where they have gained credibility and respect.

The most successful players on the new continent are those who can define its ethos on their own terms. That explains the continuing high stock price of the online merchandiser Amazon.com, despite the fact that it has never turned a profit. Investors intuitively recognize that Amazon.com has staked out a territory as the world's largest retailer with the most popular merchandising location accessible by computer. This possibility, in itself, makes the company as powerful as Sears, Roebuck, Wal-Mart, Bloomingdale's, and Lord & Taylor combined. Amazon's founder, Jeff Bezos, is no longer competing against Barnes & Noble, the other major bookseller on the Net; he has won that battle simply by not having to restructure old stores. Bezos is creating a battlefield all his own. The same is true for other new retail portal sites and information brand names: Yahoo, America Online, Value America, eBay, Brodia, Priceline, Ashford, HomePortfolio, ShoppingList, and many more dot.coms.

Third, the invisible continent is still developing its governance and infrastructure. Those who recognize this can carve out a piece of territory that will be very, very difficult for invaders to capture. Individual companies will come and go in this arena over the next few years; the few sustainable enterprises are those that migrate into consumers' living rooms through the portals of the invisible continent, and take up residence there (in the form of "mindshare" on the computer or television). For example, America Online has virtually cornered one significant part of the online market: the most attractive first point of contact for many customers. In 1998, AOL's 17 million worldwide subscribers spent as long as fifty-four minutes online every day on average. This makes AOL the "stickiest" portal site in the world, and at that level, AOL has overtaken many broadcasting channels in capturing the "eyeball" traffic of consumers. The value of this "stickiness" on the dimension of multiples became apparent in January 2000, when AOL bought Time Warner, instead of the other way around (as many might have expected).

So far, portals have been seen as online places where residents of the new continent register their addresses, contact information, profiles, patterns of behavior, shopping records, footprints, and other traits. These can be very valuable assets if used properly. Yahoo's GeoCities amateur Web home pages have defined a particular approach to orientation for people in cyberspace; once registered, people find they cannot do without this orientation. Yahoo's entrepreneurs have thus defined an indispensable role for themselves, and the market recognizes this.

How long will that definition last, however? It may prove to be short-lived; some new form of infrastructure may overtake Yahoo, America Online, or Amazon.com, just as 7-Eleven convenience shops replaced neighborhood groceries. In Japan, instead of having a computer at home, many people prefer to log in to the network at kiosks in their local convenience shops. As of November 1999, they can buy music and pictures (downloaded into a small memory card), airplane tickets and theater tickets, without paying for a large-bandwidth cable to their home. This may mean that the first company to offer an inexpensive large-bandwidth home cable—on digital subscriber line (DSL) technology using copper telephone wires, for example—will reap a fortune in Japan; or it may mean that convenience shops will stake out a highly profitable territory and keep it, offering accessories like ticket and cash vendors to Internet use that people would not easily find at home.

The flexibility of the invisible continent makes it impossible to predict now who the most prominent winners will be even five years hence. A resident of central Florida in the 1970s would have thought of the area as primarily marshland—a depressed, unusable terrain. It took the Disney Corporation to see that by the mid-1990s it could be a center of world entertainment, able to attract 40 million people per year from all over the world. And just as Walt Disney considered Maine and Wisconsin, before settling on the warmer year-round climate of central Florida, so the winners of the new continent will recognize critical features of their technological and infrastructural landscape that elude the rest of us. Bezos, for instance, recognized the value of a highly information-rich but transparent user interface; Amazon was one of the first major online entities to make it easy for customers to record their credit card numbers, mail-order preferences, and reading interests online.

Finally, as befits any frontier, *the new continent embodies highly individualistic values.* Communities and families, or old-style establishment connections, do not determine worth in this world. Nor is there one elite setting the tone for the continent's perceptions of the qualities that are worthwhile and the qualities that are not. On this continent, there are thousands of elites—rolling elites, only vaguely aware of one another's values.

In many ways, this makes the new continent a discomfiting place to be. The economic forces that exist on the new continent are so unbridled and unconstrained that they take on a hyperbolic, uncontrollable quality, compared to the "real" industrial economics of the old continents. Thus, just as the old continent fostered the communist system, and then in the long run revealed its excesses and miseries, the invisible continent is exacerbating the excesses and miseries of unbridled capitalism.

For example, invisible-continent finance embraces arbitrage and speculation at a global scale, even when that arbitrage and speculation are dangerous to the innocent people of the old continent. Trillions of dollars change hands daily in trades of stocks, bonds, currency, and various types of options. It is said that on any given day, for example, over $1.3 trillion changes hands in the currency exchange markets around the world, whereas there is only $1.2 billion in the reserves of the entire central banks of the world.[5] This churning of transaction takes place independently of production and consumption; it is, in a sense, operating entirely on a fictional plane. Yet, on this plane, fortunes are won and lost, and the success or failure of national policies is determined. The challenge of our time is finding a way to integrate the old continent with the new, without giving up the benefits of either.

YEAR 15 "AFTER GATES"

One could write a very full history of the invisible continent, because a large number of people have been involved in its development, propelled by a large number of ideas. The year that all of these forces came together, and the new continent emerged, was probably 1985. That was the year that Microsoft Windows Version 1.0 was introduced in Seattle, Cable News Network began broadcasting globally out of Atlanta, and the Gateway 2000 computer was first shipped from a cattle ranch in Sioux City, Iowa. Cisco Systems, the premier manufacturer of Internet network routers, was born in Palo Alto, California. In Austin, Texas, Dell Computers was just one year old; Sun Microsystems, in Santa Clara, California, was three years old; George Soros's Quantum Fund, based in the Cayman Islands, was four years old; and the Oracle database had been founded eight years previously.

In short, about everyone known today as a mover and shaker of the new American economy, a shaper of the current Wall Street environment, began their enterprises sometime around fifteen years ago. The companies spawned in that era—which would become as voracious in their growth as the fictional Japanese monster, Godzilla—had no precedents, either for the speed of their ascent or the unconventional ways in which they pursued their goals. Most of them did not get their start in large cities or cosmopolitan places. In their infancy back in 1985, these companies seemed to be working from an entirely new sensibility, almost as if they had a different set of chromosomes from those of mainstream American business. These new companies described themselves (or others described them) with words unfamiliar, at that time, in the conventional business lexicon: "garage," "leverage," "multiples," "cyber," "arbitrage," "networks," "platforms," "portals," and "speed." They did not seem to be concerned about the then-prevailing American economic malaise. Cable News Network, for example, proceeded with the assumption that it could create an international news channel without worrying about the limitations of broadcast radius. In those days, Americans used to license cable television city by city, and the few widespread cable channels that existed were all focused on entertainment. Suddenly CNN was serving over two hundred traditional television "territories" around the world with one signal.

Taking a maverick or counter-conventional stance was, in retrospect, the only way to thrive. But it took courage. Conventional business in America was suffering. The country was emerging from a serious recession. The federal government's deficit went to record highs of $212 billion. The dollar was continually growing weaker. Yet, U.S. demand for non-American goods was so strong that the nation's trade imbalance rose to $150 billion. Some businesses announced they were closing because they couldn't afford product liability insurance. American businesspeople generally felt hamstrung by regulations and unions; others saw businesspeople as stodgy and unable to innovate. The U.S. was coming out of its early-Reagan-years recession, but the awareness of that emergence had not yet hit public consciousness. And the quality of American products was routinely disparaged, so much so that Bob Waterman and Tom Peters's bestseller *In Search of Excellence* was routinely seen as the book that described the few excellent companies left. Even some of *those*, like Atari, were going bankrupt!

At the end of the year, the American business magazine *Industry Week* published this comment: "Few tears will be shed over the passing of 1985. The good news is that a new year brings the promise of new hope. We need it."[6] Both *Newsweek* and *Time,* meanwhile, featured cover stories that showed, respectively, Sony taking over the Statue of Liberty and Mitsubishi Real Estate controlling Rockefeller Center. Many people predicted that the dominant country of the twenty-first century would be Japan. But those who were looking more closely in 1985 could see that something new was taking shape. Instead of one country becoming dominant, the world's economy was globalizing. The stage was set for strategic alliances that would allow individual companies to serve the three major world markets: the United States (with Canada), Europe, and Japan (with several "Asian Tigers"). Instead of "cascading" from one market to another, like a waterfall, sequentially conquering key markets one at a time, successful companies now had to adopt a "sprinkler" business model: flooding the key markets in all three regions simultaneously and spontaneously. Bankers Trust and Deutsche Bank became allies; Daimler and Chrysler eventually coalesced into one company. Such alliances and mergers continue to be powerful precisely because they allow companies to serve markets across two or preferably three legs of the triad (U.S., Europe, and Japan), which in turn provides leverage for reaching the other markets around the world.[7]

Politically too there were signs that 1985 represented a turning point. That was the year the Plaza Accord was reached in New York, an agreement among the finance ministers of the Group of Five (the United States, Japan, Great Britain, France, and Germany) to allow the dollar to fall—thus ushering in a period of heavy investment in U.S. business and real estate by people in other countries, particularly Japan. Nineteen eighty-five was also the year that Mikhail Gorbachev was appointed as the president of the Soviet Union. In the United States Congress, Senators Phil Gramm and Warren Rudman championed a bill that put a cap on government budget spending, insuring that the U.S. would follow a path of relative government austerity through the rest of the 1980s and all of the 1990s. Perhaps most important of all, by 1985 Ronald Reagan and Margaret Thatcher had finally made headway in sweeping away the barriers and regulations that constrained the three critical industries of the invisible continent: transportation, telecom, and finance.

As in the earlier industrial revolution, some people and organizations naturally adapted and shifted their ways of thinking. They were not necessarily technology lovers per se, but they represented an ongoing strain of natural residents of the new continent, people predisposed to its way of life. It's as if some people had a genetic facility, a kind of innate sixth sense, to recognize old business practices that could fall by the wayside. For example, Gateway, Dell, and Cisco took a thoroughly original attitude toward supply chain management. Old-style company leaders "naturally" thought of their organizations as consisting of a series of stages of business practice: R&D, engineering, manufacturing, sales, marketing, and service. But it did not occur to the leaders of Gateway, Dell, Cisco, or other new companies to organize themselves according to a chain of functional specialization. To them, the customer was the main driver of research; research and the customers' needs were intimately connected. Their organizations looked like a web of functions and affiliated companies, rather than a traditional line-and-staff pyramid structure with a fixed span of management and vertical links to vendors and subcontractors.

As we shall see, this new approach has made these companies far less hobbled than their competitors by the bureaucratic structures of old-style thinking. These companies outsource; they work with companies like FedEx and UPS without needing extensive human interfaces between them; they change their products regularly; they focus on service. They not only use the technologies they sell, but easily and naturally design their management approaches to take advantage of them. They have no need for the endless streamlining and restructuring of a mainstream company, because they never take on the components that would make them bureaucratic.

By now it's clear how much the whole world has changed as a result of these companies. For example, Microsoft Windows has become a platform on which information, money, and even emotions and power are exchanged. In the past, the "benchmark of excellence" for corporate success was $1 billion in sales within ten years after start-up and a $10 billion market capitalization a few years after the IPO. Today, in part because of Microsoft's own example, these benchmarks have grown tenfold to $10 billion and $100 billion, respectively. The world After Gates (AG) is fundamentally different from the world that existed Before Gates (BG). Historians will call 1985 the harbinger, or *anno domini,* of the networked society.

THE NEW COLD WAR

In my previous books, I described the contradictory attitudes that many people in developed nations have adopted toward foreign trade. On one hand, they want their industries and jobs protected—a primary old-continent desire. On the other hand, they want the best products at the lowest prices, no matter where those products are made. Many Americans have voted for ardent opponents of free trade, politicians like Richard Gephardt, Ross Perot, or Patrick Buchanan. But the same person who votes for Gephardt on Tuesday may purchase a Louis Vuitton bag, a Toyota, a Sony TV, or a Taiwan-made Acer computer on Wednesday.

Now that the new continent has become more prominent, this type of schizophrenia will not be limited to trade. On one hand, people will support old-world economic and political policies at the voting booth, choosing nationalist and anti-trade candidates. Then they will vote globally with their wallets, favoring cosmopolitan consumption, and buying the best and cheapest products they can find from anywhere in the world, and seeking jobs anywhere in the world. This will undermine the politics they espouse. Around the world, people may follow the lead of the American public, with its masses of 401K-ites, who vote for any politicians that seem likely to protect the equity stake of their pensions by bolstering the stock market above all other considerations. (These people are the ones who took advantage of the Russian market's upswing in 1997–1998, but who then got hurt in the end. They may criticize the money-laundering of Russia's mob-controlled market economy, but they will be laughing all the way to the bank if the game of high multiples, known as the "new Russian Roulette," turns out to be working for them.)

If this trend continues, it could lead to a new kind of cold war, a war that takes place not just between nations, but also within our own psychologies and mind-sets. This "war" will occur between the old-world fears and new-continent demands of people around the world, and it may indeed lead to battles and eruptions as people cope with the conflict between their old view of the world and their status on the invisible continent. The weapons in this war would include derivatives, high-risk investments, currency speculation, mercantile alliances, trade blocs, copyright and trademark suits, monopoly leverage (such as the kind Microsoft has allegedly exerted over the software industry), sophisticated taxes and tariffs (and techniques for avoiding them), predatory pricing and tariff-levying, manipulation of interest rates to shift wealth from one region to another, concerted and deliberate shifts of investment capital to favor various blocs, and so on. Companies, nations, and perhaps entire regions could be bankrupted—often without a shot being fired—and forced, in effect, to surrender.

Much of the cold war, if it occurs, will be fought among entities vying for dominance in currency markets and industrial trade. These entities will not just be large corporations, but start-up businesses (growing with unprecedented speed), nations (acting on behalf of the perceived benefit of their labor force), and regional authorities. The "war" will be waged much as market wars are waged today—for example, much as Microsoft and Netscape fought over their dominance of the Web browser industry. But the stakes will be much higher because nations and regional governments will enter the game. "Winners"—including the citizens of winning nations—will prosper. "Losers"—including the citizens of losing nations—could be relegated to a new form of "undeveloped" colony. Meanwhile, some early pioneers, as individuals and institutions, can end up winning the game even though they are located in a losing country, as we have seen with Sony, SoftBank, and Hikari Tsushin in the midst of the Asian crisis.

Since most of the war would take place on the invisible continent, it would be difficult to control by traditional means, and difficult even to define. The players, and their positions, would change rapidly and continually. Outside the United States, the invisible continent may well be seen as a cyber-colony of America, an invention of American financial and computer firms. Inside the United States, it could be seen as the activities of "haves" who operate at the expense of "have-nots." But since this new continent is so open, with so few requirements for entry—except the understanding of its nature and the willingness to enter—people may find themselves torn.

The consequences of the cold war, however, would be very real. Resentment toward the United States could make it much harder for many developing nations to embrace the new continent, which could have the effect of setting back their economic development. For economic growth, in the future, will take place on the new continent far more than on the old. Developed countries, meanwhile, may find themselves surprisingly vulnerable to volatile swings of investment. Even the United States, which currently seems to have an impregnable economy, may experience a sudden shift in status. Americans may well say in the year 2020, "Why didn't we explore the new continent more carefully? Had we known its nature, we could have been on the right track. Instead, we went too far, too fast."

LEARNING TO EMBRACE THE OLD AND NEW

Issues like these cannot be resolved by Americans, Japanese, or citizens of any nation acting alone. Nor can they be solved from the point of view, in isolation, of either the old world or the new invisible continent. The purpose of this book is to offer some ways of dealing with these hybrid issues, and thus making strategic decisions that will pay off, for either a government legislator, a corporate decision-maker, or that new breed of individual who exists in ever-increasing numbers: the independent strategist making his or her living through a private one- or two-person business.

Corporate leaders in particular will find it frustratingly difficult to make the transition they need to make at all, let alone overnight. Their companies do not have the right corporate genes. To be sure, some establishments are learning to steer smoothly in new directions. They see themselves as proactive and flexible, especially compared to government agencies. Yet, it may be impossible for an IBM or AT&T, or even a GE, to become a Dell, Cisco, or AOL. You may have to be born fresh, without ties to the old system. At the very least, you have to create a whole new set of corporate chromosomes. A traditional company cannot say good-bye to its wholesalers, retailers, and marketing staff. They can't go direct to some customers, because they will alienate the rest of their distributors; nor can they bypass their distributors entirely, because they have learned to get their sales from distributors. They do not fit with the new continent; only the nimble newcomers do, like Dell, Cisco, E*Trade, eBay, AOL, and the like, in part because they helped create it and because they have little to lose by going after the market at full speed.

Does that mean that older, established companies cannot gain a toehold on the new continent? So far, there has not been a definitive answer to that question. In the rest of this book, we will look at the strategies necessary for both governments and businesses to settle in the new invisible continent more effectively.

Chapter 2, "The Golden Platforms," considers the underlying governance structure that made the invisible continent feasible on a global scale—the idea of de facto standards and agreements that set the new continent's limits and structures.

Chapter 3, "Arbitrage and the New Economy," looks at the economic underpinnings of the invisible continent and its relationship with the old, land-based continents, including the reasons the "borderless world" that I wrote about in 1990 has become more and more of a reality.

Chapter 4, a "Wake-up Call for Corporate Strategists," applies these insights to making money and finding competitive leverage. This chapter offers approaches that will allow companies to act more like the "Godzilla" companies that seem to know instinctively how to operate in a hybrid environment of the old world and new continent.

Chapter 5, "Regional Winners and National Losers," is the first of a series of chapters on the geopolitical ramifications of the invisible continent. It examines the vulnerability of nations to arbitrageurs and Godzillas, and the reasons nations are even less powerful than they were ten years ago, with power continuing to drain from them to economic forces (such as investors) and to the new regional authorities.

Then in Chapter 6, "The Long Tunnel," I turn to the problems of government in the coming years, describing the period of crisis that any national constituency must pass through if they hope to end up with a proactive strategy for the four dimensions of the invisible continent.

Chapter 7, "The New Cold War," returns to the question of the dangers of the invisible continent, and the possibilities of a global collapse—with particularly significant, and dire, implications for the United States.

Finally, Chapter 8, "Taming the New Wild West," discusses the implications of the new and old continents for participative governance in an age of overlapping and constantly shifting jurisdictions. Who, for example, should be in charge of e-commerce and taxation? Should the "multiple" transactions that are rampant in the dimension of multiples be regulated, and if so, how? And what kinds of values and education should be championed to move past the frontier period?

In all of these chapters, I do not *endorse* life on the invisible continent, per se. I don't have to endorse it. It is already here. But some routes to enter it are more effective, less destructive, and more intrinsically rewarding than others. Corporate and government executives end up wasting a lot of energy of their own and others by not looking clearly at this new interrelationship between old and new. They tend to use remedies that have worked in the old world, to no avail. Or they tend to address the new dimensions—border, cyber, and multiples—one at a time, though they are all interrelated and they are transforming the old continent's economy into something entirely new. This book will be useful for executives to reset their views before they use their power again.

By considering the cases of people who have begun to settle the new continent, I hope to show that it is not just possible to integrate the visible and invisible, it is essential. No one can live on the new continent full-time, because it is only partially sustaining. But no one can afford to push it away. We all need to integrate the two, because while they may frequently contradict each other, our lives on each of them are interdependent.

2

THE GOLDEN PLATFORMS

In 1887, a Polish ophthalmologist named Ludovik Zamenhof published a grammar for a new language he had invented called "Esperanto." This language was deliberately designed to be easy to learn, with only regular verb and adjective constructions, and a vocabulary drawn from all the languages of Europe. It was conceived in hope (its name means "hope") that people of different countries could use this language to communicate more easily. Since it was not the primary language of any particular nation, Esperanto would be accessible to all as a second language, or so Zamenhof hoped. It could thus promote global peace, commerce, and universal understanding.

In a sense, Zamenhof was one hundred years ahead of his time. His idea for a universal language seemed impractical to most people at the time; but it is compellingly practical today. The idea of a universal language has taken on greater and greater force as corporate and scientific leaders have grown more and more accustomed to communicating across national boundaries. With the emergence of the Internet as a full-scale communications medium worldwide, the need for a universal language is overwhelming.

But Zamenhof was wrong about one thing. A language cannot be decreed from a single invention; it emerges through use. The world would not settle on Esperanto; instead, it would take English away from the countries that speak it. English, as a result, is in transition. Soon it will no longer be primarily identified as the home language for the British Isles, the United States, and Australia. Its main identity will be as the primary language of the invisible continent. Thanks to the Internet and international finance, it now belongs to the world. It has become, in effect, a de facto Esperanto.

There is a generic name for standards that play this kind of role in establishing common ground. They are called "platforms." They include not just languages, but all sorts of standards: financial, technological, and cultural bases for common action. Visa and MasterCard together constitute a platform for electronic commerce and financial settlement that has altered the world. There used to be dozens of small, homegrown credit card companies around the world. They were all eliminated, absorbed into the Visa or MasterCard platforms. The platforms could dominate worldwide transactions because they allowed successful networks to form, with many more customers and suppliers than any small, independent company could handle. These networks rapidly became indispensable to the invisible continent's cyber dimension: without Visa or MasterCard, there would be no universal vehicle for making payments online, from anywhere in the world.

Visa and MasterCard, in turn, depend upon the "secure transmission" encryption and verification platforms that are built into browsers and Web software. Part of the verification is performed by yet another platform: by companies such as CyberCash, on behalf of the original card issuers such as Citibank and Bank One (through their subsidiary, called First USA Credicard). Other platforms include the delivery systems of FedEx (formerly Federal Express, but with a global reach that outgrew its old brand name) and UPS (United Parcel Service); the Wintel operating system; the electronic commerce umbrellas of AOL, Amazon.com, and E*Trade; the "dot.com" and "www" governance structures of the Internet itself; the international satellite and cellular communications systems; and the dollar. All of these have in common the mediation among a large number of people who gain capability because the platform gives them a coherent, relatively automatic, and continually improving way to communicate with each other.

In the next chapter, we'll consider the implications of universal arbitrage—the ability of most purchasers to find a better deal, most of the time, if they become dissatisfied. The presence of platforms is the ingredient that has made arbitrage so universal. Platforms are now the places where buyers and sellers meet, concurrent engineering collaborators work, lovers exchange happy notes, and policy-makers and dissidents make their points of view known to the rest of the world.

A platform is a de facto standard—not decreed by government, but settled upon by the tacit agreement of pioneers and settlers in the invisible continent. It often has been remarked upon that there is no real governance structure to the Internet. In fact, the entire new continent, the field of human behavior that subsumes the Internet, has no one in charge. The invisible continent is an emergent system—a system that takes its own shape and sets its own direction, moment by moment. Yet, this new environment is coherent. It is not anarchistic. Things get built, bought, and sold with regularity. This consistency is possible because surviving platforms are chosen by millions of users as convenient and trustworthy and can substitute for more formal kinds of governance.

The word "platform" as used here was originally a computer term. It refers to a hardware or software product that is so basic, or so popular, that many other products can be designed to work with it. Microsoft Windows is probably the best-known personal computer platform, and the one with the largest population of users. Though its development is controlled by one company (not coincidentally, the most prosperous company in the world), Windows is depended upon, extended, and operationalized by thousands of secondary companies, which produce software, chips, servers, printers, peripherals, and services related to Windows. Its viability depends as much, or more, on people's continued support as it does on any Microsoft policy. I am aware of all this, of course, because I am a Microsoft Windows platform user myself. I send e-mail, write articles and books, and create slide presentations on the Microsoft platform; and as that platform expands in capability—allowing me, for instance, to read news clippings in "pointcast" windows on my computer screen—I generally find myself eagerly taking advantage of them. Hundreds of thousands of others do the same. This, in turn, gives the platform more strength.

Platforms are not the same as the standards of the industrial era, the railroad gauges and telecommunications protocols; in most countries, those were set by government decision. Standards bodies, such as the International Telecommunications Union, still meet to decide such issues, but their decisions increasingly are irrelevant. On the invisible continent, platforms are determined by customers. Most of us, for instance, adhere to a platform called VHS when we watch prerecorded movies. It is well known how VHS, sponsored primarily by JVC and Matsushita, beat out Sony's Betamax, which was supposedly a superior technology. It also overcame another technology called V2000, which Phillips had developed. The winner was not decided by any international institution, or by a government. The consumer decided who would win. Now it seems to be shifting to a digital video disk (DVD) platform with a format originally proposed by Toshiba. This means that the other platforms proposed by a handful of companies, such as DAT and MD, will all be bypassed by consumers, at least for home entertainment use.

Because consumer decisions are rarely made in unison, platforms may not be completely consistent. There may be several competing platforms for years, each with advantages and disadvantages, each with its own effectiveness in getting people into the new continent. We see this today with the emerging platforms for telephone communication: one via the Internet (known as voice-over-IP), one via the mobile telephone (with its new global standard known as wide-band CDMA technology), and one via satellite. There are many routes to the frontier, many avenues to El Dorado, and many opportunities to make fortunes by building or controlling a platform, even if the platform has competition.

English, DVD, telecommunications, and Microsoft Windows are just four of the many platforms that dominate life on the new continent. Indeed, without control over one or more key platforms, it is very difficult to develop a profitable business on the invisible continent. Since most platforms are *not* overseen by a standard-setting authority—they are not like Esperanto or railroad gauges—they tend to favor some groups over others, and this makes the invisible continent seem inherently unfair at first glance. It seems to favor English speakers over Spanish and Chinese speakers, entrepreneurs over old-style corporate and labor leaders, Microsoft Windows users over Apple Macintosh users, and global investors over regional investors. The consumer and user choice, while free and impromptu, tends to converge to one. While there are exceptions, such as Visa and Mastercard, FedEx and UPS, most platforms end up with a winner-takes-all status, leaving only a handful of niche players. But no platform can be certain of its dominance in the long run. English speakers, entrepreneurs, Microsoft, and global investors have simply figured out how to draw more capital and customers their way. But as others develop rival platforms with wider and easier gates of entry, they too will be able to shape life on the new continent.

THE PLATFORMS OF AMERICAN SUCCESS

Consider the leverage that the English language provides for those who speak it. Over the past twenty years, in particular, the ability to speak and read English has become a critical prerequisite to international financial success. No one understands this as well as the residents of Singapore. A former British colony, Singapore was largely populated by Chinese-speaking people; but in the 1970s, under then-prime minister Lee Kuan Yew, the English language was added as a second, but equally important, official language. This clever move, avoiding the ideological (and unresolvable) debate as to which should be the national language, gave individuals in Singapore a choice. Most people, particularly those who wanted to teach at schools, chose English. This in itself was enough to give Singapore a unique role as the English-speaking hub for the networks of Southeast Asia.

Many nations with English as a national language are finding a disproportionate share of opportunities on the new continent. India has a burgeoning software industry; Ireland is known as the "e-hub" of the European market, with literally dozens of call centers. Of course, English in itself cannot guarantee national prosperity, as we have seen in Australia and Canada; but like all platforms, it provides a more solid footing than what a nation would have without it.

More than with any other nation, the use of English supports the prosperity of the United States. It reinforces the lead that the United States has in computers and communications technologies; 70 percent of the information on the Internet is stored in the English language, and 80 percent of Internet communication takes place in that language as well. This means that a disproportionate amount of high-tech innovation is first written down in English, which further reinforces the link between the language and innovation/business.

But American success also stems from the use of English in the international investment community; and that, in turn, stems from a peculiarity of U.S. political culture. Since World War II, in both Republican and Democratic administrations, the United States has been one of the most economically open countries in the world. There have been many U.S. tariffs and trade restrictions, but compared to the rest of the world, they represent a very small set of gates. As a result, whenever the rest of the world has looked for a safe haven for investments or trade, they have looked to the United States, and found "English spoken here."

And what of non-English-speaking nations? They have a more serious problem than they realize. Japanese-language material, for instance, represented less than 1 percent of the text and images stored on the Internet in 1998—despite the fact that Japan, with 130 million people, controls 15 percent of the world economy and a highly disproportionate share of the world's wealth. Before the advent of the Internet, it was feasible to translate scientific and technical communications between Japanese and English on a regular basis. But this is no longer viable; the speed of communication is too fast. Since less than 1 percent of the Internet's knowledge base is written in Japanese, inevitably those Japanese technologists and policy-makers who wish to move forward in their field will end up communicating in English—and probably speaking and thinking in English as well, if they want to succeed in the twenty-first century. A large part of the "products" exported will be transmitted electronically instead of being shipped by rail or ocean-going carriers. If the recipients of these goods and services do not understand what is being shipped, they will not pay for it. In other words, unlike the good old days of exporting cars and radios, the cyber-trade between Japan and the invisible continent is heavily dependent on English. And the same is true for trade with China, South Korea, Latin America, France, and every other non-English-speaking nation and region.

All non-English-speaking countries suddenly find themselves in the same position that Japan was in before the restoration of the Emperor Meiji in 1868. For two hundred years, the ruling Tokugawa Shogunate (dynasty) had kept Japan as a feudal society, nearly completely isolated from the rest of the world—equivalent perhaps to Myanmar today in global influence and interconnection. Then the Emperor Meiji, the first of a restored line of emperors, decreed that Japan should open itself to the West and become, in effect, successful on the West's terms—to stand as an equal to Western powers. Industrialization, railroads, telegraphs, a constitutional government, democratic elections, and a Western-style banking system all followed. The shift was traumatic for many, and took place amidst much opposition and many protests; in the end, it meant having the pragmatic flexibility to give up or adapt many cherished elements of Japanese tradition. It did not mean leaving Japanese culture behind, but it did mean that Japanese culture became markedly different in a very short time. It also meant developing a fascination with Western language and culture, a fascination that continues to flourish in Japan to this day. Japan achieved this shift so successfully that within a few decades after the Meiji Restoration, it had indeed become a world power.

Many nations arguably face a larger hurdle today than that which the Japanese faced under Meiji. The Japanese, after all, had self-consciously isolated themselves from the rest of the world, and they recognized the leap it would require to reconnect. They knew what the Industrial Revolution was all about—most of it could be seen with the naked eye and an open mind, as in steam locomotives and automobiles. But while most national leaders today are cut off from the world in fundamental ways by their language, they are not aware of the extent of this isolation, because this time, the revolution is invisible and (almost) metaphysical. Even if they recognize how isolated they have suddenly become, they know that this situation isn't their fault, or the fault of their people, and this makes them reluctant to make a leap into adopting English as more of a part of their common language. They don't see why they should have to give up their culture; and they don't recognize the extent to which the Internet, having settled on English as a platform, is making all other languages less viable. Some even hope that cyber-technology will compensate by inventing automatic translators and interpreters. While this may be possible in due course, I have yet to see a satisfactory device to help the traders and innovators who must depend on subtle nuances and perceptions among the shrewd global community of equally fast movers and shakers.

Similarly, most Americans don't understand the significance of the advantage they gain from having English as the language of international finance—the primary language used by the creators of wealth to communicate with each other. The American boom of the 1990s, much more than is commonly recognized, is a creature of English as a global language; no matter how great the American debt, no matter how capricious its policies or questionable its leadership, international investors will not rapidly leave the country whose language, which spells out the multiples and hedging techniques, is a kind of Esperanto for them. (However, when English spreads to the rest of the world, and when the unique American financial products are offered in a worldwide "e-trade" format, then America will no longer enjoy this unique advantage.)

English is not the only platform that the Americans dominate; if it were, the same benefits would accrue to the United Kingdom, Canada, New Zealand, and India. There is also the dollar. As a management consultant, I have long been impressed by the volatility of the dollar. It is the most unstable currency against the Japanese yen I have had to deal with in my twenty-seven years of consulting. In the 1990s alone, the dollar has bounced between values of 240 yen per dollar down to 80 yen per dollar; it's careened from 140 yen to 102 yen and back again in a matter of months. This is highly significant to Japanese businesses, because the U.S. is Japan's largest trading partner; the vagaries of the dollar have an enormous impact on every Japanese company's profitability. The greatest crisis that Japan has had to face over the past twenty years is the falling dollar, from 360 yen in 1972 to 80 yen in 1995; this forced Japanese companies to reduce costs and improve their productivity and product quality, simply to continue to export to America at the same prices. The price of a Toyota or Honda went from $8,000 to $24,000 during that time, while the yen received in Japan remained the same. In fact, the price of cars in domestic Japan has remained basically the same over the last two decades.

Japan and Germany are the only two major currencies that have risen against the dollar. Otherwise, the U.S. dollar, despite its enormous oversupply, has kept pretty good value against most currencies in the 1990s. As a result, Americans themselves often seem almost unconcerned about their own dollar's volatile exchange rate, even when they buy many foreign goods. They can afford to be unconcerned; unlike every other nation in the world, the United States conducts its foreign trade transactions in its own domestic currency. When Japanese traders buy American computers, they pay in dollars. But when Americans buy Japanese video players, they also pay in dollars. They pay with dollars for cheese from New Zealand, rugs from Chile, gems from Africa, or shoes from Italy.

Traditionally, given the amount of money that the Americans print annually, there would be hyperinflation in the U.S. But with the dollar's platform status, inflation is avoided. People all around the world accept the dollar as the global currency of choice for trading and savings, while the value of their local currencies continually diminishes. In Latin America, Russia, and Asia, the average man or woman may well keep a box full of American dollars in the closet. It would be illegal to keep them in the bank, but in the closet, they represent a far better hedge against inflation than anything else you could buy with local currency. Most of this money does not come out to the market again. According to C. Fred Bergsten, director of the Institute for International Economics, the dollar represents 50 percent of private savings in the world, although the American economy represents only 30 percent of global GDP.[1]

Dollar hoarders know that when the idiosyncrasies of their government lead to, say, a 15 percent inflation rate, the dollar will be immune. They don't have to enter into the unfamiliar, treacherous global banking system or rush out to buy ingots of gold. They merely need to keep adding greenbacks to that box in the closet. The result: No matter how many dollars are printed, they disappear from American domestic circulation. This represents a secret source of deflation amidst an otherwise very inflationary American monetary policy.

Of course, when international investors buy T-bills and American stocks (as they increasingly do), a large chunk of the greenbacks comes back to the U.S. But these are gathered and held in well-defined buckets of the financial market; they are seldom used for day-to-day consumption. In this way, the "homecoming" dollars are fundamentally different from the normal money supply from the Fed. This is rather fortunate for the U.S.; the $200 billion recycled back to the U.S. during 1998, for example, did not spill over to the general commodities market to cause inflation.

All of this, in fact, is a blessing for American investors and government officials; it allows them to aggressively pursue a bull market. If the U.S. runs short of money to pay for the goods its citizens buy, the Federal Reserve can put more money into circulation, printing it if necessary, without fear of inflation—because no matter how many dollars are put into circulation, there will be non-Americans who want to buy and hold on to them. This in itself is enough to keep the value high. America maintains a continual trade deficit on paper, but in reality, its exports of currency more than make up for its imports of goods and services.

But why would Japanese, Brazilian, Chinese, Russian, and other investors flock to put their money into dollars? There are two reasons: tradability and exchangeability. The United States makes it easy for them. There are very low transaction costs to buying dollars; people can buy them from anywhere in the world, without traveling to America, and sell them just as easily.

Moreover, the United States represents one of the most open markets in the world. As we will see later in this book, it has been one of the first markets to embrace the principles of the borderless economy, one of the four dimensions of the invisible continent. Americans have no ideological idiosyncrasies where commerce is concerned. They will buy the best and cheapest goods and services they can find, from anywhere in the world. They will buy products made by Chinese, Indian, Vietnamese, Brazilian, or Russian labor, as if those people were working in the States. Therefore, if another country raises its price or lowers its quality, the Americans can nearly always find an alternative source. In effect, there is a third platform that benefits America—an open "trading field" comprising the American stock and exchange markets, with its gates wide open for all legal tenders, and all trading nations free to compete for the top position. This helps to explain why inflationary price hikes have not struck the U.S. marketplace.

The net result of all this is a dollar whose activities continually reinforce its own value—and thus a dollar that is worth more than most of the goods and services it can buy, no matter what its nominal value is on the currency markets.

From the perspective of the old world, the high stock prices of American dot.com companies are perplexing. How could these companies be worth so much more than the established industries that drive the world? But from the perspective of the invisible continent, it's clear. These high stock prices exist because (thanks to the "trading field" platform of American markets) everyone in the world can invest in these companies easily, and anyone investing from anywhere in the world will find them intuitively familiar, apparently stable, yet capable of yielding the high rates of return that we expect from the cyber dimension. International investors in particular are drawn more to invest in companies like Cisco and Microsoft than to old "real-world" companies.

Figure 1 shows how Japan and Europe have financed the U.S. investments in Asia and Latin America. Beginning with the Asian financial crisis of mid-1997, the U.S. pulled out of Asia. This, along with Asian investment in the U.S., was enough to shift the net capital flow in America's favor (as shown in the central diagram). At first, the U.S. continued to pump money into Latin America. But when the crisis in Brazil flared up, Latin Americans sent their money back to the U.S. as well (as shown at right of figure). As the widely perceived safer haven, America is thus seen to have benefited from the Russian, Asian, and European instabilities. The U.S. trade deficit remained constant during this period, which is one reason the reversal of money flow had significant impact on other nations' economies. The interlinkage of the global marketplace, foreseen throughout the 1980s and 1990s,[2] is now a reality shaping the financial and political activity of our time. There is nothing wrong with this. It shows simply the nature of money, and the "honesty" of investors around the world.

Borrowing from the world to prosper...
Money Flow (excluding public money)

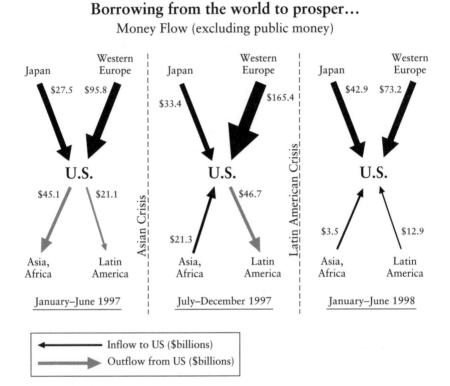

Source: Mr. Masayuki Yoshikawa, Nomura Research Institute, *Weekly Toyo Keizai*, February 6, 1999

Figure 1. This diagram shows the shift in private international investment flows throughout the Asian financial crisis. During the first half of 1997, U.S. investors poured a net $45.1 billion dollars into Asia (other than Japan) and Africa. But after the Asian crisis, the money flow rapidly reversed course, to send a net $21.3 billion from Asia and Africa into America, exacerbating the crisis and bolstering the American economy. By the first half of 1998, the money flow from the U.S. to Latin America had also reversed. The width of the arrows represents the magnitude of dollars moving into or out of the U.S. during each six-month period. The dollar's "platform" status made it a magnet for capital in a way that made instabilities elsewhere more unstable.

The dollar's platform status creates a blissful economic situation in the U.S., where job growth continues without wage hikes, in apparent contradiction of economic principles. This bliss has been attributed to the wisdom of former U.S. Treasury Secretary Robert Rubin and his successor Lawrence Summers, or to the economic fine-tuning of Federal Reserve Board Chairman Alan Greenspan. These policy-makers set a precedent for managing the money supply and interest rate—the traditional "old-paradigm" instruments of macroeconomic management—by managing other countries' economies. For instance, they press Japan and Europe to keep their interest rates low, so that there continues to be a healthy influx of capital into the U.S. By boosting American incomes through assets such as 401K-style retirement plans, they reduce American demand for wage hikes. Workers see their 401Ks grow, and hence take it easy on the labor movement to demand wage hikes.

American success, of course, is not just the result of its platform status. The American culture of creativity—the sheer capability to create the likes of a Las Vegas, an Orlando, or a company like Cisco Systems from scratch, for example—is the envy of the rest of the world. But culture and capability are not enough, in themselves, to explain the "American paradox": how unemployment can go down without an increase in wages. America has achieved the impossible by externalizing its own economy—by offering its domestic platform and its common settlement currency as a global medium of exchange. (We'll return to consider the political factors that propelled America to do this in Chapter 6.) As a result, people around the world become in effect the workers of America, twenty-four hours per day. Chinese, Vietnamese, and Latin American factory laborers work their tails off to produce goods for America at a competitive and disinflationary cost.

The benefits do not just accrue to America. The job opportunities that these laborers gain in exchange have been much more effective at stimulating growth in the long run than any government foreign aid (such as Official Development Assistance programs) would be—even more effective than the Marshall Plan of the post–World War II era. Not since the Marshall Plan, in fact, has any such system existed for spreading assets and real wealth from one country to another. And the Marshall Plan was flawed by comparison; it required an enormous administrative apparatus to create and enforce. The redistribution of the invisible continent happens all by itself. Dollars flow out of America, jobs get created around the world, and goods flow back. Dollars further flow out in exchange; they may end up in the closet, or come back to New York to invigorate the American financial market.

At the same time, the dollar's platform status creates an American economic dominance for which the U.S. is increasingly resented around the world. In old-fashioned (visible dimension) government statistics, this dominance is almost invisible; it is masked by the enormous trade deficit that the U.S. runs on paper. It is true that in 1998 Americans may have spent \$1.60 on Japanese goods for every dollar the Japanese spent on American goods.[3] On paper, this shows up as a severely high trade imbalance between America and Japan (it's even higher between America and the rest of the developed world). But Japanese customers, spending dollars on computers, have earned those dollars with perhaps twice as much of the blood, sweat, and tears of labor as the Americans who buy Japanese cameras. The Brazilians or the Indonesians borrow dollars to buy energy, foreign goods and services (not just American goods but goods from anywhere). They must pay these debts back with dollars, which are increasingly expensive if their own currency (such as the Brazilian réal) is inflationary. This vicious circle—in which debt leads to greater dependence on dollars, which in turn leads to more debt—is the source of the so-called debt's death spiral that Brazil, Russia, and other nations have fallen into.

We have seen over the past few years that any nation that can challenge the euphoria of Wall Street is severely punished or penalized. Massive exodus of U.S. dollars out of Russia, Brazil, Korea, and Southeast Asia has been arbitraged. And the resentment that these citizens might feel against the U.S. has often been displaced, in part through the clever maneuvering of the "Committee of Three" (Rubin, Greenspan, and Summers), by contempt for their own policy-makers and administrators. This in turn is helping the capital to continue to pour into the U.S. as investors continue to see their own countries as poorly managed. Investors may decry the situation in their own countries, but by treating America as a safe haven for their money, they contribute to the situations they decry.

It might seem that the three global platforms—the dollar, the open "trading field" markets, and the English language—give the United States a practically indestructible advantage in the years to come. The advantage is undeniable. But as we shall see in subsequent chapters, every platform status is continually subject to change. No international lawmaking body—not the United Nations, the World Trade Organization, the International Monetary Fund, any G-7 alliance, or even the old Bretton Woods agreement—has decreed that the dollar should be the world's settlement currency. As with all platforms, it has become so through practice. It has become a de facto standard, set by the habits and customs of traders. Similarly, platforms can often dictate behavior to their users. If the users of the American trading field start to alter the balance that has led to "Pax Americana," then the platform might lead behavior in a very different direction.

And as such, the situation could change overnight. The American platform dominance may well turn out to be unsustainable, particularly without the artful alertness of the Committee of Three that held sway during the late 1990s. (With Rubin's return to private life, it is now down to two.) If that's the case, then Pax Americana could rapidly disappear—with dangerous implications for both the U.S. and the world.

PRINCIPLES OF PLATFORMS

The reasons why platforms might collapse cannot be understood without recognizing the reasons they are becoming more prominent to begin with. National leaders may find a world of platforms disorienting, but they are not creations of nations; they exist because business needs them. Business cannot wait until the G-7, World Trade Organization (WTO), or Organization for Economic Cooperation and Development (OECD) comes up with rules, protocols, and bylaws for global investment, communication, and e-commerce. When they need new platforms, the platforms must be there, and in operation. That is the general rule of the invisible continent.

Sometimes I tell businesspeople that every time they see a woman wearing platform shoes, they should be reminded of the future of their company. (They simply have to grow four inches taller to keep the same eye contact.) For most corporations in the future, success will be intimately tied to platforms in the new continent. They will have to adjust their own businesses to meet the platforms; they can't wait for a platform to emerge that is tailor-made for them, because it might never happen. The most thriving businesses will climb upon existing platforms to offer new kinds of services that then become standard platforms themselves.

For example, Dell Computers makes its living from assembling and delivering computers at the request of customers on the phone or through the Web. In this respect, it has created a platform: a vehicle for people to more easily enter the invisible continent through the custom-made computer systems they buy from Dell. (Dell's rival, Gateway Computers, has invented a similar platform based on telephone call centers.) Arguably, the most crucial core part of this business—the delivery—is handled by FedEx. Orders come in from all over the world, but they do not necessarily travel to a central warehouse managed by Dell. They might just as easily go to a FedEx warehouse, where components, keyboards, and monitors are waiting in "just-in-time" inventories for delivery. FedEx's staff handles the shipment of modules according to Dell's specifications, and gets the product quickly to the customer, in one box to be delivered as ordered. United Parcel Service (UPS) is not far behind in establishing the same kinds of services. In effect, Dell and FedEx have formed what might be called a "virtual single company" (VSC), and so have Gateway and UPS.

In this context, FedEx and UPS are not transportation or delivery companies anymore. They have become the logistics platforms through which thousands of companies and customers gain access to each other. That is why FedEx calls its rapidly growing strategic division the "Logistic and Electronic Commerce" (LEC) division. More precisely, FedEx is poised to make its living by becoming a critical part of the supply chains of other companies. FedEx's main business is of course conducted in the real world, but at any given time, its customers can gain access to their platform through the Web (part of the cyber dimension of the invisible continent). Within that territory, FedEx can identify the location of any package—all the way from order-taking, through the procurement of components, to the delivery of finished products—on behalf of its customers.

For corporate leaders, strategy is always more effective when it seeks to create value for your customers than when it seeks merely to beat your competitors. Competitors must be taken into account, but the most critical element of strategy has remained constant since at least the 1970s: painstaking attention to the needs of customers, and close analysis of the company's real degrees of freedom in responding to those needs.[4] The emergence of a new array of platforms is most significant, therefore, because it changes the constraints on companies. In some ways, it makes you much more free; you can now fulfill customers' needs without having to do nearly as much yourself. Platforms help you concentrate what you are good at; and help you to be freed from the burdens of performing necessary but not-so-good, not-so-competitive functions.

But platforms also add constraints. Other companies will be meeting customer needs with the aid of these platforms, or creating platforms of their own; and companies that seek to go it alone, without recognizing the platforms available to them, will be severely handicapped or overburdened.

Companies that seek to establish a presence on the new continent will depend on platforms to get there. The winners in the battle for economic dominance on the invisible continent will be of three kinds: first, those who control the portal sites (i.e., the gates to the platforms of e-commerce); second, those whose grip on cyber-based payment platforms (now called "electronic wallets") is firm and sticky; and third, those who master the art of delivery (from cyberspace back into the real world). All of the winning companies will either establish (like AOL and Yahoo in portals, and CyberCash and Citibank in e-wallets) or reorient (like FedEx) their businesses so that their foremost purpose is providing platforms for others. A company with a compelling platform, on the new continent, is like the gatekeeper to a doorway that many people will want to pass through. If you become the preferred platform of people around the world, then you have an inside track to becoming one of the powerhouse companies of the new continent—the kinds that we will look at more closely as the "Godzilla" companies of Chapter 4.

Platforms Thrive by Being Open to All Potential Partners

Platforms combine two features that, traditionally, have been separate. As the creations of private companies, they are flexible and fast-moving, without being beholden to any constituencies. But as the custodians of access to universally needed goods or services or standards, they are networked to the world at large, with an implicit requirement to treat all comers as equivalent and not to play favorites. In other words, they are "common carriers." This is not a new idea; since the Sherman Anti-Trust Act, passed in the U.S. in 1890, private companies (such as railroad companies) have been prohibited from "restraint of trade"—from using their platforms to deny access to potential competitors and thus unfairly hobble the market. Reacting to the antitrust restrictions, companies like American Telephone and Telegraph built large, staid platform operations that guaranteed access to a communications network to everyone—but at the cost of hobbling innovation.

Today's platforms are much faster moving and much more flexible, but they still must heed the same restriction: they must be open to all potential communicators. The only difference is that, in the long run, the restriction will come not from government but from their own customers—who often will be their competitors as well. For example, if the U.S. Postal Service does not provide a competitive delivery of parcels, Amazon.com will have to create its own delivery system in order to (finally) make money.

This issue underlies the current United States antitrust lawsuit against Microsoft. Microsoft's lawyers argue, reasonably, that despite the company's 90-plus percent market share in personal computer operating systems, it could lose its "monopoly" position at any time to a new competitor. That argument, however, ignores that fact that "monopolies" are old-world phenomena. Microsoft is not really on trial for abusing a monopoly, but for abusing a *platform*. By pushing so hard to be the "winner" in every deal, Microsoft has provoked a groundswell of resistance among its competitors—who are also the platform's users and customers. For example, Microsoft's opponents in the software industry are not complaining about the dominance of the Windows OS per se. They are demanding that Microsoft open up access to the protocols (the technical principles and bylaws of the platform) so that other companies can use that platform to develop better applications for customers and that they can extend the platform itself beyond Microsoft's full control. They are also demanding that Microsoft's own ancillary services—such as Explorer, Expedia, Money, Office, MSNBC, and Hotmail—be completely decoupled from the basic operating system.

The antitrust suit is just one among many competitive tactics that software companies are employing. And there is evidence, with the ascent of Jini, Java, and Linux, that they have found a more effective tactic: to shift to other platforms. Bill Gates understands the threat of losing this dominant platform better than anyone else. So, his strategy will be to internalize the competitors' weapons over time, as he has done so far with Macintosh and Netscape, and increasingly with Java.

The keepers of platforms, in short, are vulnerable in ways that the keepers of monopolies are not. They hurt themselves when they violate customers' confidence, because there is always an opportunity for a competitor to provide an alternative platform. Amazon.com faced this problem in March 1999, when the *New York Times* reported that the online bookstore was charging book publishers $10,000 fees for prominent placement of information about their books on the Amazon Web site. As an author, I found this accusation interesting, because Amazon's "cyber-bribery" was typical of book practices generally. Promoters normally go out of their way (wining and dining) to get papers and magazines to feature book reviews, and many bookstores charge publishers for prominent placement of a book in stores. Amazon.com at least had the price posted in a more transparent fashion than in other bookstores.

But the article did provoke an outcry among Amazon.com's customers, who complained that they had thought the bookstore's recommendations represented an impartial assessment of the book's values. Faced with these protests, Amazon.com promised they would label all sponsored recommendations in the future. Had Amazon not acted quickly, their customers might well have taken their business to alternative sites, which could easily claim that they were less biased, more open, or less susceptible to being "bought."

Platforms Open Up New Avenues to Commerce

Amazon.com originally marketed itself as the world's largest online bookseller, and indeed they passed the size of Barnes & Noble, their largest competitor (in terms of books sold) within two years. At first glance, to many people, their platform seemed to be a base for bookselling. They defined themselves at first as not just a competitor to brick-and-mortar bookstores, but as a new form of book retailer with new possibilities for finding "books as information." If a book was out of print, they brokered with various used-book dealers to conduct searches for their customers. Many assumed that Amazon would move from there to publishing books themselves, especially amidst the emergence of electronic books.

Instead, it became clear that Amazon.com's executives were setting themselves up as a platform for electronic commerce: recorded music, videos, electronic equipment, auctioned goods, and ultimately anything that a Sears, Roebuck, a Wal-Mart, or an eBay might offer. In fact, Amazon's founder and CEO Jeff Bezos clearly announced that his wish is to become the largest retailer in the world. In all of these cases, Amazon.com had to add more value than electronic communication could accomplish on its own; it had to embody the most creative, winning approaches to merchandizing, assortment, and the price-to-quality relationship of goods sold. This is a challenge that bookselling alone doesn't offer.

The U.S. Department of Commerce has predicted that, within the next several years, one-third of consumer spending will take place either over digital television or through the Internet, at least in the United States. Others estimate that as much as 40 percent of the $800 billion per year spent by consumers using credit cards in America will shift to online sales by the year 2005. I agree with the basic thrust of these predictions. In the Christmas season of 1999, online purchases jumped a phenomenal 400 percent over the previous year, reaching an estimated $5 billion.[5]

A variety of emerging platforms exist for helping people conduct their tourist planning and purchasing. The original pioneer for this type of service was probably Traveler's Advantage (TA), one of several transactional Web sites developed by the Cendant Corporation. For a $48 annual fee (now $1 for three months), Web surfers became Cendant members. They received a discount on hotel rooms and car rentals—and more importantly, booked most of their travel (hotels, car rentals, airline tickets, etc.) online across the Cendant platform. Microsoft now has a similar travel-oriented site, Expedia. It basically does the same thing as TA but is free to registered users. Both sites are storing up information on travel-loving customers for future "business" use. Both are portals—sites that serve as platforms by providing people their first gate into the Web. The online travel business has thus rapidly become an online battleground between Cendant, Microsoft, Sabre, and several others, each vying to be a better platform for destination tourism, a large and growing global industry.

Another Cendant affiliated service, known as "AutoVantage," helps members find good prices on new and used cars. When you log on to their site, a series of forms asks you to select the car model you want, the options, and your choice of color. Then the programs, behind the scene, canvass the data banks for the best price that AutoVantage can find with a dealer. If you buy the car, several finance companies appear to offer competing credit terms, and insurance companies offer packages to select from. Cendant makes much of its income through its $48 annual fee, and can thus claim that its recommendations are unbiased and truly oriented to customers' needs.

Even more than in the case of Microsoft or Amazon, the credibility of AutoVantage or Traveler's Advantage rises or falls with its ability to live up to its promise—one-stop shopping and the supply of superior deals. Customers expect the platform to remain neutral and unbiased, while it acts as a one-stop site for wide varieties of purchases of high-end products. If the sites are seen as unreliable or duplicitous in any way, people will find alternatives to them. But as long as they are seen as trustworthy, an enormous amount of commerce will flow through them. Cendant's Web sites claim to have over 30 million fee-paying members for its executive relocation, housing, credit protection, travel, and shopping services. (In its peak year, 1997, the number was 60 million, each paying $48 in annual dues.) That roster of fees, in itself, provides a very effective source of income, enough to support the research that keeps customers well informed so they can make intelligent decisions in online shopping.

As platforms, venues like AutoVantage carry an influence that extends beyond the boundaries of the Internet. For example, Autobytel, an online auto dealer, handles over one and a half million cars annually from literally all makers. In the past, GM, Ford, and Toyota would have had relatively high control over their channels of distribution; for example, you would have to go to a Lexus dealer to buy a Lexus, though you know it is a Toyota car. But no longer. With Autobytel, you come to a cyberautoshop where all models of all makers can be researched and eventually negotiated, giving Autobytel's customers much greater leverage over any particular manufacturer.

Cendant's infrastructure is itself a platform for its fee-paying members—a de facto standard for brokering arrangements with expensive retail, built on a common set of Internet servers and software. One platform does it all. But that does not mean that Cendant, or anyone else, has to build every element of the jigsaw puzzle. All you need to do is ensure that the most competitive, state-of-the-art online services are brought in. For example, there are several real estate sites with international listings. As a customer, you type in a location and they return with a selection of houses and condominiums—along with floor plans and neighborhood guides, as in Realtor.com. Rentals and offices are listed the same way. Once you decide to buy a house, you can also broker ancillary services through the site: financing, fire insurance, burglar alarms. With traditional service providers, you would have had to carry your records and start all over again. The platform supports all of them everywhere you go—hence the name "platform."

Citibank's "electronic wallet" concept will try to take even that small level of intermediation away from individual platforms. They will become a centralized payment platform, so that you do not have to leave your footprints in many shopping sites. Your personal data can be shared across the subsections of the same platform. Or as Edward D. Horowitz, head of e-Citi, has put it: "You won't have to provide this information at any web site affiliated with Citigroup. The electronic wallet provides it for you in a safe and private fashion. In addition, with the electronic wallet, you can choose how you pay for your purchase: check, credit or debit card, or you can request to be billed."[6] Another platform exists at the commercial level, sponsored by General Electric—a procurement system that links GE's suppliers with each other, to bid for and request electronic components. This platform originated as an in-house procurement system at GE. It was so robust, and so successful, that they leveraged its cost by offering it to their clients. It has now become a more universal platform known as Trading Process Network (TPN) Post, used by manufacturers throughout the electric and electronics component business, not just to GE's advantage but to the advantage of the industry as a whole. Another good example of a business-to-business platform for electric component procurement is "RosettaNet," founded in 1998 as a nonprofit organization dedicated to promoting an industrywide initiative to set a standard for e-commerce worldwide. This stems from an effort launched in 1995 by Saqqara Systems for AMP to develop the latter's electronic catalog and order system. Another classic case is the Sabre automated airline reservation system: Originally developed as an in-house data bank by American Airlines, it is now the established international platform for keeping track of airline and travel-related reservations. Its dot.com affiliate, Travelocity, is quickly displacing Travelers Advantage and other sites because of its indepth knowledge of travel-related activities.

A more comprehensive industrywide platform is about to be launched. This is not just based on the Internet, a decentralized and router-based global network. It will use a more centrally controlled network, using ATM switches to form a VPN (virtual private network), maintained by a handful of certified service providers. It is called Automated Network Exchange (ANX) with ten auto manufacturers participating on day one, each chipping in 10 million dollars or less. It will be a global automotive component supply chain platform. Using this system, its organizer, the Automobile Industry Action Group (AIAG) hopes to link over 1,300 vendor companies around the world to, in effect, reduce the production cost of a car by $75, and the order-to-delivery cycle of components from four to six weeks down to ten to thirteen days.

Not all of these platforms will succeed in the long run, but even to get into the game, they all have one thing in common: They redefine their businesses and make new capabilities available to customers (including the abilities of "arbitrage": using competitive leverage to seek the lowest prices, fastest turnaround time, highest quality, and other most desirable features available). In that way, they outclass and outmaneuver their old-world competition. Simply using a new-continent tool to accomplish an old-world task is not enough. If you are developing a platform, you must make it possible for your customers to do something they have never been able to do before, even at the expense of having to redefine their business process (BPR) altogether.

Platforms Seek Oligopoly, But Don't Always Get There

One characteristic of platforms is oligopoly, monopoly, or semi-monopoly status. Even with Microsoft in the travel game, there isn't a second membership club that comes close to Travelocity—which gives it the clout to get better discounts for its members. Every platform seeks a similar kind of leverage, simply because it is very difficult to remain a platform without it.

Yet, no platform's hegemony is assured. The dominance of Windows as the champion of desktop computer platforms was threatened in March 1999, when Sony announced the introduction of PlayStation 2 (PSII) technology. This interactive medium ostensibly was designed to play games on digital video disks (DVDs), but it could also communicate digitally through telephone or cable lines, with a higher-quality signal than any previous game machine. Its earlier version, PlayStation I, has penetrated into 70 million households around the world.

Unlike the PC, which goes into home offices and children's studies and playrooms, PlayStation goes into the den and living room, hooked onto the TV—an ideal online shopping device. As such, PSII might become a standard platform on which those people who are allergic to keyboards might be introduced to interactive cyber-shopping, just as kids have been hooked into cyberspace through games like Dragon Quest and the Final Fantasies. Because digital video disks can hold 4.8 gigabits of information, the combination of DVD and telecommunications transmission makes possible an unprecedented degree of interactivity, speed, and fun with joysticks (instead of keyboards). A supermarket grocer could put a full raft of images on a DVD; a customer could three-dimensionally "walk" down the aisles pushing a virtual shopping cart, see high-quality images of all the merchandise, and send in an order at the end of the session. DVD, which is a Toshiba technology, solves the bandwidth problem—the problem that no matter what kind of cable people use to receive data from the Internet, it will be difficult to ensure enough bandwidth to produce high-quality real-time interactive video around the clock.

But Sony's DVD/telephone hybrid is far from the only entrant into the competition for this new platform. Sega's computer game platform (Dream Cast) is network-compatible, and Nintendo is working on its version of Net games with e-commerce compatibility. And of course, Microsoft is developing its "X-Box," a highly interactive computer with Net-game capabilities using DVD technologies. Each entrant represents a different way to occupy the living room by solving the "last-one-mile" problem: the expense of bridging the final link from every home and office to some central network by laying any new (fiber or cable TV) wire. The American cable television industry is developing a cable-modem technology that can exchange 5 megabits per second, and replace the conventional telephone for voice calls. Telephone companies such as US West and SBC have an alternative known as "very high speed digital subscriber line" (VDSL) that uses compression software to squeeze bandwidth (up to 20 megabits per second, using technology developed by Next Level Communications) over conventional ("twisted pair") telephone lines. Another American telephone technology, known as "wireless local loops" (WLL), is now available through companies like Teligent to capture subscribers without occupying the existing telephone line. In Europe, mobile phone technology, known as wideband code division multiple access (WCDMA), may well become the principal route into the new territory. Or this technology may become a global standard—now that the two primary producers, Ericsson and Qualcomm, have decided to collaborate rather than compete on the next generation of mobile phone systems. In other countries, the prevailing telephone platform may involve digital satellite transmissions; already there are dozens of satellite systems available to nations around the world. Malaysians use MEASat; Indonesians use IndoSat. The British have B-Sky-B. The Japanese are adding capacity rapidly on top of Japan's already crowded skies. More than 450 digital satellite channels are available now in 2000—enough so that even independent entrepreneurs like myself can own and operate them. Indeed, I own one (called "Business Breakthrough"), which I use for interactive management discussions in Japan. Managers watch high-quality digital television broadcasts while their computers are hooked up to the Internet through regular phone lines. They ask the instructors questions on the Internet connection, and the instructors answer almost immediately across the satellite transmission. At the same time, Japan is also investing in massive fiber-to-the-home communications lines as part of its "economic stimulus" package.

This multiplicity of large-scale, high-bandwidth networks, each using a different technology to provide universal access to the same customers, is a far cry from the industry structure of previous forms of telecommunications. In the early days of cable television, for example, permits were granted by counties and municipalities. Operators like John Malone (TCI) had to assemble their networks neighborhood by neighborhood to become major cable operators. Now a variety of global, top-down technologies vie for access. Each one is hoping to become the Oregon Trail for media distributors into the new continent, the road that more settlers use for reaching the lucrative frontier. Each of them has global reach: one world, one satellite or DVD or mobile telephone system. For a while, they will compete for the same market: the "early adopter" computer and digital telephone user. Gradually, however, they will differentiate. Their customers, voting with their dollars and frequency of use, will decide that each of the various technologies is most useful for a particular purpose. Digital satellite, for instance, may come into its own as a platform for the distribution of pictures, movies, and music to local receivers, particularly in the continually changing world of pop music, and particularly as "music-minus-one" technologies, such as karaoke, become more popular and more flexible.

Platforms tend to drift toward oligopoly status. Once a single platform has established itself—from Windows to E*Trade to Amazon.com to Autobytel—it will probably not have many direct competitors, at least for a period. There is room for a number one platform, and possibly a number two—a Macintosh counterpart to Windows, a MasterCard counterpart to Visa—but certainly not numbers three and four.

This tendency toward oligopoly is a natural function of the dynamics of networks, where part of the value that any platform offers comes from being connected to as many customers (and as many other platforms) as possible. Software developers don't want to develop for more than one platform; they'll develop programs for Windows, which has the installed base. If they have further resources, they may possibly develop for Macintosh. And if they seek the business or engineering markets, Unix or Java may be the preferred language. Similarly, customers, once they have learned to gravitate toward a single platform, will not gravitate toward another, and the platform that has attracted the majority of customers will also attract the majority of ancillary services (and therefore attract a still larger proportion of customers). That is why they are called "sticky." As computer people put it, the most popular platforms "support" the largest number of other products—including hardware, software, and services. It is always easiest to fit in with the leading platforms on the new continent, and it is generally possible to tell the most viable platforms because of the crowds. Viable platforms get noticed, written about, and spoken about.

This means that if you have a viable idea for a platform, it pays to get there first, like Amazon.com, to build a critical mass of customer base before your competitors arrive. If you don't get there first, it makes more sense to ally with an existing platform rather than to create a competing one of your own. You may be better off concentrating on niches within the category, such as tailor-made services to a special group of people; or else moving on to develop an entirely different platform where you *can* be the first. The most effective way to create a platform, from scratch, is to identify a key feature that people need to make their communications and transportation work, as FedEx has done with its automated tracking, assembly, and virtual warehousing services. From there, rather than doing everything yourself, strike key alliances that you can grow from and build upon, as Microsoft did with IBM to create MS-DOS in the first place in 1983, thus ushering in one of the premier gateways to the new continent—the personal computer. In this game, the victor is always someone who is closer to the customer, who has a higher share of customer awareness ("mindshare") or a stronger influence on key customer decision-makers. In order to make a new and winning platform, you need to have a clear positioning of your value proposition. As Amazon has done in discount bookselling, you have to have a "killer" content to become a killer platform. If you build an all-purpose platform, you may become a jack-of-all-trades without much trade—a trap that Value America apparently has fallen into.[7] Super Mario Brothers and Final Fantasy represented the killer content, respectively, for Nintendo and Sony PlayStation.

Some Critical Platforms Do Not Yet Exist

During the week that Kenneth Starr's report on Bill Clinton was released, the Cable News Network Web site received more than 18 million "hits" online—signifying that at least several million people had entered the site to request news about the report. *Playboy* magazine maintains a Web site that receives, every day, about 6 million hits, meaning that perhaps half a million people are checking the site. (By contrast, a typical visit to a Web site produces somewhere between five and twenty-five hits, which are counted each time a new page or image is clicked upon.) Potentially, this represents an enormous source of income, but there is no platform yet available that can help media to take advantage of it. Subscription fees are dubious; the experience of newsmagazines such as Microsoft's *Slate* shows that too few people are willing to pay annual subscription fees for online reading. And advertising is also seen increasingly as an inadequate and chancy way to fund electronic news.

The answer is microbilling and micropayments. If people knew that they would pay somewhere between 1 cent and 60 cents every time they pulled in a particular piece of text or image, they would meter their access accordingly—and creating valuable online information would be an enormously profitable business. Unfortunately, there is no micropayment technology easily available. Credit cards are good only for purchases of $10 apiece and more. The credit card is not a low-friction device, since it charges 3 to 4 percent to the merchant. A debit card is better, but it still charges 1 percent of the merchandise, at least in Japan. So, if you could figure out a way to generate micropayments without requiring prepayment (a method such as electronic cash or digi-cash), you could make information-providing companies very successful. In this endeavor, one needs to ask, "What do you mean by credit?"

I personally believe the credit card system itself is poised for evolution. I have believed so for a long time. Back in the summer of 1982, I was chatting on a porch overlooking the Japan Alps with the late Dr. Kazuma Tateishi, founder of Omron, the Japanese electronics components and electronic fund transfer systems company. He was already eighty years old, but quite alert and full of energy. We were talking about a then-well-known TV commercial by American Express featuring Jack Nicklaus. In the commercial, Nicklaus walks into a hotel and wants to run a tab for his room. "Do you know me?" he asks. Of course the poor clerk doesn't know him. But he need not worry, according to the ad, because the hotel knows the green American Express card. So long as they can check Nicklaus's (or anyone's) creditworthiness through the CAT (credit authorization terminal), it will be okay.

"That is fundamentally wrong," I said to Dr. Tateishi. "In a networked society, you carry your own credit. You should not need to ask an intermediary for verification. All you should do is carry with you an electronically safe way to look up your own bank account." Dr. Tateishi and I immediately sketched out a "personal micropayments" system that bypasses all the middlemen, and goes directly to the bank to ask about creditworthiness for a particular proposed withdrawal. The bank simply responds electronically yes or no, but locks the person's time deposit until the payment is made after the same period of "float" as the credit card. The system, in short, is a debit system with float—an automated system with the same result as paying off all your credit card bills every month. Unlike an ordinary credit card transaction, there is "friction"—no extra percentage of the transaction is billed to the merchant but ultimately charged back to the customer. All the micropayments are tallied up on the platform until the one lump sum payment is made at the end of the month. (A patent for this system was granted to me in Japan in 1983, but banking regulations prohibited such a debit system until January 1999. Thus, there are only four years left in the life of this patent!)

Putting this, or any micropayments system, into practice would mean a significant behind-the-scenes shift in the credit card business. Currently the business has two functions. First, it facilitates transactions, charging merchants a small fee (often 3 percent) for this. Second, it extends credit (and, by extension, recognition) so that people who are unknown to the merchants have American Express, Visa, Mastercard to vouch for them and guarantee their payments (as AmEx did, famously, for Jack Nicklaus). If these two credit card functions—credit and transaction—could be decoupled, then intermediaries such as American Express, Visa, or MasterCard would shift their roles. They would no longer be needed as intermediaries, offering a voucher for individuals. Every vendor could use automated credit rating systems, built into the network, hooked directly through the Web to the customers' banks.

In that kind of freewheeling environment, different types of accounts might become available as banks and vendors compete for customers. Banks might offer checking accounts with a thirty-day float after every debit, or they might allow a customer to decide the amount of float—to decide how long to allow before a transaction shows up on the books. Credit cards might be offered with different interest rates for different types of purchases, again set by the customer with different ramifications for each interest rate.

At the same time, the other side of the credit card business—facilitating transactions—would probably remain a platform activity. The organizations that have built the transactional and settlement platforms of the new continent, including Visa, MasterCard, and American Express, would probably hold on to that central role. They would, in effect, become settlement banks and common carriers of transactions. They would, in other words, administer the networks that linked banks and merchants together, and they might retain and license out the global brand names they have developed.

This is an example of a platform that inevitably will come to exist, disruptive though it may be—only because it is much needed. Another such platform already came into existence in April 1998, when a site named Priceline.com was launched. Like Jeff Bezos, the chairman and CEO of Priceline comes from the investment banking industry; his name is Richard Braddock, and he is an ex-Citibank executive, working with a seasoned entrepreneur, Jay Walker. (As with many of the new continent's most powerful platforms, experience in the financial world is proving quite relevant here.) In April 1999, after less than two years of operation,

Priceline.com had a market capitalization of $20 billion. Only five companies in all of Japan were worth more than this company at that time, and it had taken most of them forty years or more to get there. Yet, according to the analysts' forecasts, the company was expecting to earn only minus 0.25, .002, and 0.13 cents per share, respectively, for years 2000, 2001, and 2002. These are for shares that were trading at about 100 dollars in mid-1999.[8]

What could this new company, without many tangible assets, possibly have to offer that is worth that much to the market? Priceline has only one product: a platform for bringing sellers and customers together in all arenas. They provide a bidding process for industries that are capacity dependent. Priceline's well-known first service involves airline tickets. Customers announce the price they are willing to pay for air travel to any destination on a particular day, guaranteeing with a credit card that they will take the seat offered to them no matter what time it leaves. Then the airlines bid for that traveler. Priceline solves the airlines' utilization problem by letting people decide how much they are willing to pay to fill up the seating capacity minute by minute or day by day.

For the first time in the recent history of commerce, the customer sets the price, and sees if there are any manufacturers or service providers who are willing to accept the price. This works pretty well when there is always high fixed cost and fluctuations of capacity utilization. In any given day, some half a million seats are flying empty over the U.S. skies, so even a token cash revenue represents an additional marginal contribution to airline companies' fixed costs. The same is true for railroads, cruise ships, hotel rooms, machine tools in factories, theaters, theme parks, hospitals, scientific and measurement instruments, and increasingly, schools, as the number of students declines. (If I were Priceline's management, I would offers these services, rather than new cars and groceries, which are basically "me too" services.) Instead of buyers shopping for a producer who can provide them with products, producers now come to Priceline.com to shop for customers. And that is why this concept is unique, made possible only on the new continent. This is a much more efficient way to run a market, because producers are more skilled at getting the information they need about customers than customers are at getting the information they need about producers.

If Priceline.com became a common platform for buyers to come in for literally anything—ranging from consumer to industrial products and services—its extraordinary market capitalization could be justified. Priceline's billions in market cap thus represent a tiny percentage of the savings it can potentially produce for both buyers and sellers who meet directly on the invisible continent. On the other hand, there is always a threat to the Amazons and Pricelines from more specialized challengers. The winners will be those who can attract more traffic and those who are sensitive to the specific needs of the ask/bid participants (the customers), using the time-honored marketing techniques known as clustering through segmentation and resegmentation. These new companies face daunting challenges: to keep reminding customers of the reasons they came to the portal to begin with, and to keep looking for other clusters who would find the basic value proposition attractive, as opposed to offering nondifferentiated products available through any portal sites.

Another platform that is still in the making is the inexpensive, easy-to-use network telephone/computer/television: the single device that will circumvent the difficulties of personal computers for people who want to go online. This may evolve from the Sony PlayStation, from Windows CE, from the Macintosh iMac and iBook (whose popularity obviously stems from the fact that they represent a move in the direction of creating this platform), or from some other device, like i-mode. The i-mode is a service offered by DoCoMo, Japan's NTT affiliate, which transmits Internet service, including color video images, through mobile phones. A variation of this is already available as a wristwatch using voice prompt, meaning there is no longer a need to push buttons or keys. The mobile phone thus becomes an electronic wallet itself, replacing most of the things that people currently hold in their wallets and even briefcases. Credit cards, driver's license, health insurance, airline tickets, and concert reservations, as well as bank notes and a music-listening Walkman, will all be internalized in the i-mode. We do not know what particular combination of conduit, hardware, and software will finally make this device ubiquitous, so that homes have as many of them as they have radios and television sets now. All we can say for sure is that the emergence of this type of "wearable" platform is inevitable because the rest of the world, the platform's partners in the dance, is calling for it to emerge.

Platforms Are Vehicles for Community

In Japan, one of the most common platforms for the new continent can be found in any 7-Eleven convenience store. This chain is owned by Ito-Yokado, which also owns Southland, the company that operates 7-Eleven stores in America. In each Japanese 7-Eleven is an information kiosk, hooked to a national network. Through a voice-prompted interface, people can retrieve entertainment and travel information (in the form of downloaded music, games, and pictures) and purchase tickets on the spot. Other franchised convenience shops, such as Lawson and AM/PM, also compete for this portal position in location-based electronic commerce. Lawson, owned by Deiei, offers a matchmaking service, which has become known as (arguably) the best way in Japan to find a date that might lead to marriage. Girls in Japan spend 3,000 yen (about 25 dollars) to get listed, and there is often a long queue of people waiting to use the system.

Nearly every platform, in one way or another, becomes a vehicle for linking people together—and thus for creating community. It may not involve as intimate a subject as love and marriage, but it frequently will involve long-standing human loyalty. A satisfied travel or automobile purchaser *who has been drawn in through software to participate in the core of the transaction as never before* will be an extremely loyal customer. Paradoxically, this customer will perceive a closer and deeper relationship with the enterprise than if he or she "only" had contact with human beings, because the software gives customers a feeling of more control. Ideally, it gives them more genuine control during the transaction, and thereafter.

Of course, if something goes wrong, there must be a human-staffed help desk or complaint service to deal with issues too complex for software. An effective way to address this issue is to use a one-way teleconferencing facility. Instead of hearing a voice at the end of 1-800, if you can see the service rep (not a telephone operator) on your screen, your level of frustration is vastly reduced. I have not seen clear evidence of a need for (two-way) videoconferencing in business-to-consumer applications, but one-way video on CTI (computer-telephony integration) has proven extremely useful in our experiment of introducing Internet on TV to Japanese households.

Platforms eventually will provide this and many other good ideas, because they will naturally keep improving. Without improving, they can become irritants, and customers in a close relationship with an irritating company can easily feel betrayed. In that case, the customers will drop their loyalty and move to another platform. For example, some package carriers (DHL and Airborne) have weakened their position as potential platforms through poor customer service. Many credit card companies have disappeared for similar reasons. Japanese postal services are gradually being replaced by faster and cheaper parcel delivery companies like Yamato, Akabo (Red Cap), and Sagawa.

A few real communities—civic establishments such as towns or cities—are beginning to recognize the value of developing this kind of relationship with their population. One such project, "Smart Valley," launched in 1994, is an initiative to build a platform of Internet access and local information pages, linking community groups, governments, schools, and local corporations. Eighteen municipalities in Santa Clara County, south of San Francisco, teamed up for this regional effort. By making online connections in multiple directions, they facilitate telecommuting (and carpooling), they give schools more opportunities to learn directly from the community, and they open up local government (making it much easier, for example, to get local permits). This system has become a prototype for other community projects around the world.

Another such project is under way in Malaysia. Despite the economic depression and recent political unrest in that country, the Malaysian Multimedia Super Corridor (MSC) is under construction in Selangor State. So far the project has been pursued on schedule. If it is successful, this will be expanded to two other states in 2005; and after 2010, it will be expanded to the entire country. MSC has attracted over 275 companies to this community, including 29 world-class corporations; and already 139 companies are in operation in the MSC-designated areas.

I was personally involved in the original concept development of MSC from day one in 1993. I tried hard to figure out how a developing country like Malaysia can keep pace with the development of the invisible continent. I came to the conclusion that throwing the whole country into the twenty-first century across the board would be not only impossible, but unwise, given the complexities of a multiracial society with a dominant Islamic culture. So my recommendation to Dr. Mahathir, prime minister of Malaysia, was to carve out a large enough area to experiment with the future. A body of appropriate laws was put in place, governing "Cyberjaya," a new "fully intelligent city" named after the Malaysian word meaning "cyber-community." An area fifteen kilometers wide and fifty kilometers long immediately south of Kuala Lumpur was chosen as the Corridor. We chose nine flagship applications to demonstrate how new continents were different from the old ones. The Cyber Law (Communications and Multimedia Act—1998) has passed the Parliament, and the first group of the Electronic Government "moved" to Putra Jaya in June 1999.

At the same time, of course, Malaysia was hit hard by the Asian financial crisis, and Dr. Mahathir later found himself in a political struggle with the former deputy prime minister, Anwar Ibrahim. As a longtime economic advisor to the Malaysian government and particularly to Dr. Mahathir, I find it a great pity to see the country's efforts to move into the invisible continent, with due planning and preparation, suddenly slowed as a result. This shows once again that, like the Oregon Trail, the road to El Dorado is arduous.

SEEING THE CEO AS A CIO

It's one thing to understand the value of platforms, but the true test is putting that concept into practice. As with most corporate strategy issues, creating a corporate strategy around platforms cannot be approached in a one-size-fits-all standardized way. It requires a careful assessment of the needs of your customers and your own capabilities.

The critical challenge is to find the best mix of platforms among those offered by other companies and those that exist within your own proprietary systems. As you look at other people's platforms, pay particular attention to the capabilities that your organization has chronically lacked. Is there an electronic commerce capability, payment and settlement, or some aspect of logistics, that would fill in a missing piece of your business? If so, building someone else's platform into your business may be the most effective way to gain that capability.

Contracting with a platform is not like developing an exclusive alliance. The platform is available to all; your competitors can use it too. But they cannot duplicate your relationship with the platform provider. If you are a prominent user of the services involved, then the provider will change to meet your needs, in the same way that FedEx evolved to meet the demands of Dell and other critical accounts.

Also look internally for those aspects of your business process that could be adapted into a platform for others. Does the structure of your supply chain suggest ways to broker your logistic expertise? Could you turn your payment system or sales management approach into a generic service? Have you got a form of concurrent engineering and R&D administration, human resources, or electronic commerce that other organizations might use? If your answer is no, then perhaps you would be better off shifting to an external platform yourself. Then you might investigate the growing number of business process platforms, such as sales force automation (SFA, offered, for example, by Siebel Systems on their "sales.com" site), customer relationship management, or one of the shared application platforms, called "ASPs," that make complex software available in semi-customized form without the expense of having it tailor-made to your specific purpose.

Since the effectiveness of your use of a platform depends on the technological capabilities of your decision-makers, it's vital for the CEO of your organization to also be your chief information officer (CIO). Of course, there could be a CIO staff position separate from the CEO's position, but the CEO should have the knowledge, interest, passion, and capability to double as CIO at any time. Information technology, network computing, effective telecommunication, and knowledge of state-of-the-art corporate benchmarks have become so central to corporate strategy that the life or death of the company may depend on the judgment of senior leaders in this area, particularly as companies get more and more involved in electronic commerce. If the company must be reorganized to fulfill the "cyber" imperatives of the invisible continent, as most large established companies will, then the reorganization should be informed by a technologically savvy perspective. For all these reasons, the CEO should be keenly, personally aware of the technology, and a direct user of the sort of systems that he advocates for his employees. This point was really brought home when Bill Gates announced in January of 2000 that he would step down as CEO of Microsoft and become chief systems architect. Some CEOs of large companies still refuse to use computers. "My staff is my computer," they say. They will never gain a foothold on the invisible continent unless they change their attitudes and become at least a partial resident of the new continent, breathing its air day in and day out.

This point came home to me in a conversation I had in the 1980s with Walter Wriston, then the chairman of Citicorp (since merged into Citigroup). Wriston mentioned that he had picked his successor, John S. Reed. I knew that Reed's background was not in traditional banking, but in technology, and I was very surprised. "Why have you chosen him?" I asked Wriston, "when there are so many other potential heirs apparent?"

"The future of banking," Wriston said, "is going to be determined by nanoseconds. It's a technology game, and it's very, very hard to teach bankers the technology. It's easier for a technology guy to learn banking, so I actually need this guy."

Later I had occasion to ask John Reed himself about whether Walter had indeed picked him for that reason. Reed confirmed it and said, "I was reluctant at first. I said I would not be a good CEO of Citicorp because I don't know anybody in Washington. I don't know anybody in the industry. All I know is technology." But Wriston, Reed said, had told him not to worry: "If you are the chairman of Citicorp, all the important guys will either come to you, or you'll have no trouble meeting them and you'll get to know them very well in two or three years. That problem will be solved as time goes on."

Has it paid off to invest in technology for that bank, and to choose a CEO who could also serve as chief information officer? In Citicorp's case, it's made an enormous difference. It's particularly obvious in Japan, where most other (homegrown) financial institutions are in crisis, but Citicorp is experiencing breakthrough performance even in domestic retail. To be sure, you don't have to be a Citicorp-sized company to develop enormous reach on the invisible continent. But you do have to know how to use the tools of the cyber dimension, how to reach out to customers, and how to leverage your products and services through technology. Companies that can develop these capabilities without too many growing pains and stresses are poised to become the kinds of companies that I will describe in Chapter 4—the "Godzilla" companies, with voracious appetite and rapid growth.

3

ARBITRAGE AND THE NEW ECONOMY

During the past few years, business writers have increasingly drawn upon images from quantum theory to explain the new economic environment. To be sure, even on the new continent, business is much less complex than the subatomic behavior of quarks and gluons. But there is an extremely useful metaphor at the heart of quantum theory. It stems from the famous "uncertainty principle" articulated by physicist Werner Heisenberg in 1927. Heisenberg postulated that a given bit of matter could be measured either as a particle (in terms of charting its position), or as a wave (by measuring its velocity), but not both simultaneously, because the act of measuring one characteristic would render the other measurement uncertain. This meant that it was not possible to say, once and for all in terms of measurement, whether the particle or the wave state was closer to the essence of matter. Metaphorically, at least, there is a fundamental dichotomy at the root of all things, an ability to be two contradictory things at once.

The same is true for every person and institution that gets involved with the invisible continent. Hundreds of times per day, people shift between the old world and the new continent in their daily activity. These two worlds are governed by fundamentally different economic principles, and they require people to operate with two completely opposed sets of economic strategies. Most people who succeed on the invisible continent manage to navigate these constant shifts of economic identity without ever explicitly acknowledging the types of shifts that are required. This need for a dual identity is the source of much of the confusion that people feel around recent economic events.

Back in the old world, the political and economic system has an implicit goal: to create jobs and employment, so that people can make purchases, save, and become prosperous. Many decisions in this economy are geared toward providing "flow-through": moving money into the hands of employees, through them as consumers, and back into production. For old-world governments, the theories of John Maynard Keynes, and the various Keynesian economic policies and their offshoots, are all geared to regulating the *flow* of cash: controlling the supply of money and the interest rate to either speed up or slow down the flow at any given time.

But on the invisible continent, the volume of wealth that flows, migrates, and dissipates is unprecedented—and unlinked to the flow of tangible goods. As we saw in Chapter 1, this dimension of high multiples on the new continent is driven by financial practices and by technologies that multiply the flow (or pseudo-flow) of capital, commodities, and assets, in the form of derivatives and financial multiples. In the mid-1990s, in my book *The End of the Nation-State,* I described four forces underlying this shift, all of which have become more global and flexible in their activities: investment, industry, information technology, and individual consumers.[1] These four forces are the primary building blocks of wealth today. Wealth no longer exists as an accumulation of real estate, gold, or objects of any kind; it is stored in the form of notations in networked data banks (information technology) that track investments in those industries that target and serve individual consumers.

Thus, on the invisible continent, the movement of wealth often dramatically outpaces the normal monetary "flows" of a traditional Keynesian economy. The difference in economic behavior from the old world to the new continent is as starkly different as the difference between a wave and a particle. Keynes's theories (and the theories of post-Keynesian economists, such as the supply-siders) are highly inadequate to help people predict and deal with new-continent behavior. The analogy to physics holds: Keynesian economic theory (of cause-effect relationships) is to the theory governing the new continent as the Newtonian Theorem (of cause-effect one-to-one relationships) is to the Heisenberg Theorem.

Specifically, the multiples and market capitalizations seem to follow the principles of uncertainty. As measurements of net worth, they have little to do with the actual goods and services offered by either Amazon or Priceline, for example. At the end of April 1999, Priceline.com was only one year old; yet, its market cap was already $24 billion, an equivalent to the fifth-largest company in Japan. Amazon.com is known for its extraordinary market capitalization and stock price, despite never having turned a profit on product sales. If you measured the books, music, auction items, and other goods that Amazon.com sells, or the value of airline tickets or other brokered deals offered through Priceline, you would come up with a "particle," or objective, value. But if you took your measurement of the worth of Amazon.com and Priceline.com from the market cap, then you would have a kind of "wave" measurement, based entirely on financial interrelationships. The difference between "value of goods" and "value of stock" may be unresolvable in the real world, but it has enormous real-world effects. When the multiples are big—say, 700 times earnings, as we have seen in some of the dot.com companies—then they can buy other companies by offering their own stocks. WorldCom grew to become one of the major telecom companies in the world with this method. So did Global Crossing and Qwest. AOL bought a number of cable TV and telecom companies before it absorbed Time Warner. Yahoo, a champion of portal sites, bought several companies, including Broadcast.com. Each of these companies has converted its multiples into real companies and properties. At that point, the company is no longer cyber- and portal-based; it is a group of companies comprising both old-world and invisible-continent entities. Cisco Systems, using high multiples, has acquired literally dozens of technology companies, and now is positioned as one of the largest broad-ranged Internet equipment producers in the world. Multiples are thus like signals from investors to managers, giving them new ammunition and telling them to use it to conquer the world with—or to conquer whatever they see en route to success.

If a company doesn't make use of this ammunition, then the multiples can end up as multipliers of nothing. When the market expectation of the company subsides, it is no longer worth much. Netscape did not take advantage of its initially attractive multiples, and fought head-on with Microsoft; only to be absorbed by AOL when its future seemed no longer viable on its own.[2]

In this chapter, we look at the reasons the invisible continent's economy is different from that of the old world—and the forces that might bring the new and old business environments into a costly and destructive long-term economic conflict, if the decision-makers who straddle the two worlds are not careful.

THE ESSENTIAL NATURE OF ARBITRAGE

Where does all of this multiples-based wealth on the invisible continent really come from? Some argue that it is purely speculative wealth, without any real grounding in producing goods and services, and without any boost in productivity. But in fact, the productivity gains on the new continent are both tangible and remarkable. They do not come from the kinds of competitive strategic moves of the old world: the quality and reengineering efforts, or the cost-cutting that leads to productivity gains within corporations. The productivity gains of the new continent come from the interrelationships of the network itself. They come from arbitrage. That's why they often seem so cruel, so unmanageable, and so unfamiliar to people who are trying to protect jobs and industries.

The English word "arbitrage" is fairly recent; it was coined in the nineteenth century to refer to the then-novel act of speculating in shares of stock—buying them from one exchange, selling them on another, and pocketing the difference in prices as profit. The word derives from a French word meaning "arbitration," and it has thus always conveyed a meaning of "making a judgment outside of the established courts." The word took on a connotation of greed and duplicity in the 1980s, when the "arbitrageurs" of Wall Street included convicted insider traders like Ivan Boesky. But arbitrage, in itself, is not a greedy or corrupt activity, although it can be amoral and its effects can be demoralizing, especially to people whose security is arbitraged out from under them.

Arbitrage simply means the playing off of one supplier against another, to continually bring the price of goods and services down, and the quality up—not through control or negotiating, but simply through choice. If you are dissatisfied with the old sources of supply, you eliminate the difficulties by finding new partners that operate in a less fettered way. Giving up your fettered partners may mean making some people unhappy, eliminating some middle people, or changing your habitual practices, but the savings are so great that the new choice is necessary. No business can justify refusing the advantages of an arbitraging choice.

In the past, lack of information was the reason for not being able to make the best judgment. On the invisible continent, because of the continuing proliferation of new platforms, there are many more opportunities for arbitrage, and more emerging every day. Thus, people find it difficult to maintain loyalty to any single supplier or customer. Arbitrage provides golden opportunities to establish new partnerships and create new businesses, but unless you understand the full scope and dynamics of the invisible continent, you may not be able to take advantage of these opportunities.

Arbitrage represents the new continent's way of making judgments about the worth of goods and services, outside of any established regulatory body. The network of opportunities is so large, so flexible, and so uncontrollable that it is not just possible, but inevitable, that customers will move rapidly to find the best and cheapest opportunities for themselves. In a world of constant arbitrage, buyers always have more opportunities, but no entrenched professional or institution is safe.

Arbitrageurs manipulate the paradoxical ambiguities between the "particle" identity of the old-world economy and the "wave-like" identity of economies on the invisible continent. If you understand the relationship between the two worlds, you can find opportunities for arbitrage by seeking venues that can provide services via the invisible continent for much lower costs than their old-world equivalents. A traditional old-world credit card company, for instance, might find itself only able to offer you 3 percent handling costs. They could not go lower because of the expense of checking credit ratings through the established credit rating services. But an invisible-continent credit card company could use the platform of the Internet to check directly with customers' banks, assess potential customers' bank balances or time-deposit, and assign their own credit rating on the spot—offering lower than 1 percent rates with the money they don't spend on "credit" services.

A FIELD GUIDE TO THE NEW ARBITRAGE

There are seemingly infinite varieties of arbitrage, with many, no doubt, yet to be invented. These are some of the most common and most noteworthy:

Evading the Traditional Value Chain

One of the largest Internet shopping sites, Value America, has no warehouses or distribution centers. They send their orders directly to manufacturers and distributors, who send the products directly to customers. The Value America Web site looks like that of a department store (visitors often ask where the nearest location is, only to learn that the company has no physical locations). But the business itself is much more like that of a broker. Value America does not "buy" goods to mark up and sell on; in effect, it refers customers to products, promoting the products it deems worthwhile, and collecting a broker's fee from every sale. It also performs another vital service—monitoring the quality and responsiveness of the transactions it facilitates. When there is no direct contact, being able to guarantee trust is paramount.

In short, Value America has arbitraged the traditional value chain. The conventional problem with retailing is the narrowness of margins after everyone takes their cut: manufacturer, warehouse, wholesaler, distributor, buyer, and sales staff. In addition, most supermarkets and department stores are engaged in the expensive business of buying, selling, and maintaining real estate. Perishables also add costs for retailers, as meat, milk and vegetables get rotten on the shelf. Most of that is dispensed with in the Value America system (or the system of BayNet, its recent competitor).

This approach wreaks havoc with the conventional corporate attitudes and structures. In traditional hierarchical systems, corporate leaders seek to dominate the "value chain," as Harvard Business School professor Michael Porter calls it—generally by buying up their key suppliers and industrial customers, to put them all under one hierarchical umbrella. A typical company might establish control over a chain that stretches from R&D to engineering to manufacturing to marketing to sales to after-sales services. In each major market, and in each important country, a similar structure is established. IBM USA, IBM France, and IBM Japan are all organized to exert as much control as possible over every step of the value chain.

But companies that thrive in the new continent don't need that structure. They tend to develop a very small central group of decision-makers, like a brain trust, and they cheerfully arbitrage every other function, looking for the best possible deal, with the highest quality for the lowest cost—from inside or outside the company. For example, a Silicon Valley firm may contract out its R&D development work to a group of engineers, and then send the implementation of software detail to another group of engineers in Hyderabad or Bangalore, India. Component procurement may be handled by a Singapore firm, and the product may be assembled in low-cost factories in Vietnam or northeastern China. The final assembly of modules may take place through FedEx or UPS, the billing and accounting may be completely handled by a credit card company, and commercial advertising may be outsourced nearly entirely to J. Walter Thompson. A company managed, essentially, by only a tiny cadre of people could generate billions of dollars in sales. The result, shown in Figure 2, is the web-shaped company as opposed to the pyramid-shaped or value-chained company of the twentieth century.

Removing the Middleman from Brokerage and Sales

In the last decade, a satellite-based auction system called Aucnet has emerged in Japan. Anyone, anywhere in Japan, can offer their car for sale to everyone who tunes in. Since the auction is not local, the price is perceived as fair—after all, the car fetches the highest price that anyone in the country would pay.

As we saw in Chapter 2, Priceline.com has applied the same principle to airline ticket prices in the United States. The Priceline Web site invites

...migrating toward a web-shaped corporation

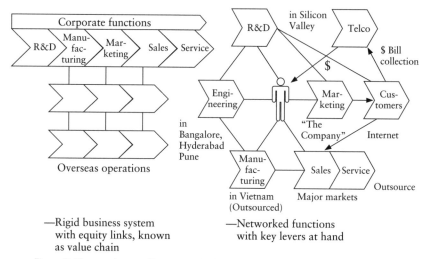

A 20th-Century Company   A 21st-Century Corporation

—Rigid business system
  with equity links, known
  as value chain

—Networked functions
  with key levers at hand

Figure 2. Changes in prevailing corporate structures, migrating toward a web-shaped corporation, show the influence of the invisible continent. At left, a conventional company of the 1980s is shown: a rigid business system with corporate functions in a well-ordered chain of routines, with equity links that allow the "central" corporate functions to control the overseas operations at the "edges." At right, a new-continent company of the twenty-first century is shown: All of the scattered functions are out-sourced, all with links (direct or indirect) to the individual who is overseeing a particular product (just to the left of Marketing), with a web of cross-ownerships and equity stakes. The networked functions are outsourced with the key levers at hand, but the whole organization works as a virtual single company (VSC).

would-be travelers to suggest the price they would be willing to pay for a seat. The airlines bid for the most desirable purchasers with their commodity currency—empty seats on flights, seats that would otherwise not be sold. In a system like this, the consumer has the upper hand, at least as long as there is a surplus of empty seats.

The growth potential of arbitrage in this field is enormous, when you consider that the world's largest industry is destination tourism—it is bigger, in revenues, than the automobile industry. Many travel purchases—airline tickets, hotel rooms, car rentals—are essentially commodity purchases with a large amount of leeway in prices.

Any field is ripe for the arbitrage of traditional sales forces. Industry Net was set up to use the platform of the network to replace the brokers of wholesale electrical and mechanical components—in effect automating what used to be a highly labor-intensive task, the task of procurement. Thirty thousand companies had registered their catalogs on this system, before it went belly-up and was reabsorbed by Perot Systems in 1997. While this particular effect has not yet materialized, it is certainly a field in which global arbitrage is attractive. Electronic, mechanical, and automotive components, particularly spare parts, are 75 percent "air"; the prevailing system of distribution is so inefficient, rife with unproductive inventories in a long supply chain, that directly connecting suppliers to buyers around the world makes enormous sense.

Arbitraging Communications and Reinventing Distribution

In the mid-1990s, the Japanese government raised its postage rates for direct mail from 62 yen to 80 yen for a first-class letter. Within weeks, a number of arbitraged solutions became commonplace. Many direct-mail vendors discovered it was cheaper to carry their mail to Hong Kong and air-mail it back to Japan from there, than to send it within Japan. The government responded with a law banning bulk mail leaving Japan. The result was a loss for the Japanese printing industry; circulars are now sent electronically to Hong Kong, printed there, and mailed back to Japan. Arbitrage has effectively checkmated the Japanese government's attempt to raise postage rates, and it is doing the same to governments around the world.

The fax machine has long been known as a vehicle for arbitraging postage rates—and making real gains in speed of transmission as well. This has provided broad new opportunities for such well-known retailers as L.L. Bean, J. Crew, and Land's End. All three of these companies make more than $120 million per year of sales in Japan alone. Most of them send catalogs to Japanese consumers, who in return place orders by fax. The companies then use either UPS or the U.S. Postal Service to ship directly from the U.S. The expensive Japanese distribution and transportation postage rates are arbitraged. But the fax is impractical for bulk transmissions, so it in turn is being arbitraged by electronic mail, and in particular, by electronic transactions. Currently the i-mode, the Internet service established by Japan's largest mobile phone operator, DoCoMo, charges only 1 yen (1 cent) for sending a packet of data via e-mail. Almost all critical communications fall within this limitation, and the phone is selling literally by the millions.

Something similar is taking place across the world with long-distance communications. For example, 70 percent of all trans-Pacific telephone calls are logged as if they originate in the United States—even when they are placed from, say, Japan. This is because the United States telephone system, being deregulated, is a far less expensive place from which to originate international calls. People from Europe, Asia, and even Canada routinely find services that will simulate the origination of a call in America. This is so prevalent that it is threatening the survival of established long-distance telephone companies, such as KDD. In December 1999, KDD was indeed absorbed in a three-way merger of DDI and IDO to form a new DDI, controlled by Toyota and Kyocera.

And this innovation is also short-lived. Within a few years, Internet-based telephone calls will probably be commonplace, meaning that all telephone calls through the switched network will become essentially local calls. On the Internet, with its digital packet-switched platform, it costs no more to carry a voice around the world than to the next block. The charge will be a fixed rate, regardless of how far the call travels or how long it lasts.

Less visible than the arbitrage of postal and telephone rates is a far more significant shift—a much larger change in distribution in general. During the past twenty years, in most developed nations, the costs of basic goods such as food and clothing have continually fallen. The reason has nothing to do with improvements in agriculture or manufacturing. Distribution is much more efficient today, and the reach of fast distribution systems is global. A grocer in New York buying citrus fruit need not choose only between California and Florida oranges; the grocer can leverage access to Brazil, Israel, and Central America. Local farmers everywhere must be humble, because the cost of bringing new foods to compete with them is continually getting smaller. Japan has established networks for transporting perishables, particularly fish and sashimi, in chilled and frozen containers from all corners of the globe. Similarly, local labor unions will soon discover that their most effective weapon is not fighting overseas competitors, but joining the new continent themselves, and seeking to develop unique capabilities that will impel customers around the world to want their goods.

Losing the Limits of Time

A growing number of Japanese businesspeople are switching their accounts from local banks, which close their shutters at 3 P.M., to Citibank—an American bank that never sleeps. Operating outside of Japanese regulations, Citibank is open twenty-four hours per day. This gives Japanese people capabilities that they never had before, such as telephone banking and access to automated teller machines. And it's the bank's overseas branches, located in the U.S., Taiwan, and Singapore, that offer high-risk/high-return instruments through the Internet that are not available in domestic Japan.

Because the new continent circumvents global time zone limits, it allows people to arbitrage their efforts past the ordinary constraints of time. Most Japanese financial institutions, in addition to subsidizing the payback of bad debts from the bursting of the bubble, must compete with a Citibank that has no need for extensive physical branches and thousands of clerks at the counter. Citibank is no longer a network of branches, but products and services offered on the network. The bank does not even have to exist within the country where customers reside.

In a traditional company, employees punch in at nine o'clock, punch out at five, and collect overtime if they leave at seven. Those companies will change their practices very quickly when they enter the new continent, because they cannot compete on a nine-to-five schedule. On the new continent, if an American engineer is sleeping, his counterpart in Bangalore, India, is up and working. Projects that can be organized in global teams can be completed faster, simply because they need not wait for all the team to come to work and leave at once. The concepts of overtime and commuting rush hours will soon disappear as Web-based companies become more or less standard.

Already companies on the new continent are finding it difficult to pay people for the time they spend at work. They operate much more effectively by paying people for the results they produce. This provides a negative incentive to people who spend much of their time at work looking busy or doing nonessential tasks. A corporation can now arbitrage R&D, production, personnel, finance, information systems, and even a sales force on a global base.

Unfolding Currency

Whenever I earn money in Japan, I divide it into thirds. I convert one-third to dollars and another third to euros, and I leave the rest in yen-denominated instruments. No matter what happens to each of these currencies' economies, the chances are that some of these will do well, and my retirement savings will be protected. In essence, I have arbitraged my way around the insecurities of any particular national currency.

At the same time, I carry in my wallet a universal financial settlement instrument. It is called a credit card. I continually monitor the relative strength of my holdings' three currencies: the yen, euro, and dollar. Whenever I buy goods, I settle with the strongest currency. I pay with the dollar when it is strong, and with the euro or yen when the dollar is weak. This makes me, as a consumer, independent of the policy mistakes of any particular government.

Any credit card purchase is a kind of arbitrage, because it technologically bypasses the need for currency conversion at a border crossing. The transaction exists purely between the buyer and seller, and government oversight of the transaction exists only in the most perfunctory manner. Nor would it be easy for governments to impose more rigid oversight, because most of the transaction takes place outside any particular government's jurisdiction. Most efforts to deal with this so far have posited that the location of the vendor should determine taxation—so that if Amazon.com stays in Washington State, the state of Washington and the United States government should be able to tax all transactions. But if those governments exercise that right, then it's only a matter of time before Amazon.com and other vendors arbitrage their locale, by moving to some offshore location, or a new cyber-equivalent to Delaware, a state with lenient tax laws. Before long, local governments will compete to give tax breaks to electronic commerce retailers, in the same way that they now give breaks to companies that build factories in their locale.

Conceivably, credit card companies, or any institution conducting cross-border transactions and settlements, could take on the responsibility for taxation themselves—holding 5 percent from each purchase and allocating the amounts according to the source and destination of traffic. "This month, 30 percent of the transactions began or ended in America, so the U.S. gets 30 percent; Japan gets 15 percent, and Germany gets 10 percent." This approach would be popular because it would reduce the "friction" that might slow down transactions otherwise; it would allow people to make purchases without worrying if the sales tax is included. But it would also put the jurisdiction and decision-making over taxation in the hands of credit card companies, or any companies performing settlement functions. At that point, these companies will be the most sovereign entities on the structure of international consumer trade—at least as influential on the invisible continent as most governments and central banks. Arguably, they are already more influential in the cyber dimension.

What checks would then exist on the power of credit card networks? What would prevent them from abusing their information about transactions, or from favoring some clients over others? If they abused their monopolistic positions then they, too, would be arbitraged. People would switch to more transparent and accessible financial transaction systems, which would emerge as soon as there was a need—because the platforms of international telecommunications, particularly what is known as "secured networks," would make it easy for new and cheaper systems to emerge when needed.

Bypassing Trade and Tariff Restrictions

To the arbitrageurs of the new continent, trade and tariff restrictions are irrelevant, because they are so easy to bypass. People living in Japan have a clear reminder of that reality every time they sign on to Bargain America, a shopper's Web site on the Internet. Originally set up to help Japanese people find mail-order catalogs from the United States, Bargain America reconfigured itself as a direct-shopping source for products that are hard to find, highly taxed, or restricted outside the U.S. The company, based in San Jose, California, was founded by a former manager of Microsoft's Japanese operations and a former marketing executive at Apple Computer and Regis McKenna, the premier Silicon Valley public relations firm. In other words, this was not a venture by conventional retailing or mail-order people, but a venture by computer-savvy people who recognized a potential gap that they could capitalize on as arbitrageurs.

Japanese people, in particular, use Bargain America to order American products without having to clear them through Japanese wholesale import restrictions. The products include drugs and cosmetics (Nicoderm, Nicorette, Rogaine, dietary supplements, cold medicines, vitamins, and skin care products are popular), Coleman stoves and outdoor jackets, and brand-name fashions. (Chances are that by the time you read this, the product mix will have changed.) The company is popular enough that more than a hundred thousand people have requested its e-mail newsletter, and it has taken on the role of translating the Japanese and American consumer cultures to each other.[3]

By now there are hundreds of participants in this kind of cross-border arbitrage. Due to the pressures from companies like Bargain America (along with many others, including U.S. catalog houses, and local discounters and outlets), Japanese consumer prices have started to come down in the mid-'90s and have descended almost to match those in the U.S. In the 1980s, when the Japanese Ministry of International Trade and Industry (MITI) and the United States Trade Representative (USTR) negotiated to the point of exhaustion over Japanese import tariffs, not much change resulted. But then the prices of American goods started to fall in Japan on their own. The brutal face of arbitrage by many types of participants had succeeded where decades of negotiations had failed.

Those who argue for curtailing free trade, because they believe that free trade curbs the right of countries to offer environmental and labor protections, are actually arguing against the effectiveness of arbitrage on the invisible continent. And they are quite right in their assessment of its potential impact on government power. There is as yet no effective police in this frontier territory. A government that restricts political literature or pornography cannot stop its people from ordering those materials from an online book service. A government seeking to impose tariffs or consumption taxes cannot implement them in a world of multiple vendors and full electronic (including telephone and fax) access to them. If a man imports Viagra or Nicoderm on the Web, into a country that has not yet approved the drug, there is no agency that can fully enforce that restriction. And if there is a grievance over something that happened on the Internet, there is no cyber-court with jurisdiction, because no body of international law has yet agreed on the parameters of cyber-crime—and even if such a body did agree, there is no consensus on whether and where that court would have sovereignty.

Is it a crime, for instance, for residents of one country to cross national borders to shop and not pay tax? It could be a crime in certain countries. But there is no court to enforce the law if it takes place outside the established customs apparatus. And during the hiatus of the next decade, before the governing law of the new frontier is established, the earliest settlers are establishing precedents and stakes that will be very hard to uproot later. For instance, new retailers such as Value America, eBay, and Amazon.com have become established enough to be influential. Part of their business proposition includes the avoidance of local tax. It will be very hard to reimpose national customs agents on the new continent after the fact.

Belaying Bureaucracy

Personally, I can't wait until bureaucrats are replaced with machines. That's because, as a small business owner operating in Japan, I am continually stifled by Japanese bureaucracy. Many of the consequences of this bureaucracy are so absurd that they have become part of our national folklore—stories we tell ourselves to show how absurd life can be. For example, a local group in Osaka wished to install a sculpture on Route 2 as it entered the city. This required the approval of the national government, which technically owns the road; a bureaucratic commission in Tokyo, five hundred kilometers away, voted the statue down. After five years of negotiation, the mayor of Osaka won the right to put it on the pedestrian path near the road.

But people have been bumping into the new statue when they walk at night, so it needed to be illuminated. Once again, the central government in Tokyo had to grant approval. This time their answer was no, because "It would unfairly drain electricity from the power utility." It took another several years to get illumination for these sculptures. In the end, residents on both sides of the street offered to run cables from their buildings, and volunteered their electricity.

Not long ago I heard from a representative of an American luxury retail chain. He was complaining because in another Asian country (not Japan), they had begun efforts to build a new store. It took three years to get the permits, and three years to navigate through construction, because of the bureaucracies they encountered. "By the time it opened," he said, "the customers we counted on had all found other places to go."

Fortunately, being a bureaucrat is destined to be a short-lived occupation, at least on the invisible continent. Voice pattern recognition, for example, may be used as an "electronic signature" and may thoroughly change the technology of interaction with democratic governments—in effect, arbitraging bureaucracy. When a citizen registers to vote, he or she would now become eligible for getting permissions and other government approvals via the telephone. Those who cannot speak would be given special personal identification numbers (PINs) to key in. Any sculptor who needed a permit would simply submit the appropriate information and receive approval through an automated process. Nor would it be necessary to go to government offices to get, for example, a driver's license or building permit—and the security of the system would be tighter than it was under the old paper-bound approach. A prototype form of this system, called "Easy Permit," is being developed as part of the Smart Valley initiative in Santa Clara County, California. Singapore's IT2000 project and Malaysia's Multimedia Super Corridor have their own versions.

Why would governments offer such services to captive populations? Because populations may not be so captive. Soon many of us will be able to choose the location of residency and citizenship, depending on the "service offerings" of different governments. Today some companies locate themselves in the state of Delaware, Grand Cayman, Ireland, or in the Isle of Man. Some wealthy individuals "live" in Hong Kong and Zug, Switzerland, though they may work or keep their families elsewhere. Likewise, soon there will be governments issuing passports, driver's licenses, and the like on the Web in exchange for collecting tax. In effect, they will offer sovereign services online. Some corporations purchase medical insurance for their employees around the globe, making it available to them wherever they go; in a similar fashion, most public services could be purchased and offered around the globe for expatriates everywhere, and ultimately perhaps for noncitizens as well. This means that even government health services can be arbitraged when the security of the network and transaction become commonplace. The first step is developing a widespread platform for recognizing fingerprints, palm-prints, irises, or voice patterns, so that an individual's "online presence" is 100 percent guaranteed.

To be sure, any arbitraging system that threatens to bypass account-able government officials will raise legitimate concerns about invasion of privacy and abuse of power. For the moment, let's not lose those concerns, but let's hold on to them until we can explore the ramifications of the new continent in more detail. In Chapter 7, on the evolution of democracy, we'll return to the question of effective government.

Arbitraging Professions

People of an earlier generation often believed that knowledge-based professionals, such as teachers, lawyers, doctors, accountants, and consul-tants, had the most secure and rewarding jobs. But on the new continent, the life of a professional is uncertain, and the security of "certified" pro-fessionals is highly precarious—unless they learn how to add value to the customer's intrinsic hidden needs.

The arbitraging of traditional teachers, for example, is taking place suddenly and dramatically. Observers have predicted for decades that access to telecommunications would transform education. Only now is that prediction beginning to come to pass. It turns out that telecommuni-cations in the classroom was not as significant a factor as people expected; the critical factor was the ability for parents, communities, and students to find more cost-effective teaching approaches. Schools, traditionally the venue of government, will increasingly be arbitraged into the private sec-tor, at least anyplace where the invisible continent is influential. The result, explicated more fully in Chapter 8 of this book, will be a shift in the way people think about the function and purpose of education.

One of the most prominent Japanese college-preparation companies uses the platform of digital satellite transmission to send the same recorded lessons to students all over the country. All their high school math courses are conducted by one person. He is the most popular math teacher in Japan, the Michael Jordan of high school math teachers. Every student wants to follow his lectures. This, in turn, makes his lectures more powerful; because people are predisposed to think of him as the best math teacher in Japan, they are more likely to learn from him, no matter what he does. His annual compensation is $1 million. This represents fifteen to twenty times as much as the average Japanese high school teacher gets. It's a salary so high that it must be individually approved by the company's board of directors each year. And each year, when his salary is renegoti-ated, he commands a significant increase, just like a star NBA player. Yet, to the students, he is a bargain; each student pays only $10 or $20 of his salary.

I personally became curious about this high school teacher because, as a member of the board of Nike, I have come to know how a contract is developed for the likes of Michael Jordan, Tiger Woods, and Michael Schumacher. I knew firsthand about the value of an international brand, and the way in which that person can accrue a disproportionate share of wealth to him- or herself. In the global mass media, enthusiasm (what Nike chairman Phil Knight calls "emotional attachment") is the driving force behind these deals. Michael Jordan is just one of the celebrities involved in Nike sponsorships or endorsements, but his status as a celebrity is so singular that it devalues the status of all *other* athletes, even after his retirement. Consider the fate, then, of the *second*-best math teacher in Japan. He or she, whoever it may be, probably earns around 10 percent of the best math teacher's salary. Everyone but the "Michael Jordan of math" has been devalued, cast in a support role, to fill in the gaps that, for one reason or another, the top teacher cannot or will not cover. And as interactive technology gets more and more sophisticated, and people come to trust the brand name of the "emotional leader" math teacher in Japan, those uncovered gaps will get smaller and smaller. Every other math teacher will be reduced, in essence, to an assistant, helping students make sense of the most brilliant professional's lectures. In the networked society, not only has this begun to happen in math, but it will also happen (with some variation) in every subject.

On both the new continent and the old world, celebrity is compelling, in part because it is much more cost-effective than individual relationships. An actor in a worldwide drama might make millions of dollars, but each viewer pays only a small part of that price, while theatergoers each must pay a much larger fraction of the cost of seeing an actor on the stage. But celebrities in the old world have a severe limitation; they can deal with their audiences only on the most superficial and lowest-common-denominator levels. A teenager might buy a film actor's poster to hang on a wall, but the actor will not have the teenager's poster on *his* wall; the actor and teenager relate in only the most superficial, mass-oriented way. On the invisible continent—thanks to the power of interactive media technologies, simulated conversations, rapid software response to individual requests, and high bandwidth—celebrity can provide a much more individually tailored relationship. It still comes nowhere near the fine-grained depth of a real human relationship, but it is certainly fine-grained enough to provide the same level of care that most people get from most professionals most of the time.

In the same way, computer-network-augmented professionalism is far more cost-effective than traditional face-to-face professional services, once a threshold of interactivity is crossed. Once a significant amount—not the full amount, but enough—of a professional's expertise is embedded in electronic systems, then the professional's uniqueness is arbitraged.

A CD-ROM called Family Lawyer sells for $98 in the United States. It has all the legal language, in electronic form, that anyone needs for the routine tasks that a lawyer performs: rental agreements, borrowing money, employment, divorce agreements, birth certificates, wills, joint ventures, partnerships, and more. Lawyers who merely shuffle papers and fill in forms have been replaced by that CD-ROM. Lawyers who want to remain in business must cultivate a greater depth of expertise, and the capability of giving valued advice or introspective consultation. They must be able to give advice that moves beyond mere boilerplate.

Quicken originally was marketed as a replacement for accountants. The backlash from the profession was so strong that the company's marketers hastened to change their position: "No, we work with accountants to make sure that this program augments their work." The software, nonetheless, has sold over 10 million copies. Thirteen million households in the U.S. alone use some form of electronic accounting. Accountants, to be worth a premium over the software, must be able to give advice. Quicken has reduced the commodity value of tax preparation, the arbitrageable value, to 100 dollars plus some fraction of the cost of a computer. Ultimately the same thing may happen in medicine, particularly at the diagnostic phase. It has already happened in certain aspects of architecture and contracting, such as evaluating buildings for earthquake-preparedness.

None of this requires the kind of "expert systems" that would replace professionals entirely. Such systems, ballyhooed during the 1960s and early 1970s, will probably never exist. But one or two professionals, augmented by electronic networks and packaged software, can now do the kind of work that hundreds or thousands of professionals did before. Given that level of arbitrageability, we can expect to see more and more "consumer-crowds" flocking to the few charismatic professionals whose electronically mediated service feels as compelling as the one-on-one service that professionals expensively provided in the past.

Awareness of this possibility for arbitrage has influenced my own work as a professional consultant. In October 1998, I launched a digital-satellite-based television station in Japan. This company, named Business Breakthrough (www.bbt757.co.jp) broadcasts management programs around the clock. Several hours a day, particularly at night, the top consultants and professionals come on air live through a high-quality digital satellite, responding to questions that come in from viewers over the Internet. In other words, the best professionals are available for Q&A on management issues, including personnel problems, finance matters, IT, logistics, operations, organizational dynamics, and strategy. I personally appear every Sunday evening for two hours; one hour of lecture and another of active Q&A. This way I can leverage my twenty-seven years of experience as a management consultant with thousands of executives and also make myself available to their needs. Before, the maximum number of clients I could possibly serve was around a dozen. Now it is unlimited. The members also get the benefit of cross-fertilization with other members with similar interest.

In September 1999, Business Breakthrough added a broadcasting of MBA programs by prominent schools around the world. In order to ensure attendance, the program requires enrolled students to log on to the Internet, and to punch in certain keys at certain intervals. The instructors can check the attendance as well as conduct tests. An MBA used to be available to a handful of wealthy students, but now quality courses can be made available to literally thousands of earnest students around the world. Now the certificate itself won't mean as much in the future, just as the lawyer's and accountant's license will mean less, but the question remains: What do you do with it? It turns out there is a lot to do. In the twentieth century, most industry needed only a handful of smart people to figure out what the rest of the company or troops needed to do. However, life in the invisible continent is fundamentally different. Value is added intellectually. This means that the Harvards and Stanfords should produce millions of well-educated and trained students, not hundreds and thousands. Unless they respond to this demand, they will not produce what the invisible continent needs: people by the millions who can think and act effectively across the four dimensions of the new economy. We need to empower more people who can take initiative beyond the manuals, not merely memorize and obey them.

A PRICEABILITY-BASED ECONOMY

The ease of arbitraging professionals, and the "Michael Jordanization" of capability on the new continent, have profound implications for jobs and education around the world. When the single highest-ranking player gets the bulk of the reward, what happens to the rest of the team? They cannot continue to make a living as the imparters of "canned" or rote information. That role has been taken from them. They can now survive only by becoming partners and counselors in discussion with their customers (or if they are teachers, with their students).

Moreover, their capability for setting prices has gone through a dramatic change. The price is no longer based on a credential shared with other professionals. It is based on people's willingness to pay for services, which in turn depends upon the extent to which a professional—or anyone in the new continent's economy—can create perceived value, based on real satisfaction.

That may sound so obvious that it's trite—"Of *course*, the price is based on the perceived value"—but in the old world, prices are rarely set that way. They are set through systems of control. Most professionals in the old-world economy are accustomed to establishing basic prices through professional associations: teachers through their unions, doctors through groups like the American Medical Association that lobby for limits on new entrants to the profession, accountants through CPA firms. This system, like the medieval artisans' guilds, assured members of the profession that their earning power would be sustained at some minimum level, by collective bargaining or by controlling the supply of professionals. Suddenly an arbitraged economy has destroyed that assumption. In other situations where the supply of professionals has been abundant, as with the American Bar Association, they have collectively become very innovative and expanded the market itself. More and more professionals on the invisible continent will probably follow that example.

Corporate price-setters are also accustomed to setting prices based on their ability to control and dominate their value chain, and thus reduce their costs. On the new continent, prices have less to do with costs and more to do with uniqueness of service. For example, I know an MIT professor specializing in Africa who offers three-week tours of the jungle for $15,000 per person. This package is probably three times more expensive than conventional package tours of the same terrain. Nor does he provide luxurious accommodations—for part of the tour, people sleep in camps in the "bush." But conventional tours don't have an extremely learned, fascinating speaker who can expound entertainingly for days about the animals, vegetation, human history, and tribal cultures—and how they all fit together. His tours are continually filled up, with a long waiting list. His "priceability" is high because he is not selling a tour, per se. He is selling a unique opportunity: to become an instant expert on the life of Africa.

It's like the difference between a marine-mammal-watching expedition and a trip to an aquarium. At the aquarium, if it's large enough, seeing dolphins and whales is expected. Each time you go, whales will be there. You will always see the same whales, doing the same things. But out on the boat on the ocean, the experience is more valuable, even if you don't see the mother and child whales. You know that whatever you see, it is a once-in-a-lifetime experience. You could go every week and never again see this set of whales in this kind of sunshine or twilight, in this kind of mood. That is the kind of experience for which people will pay a premium. The whole island of Maui, Hawaii, nowadays lives on this expectation. Whale-watching literally brings Maui hundreds of millions of dollars per year, year in and year out, far more than Lahaina, its well-known mecca of whaling, earned during its heyday a century ago.

Michael Jordan, when he was playing, provided a unique experience. His games, distributed in real time throughout the world via satellite broadcast, were events. The same was true for Michael Jackson concerts when Jackson was in his prime, and for Mike Tyson's boxing matches; and the same is true now for Tiger Woods's golf matches. Even if Tiger is playing poorly in a tournament, people want to watch him play. They want the camera to spend more time on Tiger than say, David Duval, who may be winning the tournament. People around the world will watch these events precisely because they are emotion-triggering events.

And because millions and millions of people watch this worldwide, each guy paying a dollar, the producer can afford to pay Michael Jordan (not Karl Malone, though his records are impeccable) or Tiger Woods extraordinary amounts of money. They use their uniqueness as a form of leverage. If they lose their uniqueness—as, arguably, Michael Jackson and Mike Tyson both did during the 1990s—then their earning power will rapidly diminish.

Nor is this priceability limited to unusual services such as ecotourism, spectator sports, or live popular music. As food, transportation, clothing, and communication drift toward commodity pricing, simply because they are so easy to reproduce elsewhere, producers can find a competitive edge only through unreproduceability. This means either creating a platform that others depend upon exclusively, or providing a good or service that no one else can provide. If you have a monopoly of insight or know-how that no one else can match, you may not need to compete in the dog-eat-dog situation of arbitrage.

To be sure, this is not the universal approach that everyone will need to take to make money. Most people still spend a greater proportion of their income on commodities than on unique experiences. But the providers of uniqueness have a much greater claim on the fastest-growing part of the economy on the new continent—disposable income. Consider, for example, a U.S. citizen earning about $50,000 after taxes—which is a comfortable, typical family income in the States. It is possible to cover the basics of life—food, clothing, shelter—for about 70 percent of that income, or $35,000. The rest of the income is disposable—it can be used in any way that the individual or the family desires.

Now suppose the citizen's income goes up to $90,000. The subsistence income is still at $35,000, but the disposable part has jumped to $55,000. More than 60 percent of that person's income is discretionary.

On the new continent, larger numbers of people cross that threshold. They are not rich, but they have more disposable income. They are interested in spending money on satisfaction, on Abraham Maslow's "self-actualization," on becoming the type of people they want to be. They will make purchases in this realm that seem to elude common sense—at least when seen from the perspective of the materially driven old world.

Paradoxically, as people make more disposable income, they are increasingly aware of their choices—and thus more determined to make that money count. So there isn't much opportunity to offer commodities at inflated prices, because commodity prices can always be arbitraged lower. Sears, Wal-Mart, and all the other established retailers have a lock on this part of the market. A new entrant is unlikely to succeed in this sphere. Heinz and Del Monte are already competing for the position of dominant supplier of ketchup; another ketchup supplier has an enormously uphill battle to fight to establish shelf space there.

In a world where people have more choices, they tend not to choose. They wait for those vendors who will make the right choices for them. For example, a movie like *Titanic* becomes a hit rather quickly, based on the buzz that it generates, which then accelerates its ability to become a hit. To be sure, there were hits in the old world—*Gone With the Wind* was nearly universally seen in its time—but not with the overwhelming acceleration, the sweeping wave of buzz, that takes place today.

Nor is the phenomenon limited to popular culture. Not long ago I was asked by the Japanese daily newspaper *Asahi Shinbun* to critique a traveling performance of the Vienna Philharmonic in Tokyo. I was obviously chosen as one of the few people who professionally practices both consulting and the clarinet. It was an enormously popular event; media paid easily a hundred times more attention to it than they would to an equivalent performance of the local NHK Symphony Orchestra. Yet, I personally believe that for nearly everyone in the audience of that performance, if they heard the performance by the NHK Symphony Orchestra of the same pieces of music, *they would not be able to tell which orchestra was which*. The quality of music was indistinguishable, yet the price was ten times as much for the Vienna Philharmonic. It was more valuable simply because, as a hit performance, it represented a unique experience; they even advertised as a "once-in-your-lifetime" performance.

Recently in Tokyo, I also went to a concert by the "three tenors" in Korakuen Baseball Stadium. Since the three tenors were using electronic amplifiers and were not necessarily in their top condition, I would rather have heard them on a CD in my living room. But the fifty thousand members of the audience, who paid several hundred dollars each, all seemed enamored. The popularity set the price—not the quality, not the cost, and certainly not the competition. In the field of emotions, price can be set to exclude the mass. In the field of commodities, price is set rationally or else it is arbitraged. Emotions are thus the great money-maker of the new continent.

THE GREATEST ECONOMIC STRENGTH

In the old world, producers dominate the economy. They set prices, they control distribution channels, and they dictate the terms of alliances. On the invisible continent, all of that power is in the hands of consumers—who, because of the new role that their arbitrage gives them in the structure of commerce, are becoming more enlightened as consumers, and better judges of their consumption, than they ever have been before. Ordinary consumers already dictate the practices of the companies that serve them directly. These companies, in turn, have unprecedented power over the decisions of their industrial suppliers. And in disputes between nations of industrial producers and nations of industrial consumers, the consumers always win—just as, in the past, producers of manufactured goods inevitably trumped producers of natural resources.

That is one reason for the paradoxical strength of Japan. As a producing nation, Japan may have declined—at least in the minds of *Time* magazine and *Newsweek*. But it is still, by far, the second-largest *consumer* economy in the world. The third-largest, Germany's, is less than half the size of Japan's in terms of GNP. Japan also has the largest trade surplus in the world, reflecting its competitiveness. It is also the world's largest creditor nation, and the nation with the largest amount of savings.

China is still far less important than Japan economically, despite the potential that Americans talk about. IBM Japan is a company with $25 billion in annual revenues. IBM China is, at best, a $3 billion company. The same proportions hold true in the automotive, tire, financial, pharmaceutical, and petroleum industries. If you are looking for markets to enter that will help you succeed on the new continent, seek the markets with the greatest consumer power and discretionary income. That is much more important than pure population, or than the potential for production. If I were starting a business, I would go to India to help with my software production—indeed, I have done exactly that. But I would not seek out India as a site for locating the business. I would reserve that for a country with a more advanced, or more rapidly advancing, consumer presence.

This is the greatest argument in favor of free trade, and it is an argument that could not have been made before the onset of the invisible continent. The Richard Gephardts of the world presume that jobs will automatically follow investment; and that investment will automatically migrate to the places where labor is cheapest, and where environmental controls are most lax. That was true (and continues to be true) in the old world. But it is no longer true on the new continent.

On the invisible continent, jobs can be anywhere—and jobs are most needed wherever they can most effectively, most efficiently provide high-quality contact with customers. Therefore, jobs inevitably will go wherever the market is. Instead of following the cheapness of labor, jobs will follow the discretion of customers. This is as true for high-paying manufacturing jobs as it is for low-paying service jobs; indeed, on the new continent, the manufacturing and service components of a job blur together, and the value of a job no longer depends on the distinction between manufacturing and service.

There are several reasons for this. First, with the speed and cost of distribution arbitraged, the typical supply chain may take two weeks to get from investment to product delivery, instead of two years. Second, the reliance on alliances instead of equity-based control (arbitraging corporate functions) means that it is possible to assemble a skilled team to solve a problem more quickly. And third, the higher levels of communication allow for the direction of labor forces with much less expensive controls. All of this means that investments in labor can be much more fluid than they were in the old world. The companies that develop the capability for fluid labor find they save on transportation costs by having items assembled either on the fly, or near the customers. This is one of the reasons Dell can still assemble in Austin, Texas, and Gateway in South Dakota. In the logic of the old world, they would long ago have moved into China for production.

Ultimately, if you have the full control of the customer interface and the logistics of distribution, you can do anything between them. In other words, the winners in the twenty-first century will be those who control the customer interface (known as "portal" sites in the online world), and the delivery of goods and services. Examples of the former are Yahoo, AOL, and MSN, and the latter are UPS and FedEx (both U.S.), and Yamato (in Japan). These two functions are essential to close the order-to-delivery circle of the new continent, but the rest of the value chain functions—engineering, manufacturing, retailing, after-sale service, and more—can all be either lumped, or outsourced to the best vendors and alliance partners. As we move to the next phase of the business-to-consumer battle, electronic wallets will replace credit-card-based settlements. Soon the winning e-commerce operators will have to possess a trinity of services: portal, settlement, and logistics operations.

The greatest argument against Gephardt is the recognition that America's strength since 1984 lies with the businesses that have looked precisely for niches next to their customers, wherever their customers happen to be. That's why unemployment is at a historical low at the same time that basic manufacturing jobs have fled America for other nations that can produce products more cheaply, although final assembly may still remain in the U.S. In the end, the residents of the old continents, known as "protectionists," have lost their arguments because the survival of community depends, now, more on the happiness of consumers than on the location of producers.

A PORTAL REVOLUTION

Increasing amounts of flexibility will be needed in the years to come to enter the new continent, because consumers are also becoming more unpredictable. The level of choice they will face is going to expand far beyond the choices they have today, as the Internet becomes a more popular purchasing medium. As suggested in Chapter 1, the sales numbers ($5 billion) for the 1999 Christmas shopping season in America were notable. But the 1998 season, with sales of $1.5 billion, was more notable still. Because the stock market had had a turbulent year in 1997, many observers had expected weak Christmas sales; instead, they were very strong. But that was not the most significant aspect of the season. Typically, 30 percent of the purchases of all American consumer durables occur during the Christmas season—and there is a sharp drop of sales thereafter. This time, however, the online shopping "boom" continued through the spring of 1999, and on into the rest of the year. As a result the Internet-related stocks, such as Yahoo, eBay, AOL, and Priceline, shot up sharply in the first half of 1999. Some of these companies recorded unprecedented price/earnings ratios (PEs) of 700 times earnings. I think of December 25, 1998, as "Portal Memorial Day," memorializing the war among companies vying to become the consumers' first port of entry into the world of the Internet. This role, as a portal, has become a vital foothold for staking a claim on the new continent.

In the old-world (and the visible-dimension) ways of thinking, it doesn't make any sense that a consumer-driven economy would be healthy. Consumer demand, according to the old economic maxims, leads to producer shortages, which leads to higher wages and prices—and thus to a spiral of inflation. The new continent does not operate according to those rules. On the new continent, by exercising their ability to arbitrage, consumers keep inflation from overtaking the economy. In other words, the continual availability of new sources of production, and consumers' ability to arbitrage across them, means that no producer can set prices too far above the floor, at least without adding significant value. Otherwise, his customers will simply leach away from him.

At least, that's true in the consumer economies. But there is another side to the coin: Less-developed economies and newly industrialized nations will find it increasingly difficult to catch up with this customer-knowledge-intensive, consumer-driven world. That is why their perceived purchasing power has gone down in the last few years in relative terms; and that is why they find it so difficult to escape recession or depression. Furthermore, the mindless arbitrageurs and speculators come into the economy in a hurry, and go out quickly after "short-selling" their currencies and stocks. (Even the United States has difficulty in maintaining economic equity under these pressures: The income spread between the top fifth and bottom fifth in America has widened during the Clinton "cyber-euphoric era.)[4] It is part of our responsibility, as citizens of the invisible continent, to provide equitable pathways through which developing nations (and the less blessed in developed countries) can come aboard. For the consumer economy is not the same as it was thirty years ago in countries like the United States and Japan. Then people were trying to buy the things they needed as members of the burgeoning middle classes. Today there is nothing left to buy for many of these people—except the experiences and opportunities to make their lives better and richer. The most successful businesses are those that give people choices that make their consuming, and their personal investing, more effective and satisfying. In the past, people assumed that having a strong economy would lead to a more educated population. Today we see the cause-and-effect operating in the opposite direction. In any nation where enough people exist with the wherewithal and education to do this type of intelligent consuming, the economy itself has an innately strong foundation.

THE INVISIBLE-CONTINENT DOG AND THE OLD-WORLD TAIL

In the next chapter, we will consider further what this means for companies. But what does it mean for countries and governments? It would be wonderful to leave the chapter on an optimistic note derived from the rosy outlook of consumers. But the consumers of the invisible continent do not operate in isolation. Their world, in turn, is shaped by the flows of investment and competition. Those flows, in turn, continue to threaten the viability of the new continent's economy, and of the economy of the old world as well.

The basic disparities between the finances of the old world and those of the invisible continent are scale and speed. Operating in the "dimension of high multiples," a full-scale capital transaction (raising money, creating something new, and receiving enough return to pay back investors) takes place in multiples of 10 to 25 times the size of its old-world equivalents. And it takes place in a much faster time span, in the course of a day or an hour, or in an extreme case, in seconds. The size and speed of transactions are amplified on the invisible continent by several factors: by currency speculation, by banking practices, by the oscillating property markets (which, in a borderless world, make it easy to borrow money against moribund but overvalued real estate assets in one city and invest that money elsewhere), and by the electronic capabilities of the stock market.

These changes in speed have many effects, some more subtle than others. In his book *The Age of Heretics,* Art Kleiner describes how the increased speed of the new continent led to a dramatic shift in the density of transactional relationships.

> In the 1400s, a business transaction might take eleven years to complete. Families dominated business, simply because business moved too slowly for individuals to master it. In the 1930s, a transaction took a week, or a quarter, or perhaps a couple of years to complete, and individuals created their own large-scale enterprises. They threw away the vernacular ties of family and community. Now [we live] in a world where a transaction took only a few seconds to complete; or if it took more than a few months to fulfill an order, that was a sign that something was wrong. As a culture, we were not prepared for the ways in which this speedup would allow the vernacular spirit, the spirit of [community], back inside the belly of the industrial beast.[5]

This fine-grained web of new relationships, made possible by the increased speed of transactions, gives power to those who know how to build such relationships. As Kleiner notes, traders who work the networks of the invisible continent no longer depend on established sources of capital. They draw it from a variety of places, taking only minutes to develop the kind of trust that once would have accrued to a family over generations.

At the same time, the weight and speed of capital shift in the new continent inevitably affect the direction and flow of capital in the old world. Moreover, the new continent's economy is "fictional" in a way that the old world's economy is not. Many of its transactions are decoupled from the genuine buying and selling of goods and services. For example, an investor may own property in Tokyo. In the old-world economy, this property may be rapidly moving toward bankruptcy; its owner most likely cannot find tenants who will pay enough rent to support its expenses. But in the new continent, the property is collateral for a loan for money which, when invested in another city, can help pay for the property—and more. The property isn't needed, strictly speaking, to borrow the money, but the bank believes that it is needed.

If the property owner starts to borrow against the money the bank has loaned him, however, then a vicious cycle begins. To cover the interest on the property loan, ever more money must be borrowed. If the investments are slow to be realized, the cash flow must be maintained. As long as the boom around the investor continues, there will probably be just enough money coming in to cover immediate expenses. But sooner or later the bubble will burst. At that point, the cycle will reverse. The negative cash drain will become overbearing. Taxation and pension laws will tie up more money than is necessary. The big losers will not be the property owners (whose bankruptcy is also, in a sense, "fictional") but the governments that have depended on those "fictional" revenues as if they were real.

Recently even some economists who have discounted the impact of information technology in the past now agree: The productivity from information technology is directly causing the overheating of the economy. As I noted at the start of this chapter, the productivity gains on the invisible continent are real, but I find myself skeptical of the influence of technology. To be sure, there are some productivity gains from information technology and new economy, but most of those gains come in the form of arbitrage. Unfortunately, that means that many of them will not show up in the records that governments use to determine taxation. They will not be taxed, and they will not contribute to national services. Governments wanting to keep up with their business counterparts, or to meet the demands of the new continent's corporations, will borrow to do so. The borrowing will look reasonable in boom times, but when or if the market falls, the illusions of wealth will become visible. All the extended giants will feel their crunches at the same time. And governments, weakened by the forces of the invisible continent itself, may not be adequate to the task at hand. We will return to consider their dilemma in Chapter 5, but first the perspective of the new corporate players must be understood.

4

WAKE-UP CALL FOR
CORPORATE STRATEGISTS

One of the best-known motion picture series first came to the screen in Japan in 1954. The plot was simple: A remote Japanese island is besieged by a monster—a long-dormant dinosaur awakened by radioactivity, more than 150 feet high, with a vicious and unpredictable temper. Through a series of movies during the next thirty years, the monster and its progeny continue to grow at an accelerated rate, ultimately reaching 328 feet tall. The Godzillas consume everything in their path, moving quickly and destructively through inhabited areas, and setting neighborhoods ablaze with their breath or with rays from their eyes. Their motives are inscrutable, their power unfathomable and uncontrollable; yet, they are beloved as well as feared. Their most notable feature—a constant characteristic recognized throughout the twenty-odd Godzilla movies—is that their chromosomes are innately different from those of any "natural" animal. Godzilla has genetic material unlike that of other reptiles or animals; its fate, therefore, is to grow and consume voraciously.

During the twelve-year period between 1975 and 1987, a new group of companies came to life in America. They represented a new kind of corporate species, seemingly genetically programmed to grow and consume markets and resources at rates that would have seemed unthinkable before. These companies are voracious. Their leaders and employees know how to take advantage of the components of the new continent. They suck up the world's investment capital; they drain Wall Street and NASDAQ. Money that goes to them is not available for investment elsewhere. They are corporate equivalents to Godzilla; they hatch fast, grow fast, and consume everything they can. Their size and speed make it impossible to deal with them strictly from an old-world mind-set. The only way to explain their phenomenal growth is to believe that these new corporations have different corporate chromosomes. They represent a more advanced evolutionary form.

The first "Godzilla"-style company was probably Microsoft, whose founders (Bill Gates and Paul Allen) made their first contract as college dropouts. They produced a version of the Basic computer language for the first personal computer, the Altair. Microsoft started small, with an initial market limited to diehard computer hobbyists; it was not even a full-time business for Allen and Gates until 1977, and its first consumer product, the operating system for the then-new IBM personal computer, was released late in 1981. Christened PC-DOS, in its IBM incarnation, and MS-DOS in its "open-platform" Microsoft rendition, it laid the foundation for Microsoft Windows, whose Version 1 came out in 1985. Since then the whole world has changed as a result of the emergence of Windows, a platform on which information, money, and even emotions and power are exchanged. Throughout all these years, Microsoft doubled in size every year—in revenues, stock price, and number of employees. It currently enjoys the world's largest market capitalization of any corporation—at $575 billion, an equivalent to South Korea's GNP.

But Microsoft was not the only company to grow at an extraordinary pace. The Oracle software company, formed in 1977, also grew at dramatic rates, not going public until 1986 but ultimately becoming the software force behind the data banks that sort and organize the information and connections of our networked society. Sun Microsystems, a voracious maker of highly powered Unix computers, was born on the campus of Stanford University in 1982. Dell Computers was founded two years later in a dorm room at the University of Texas at Austin. Cisco Systems, also founded in 1984, manufactures Internet routing hardware and software. It has had nearly 100 percent annual growth in income since its current CEO, John Chambers, took office in 1995. It currently has sales of $14 billion and a market capitalization of $320 billion—far beyond many other companies with a better-established industrial pedigree. Quantum Funds, Gateway 2000, and Cable News Network also emerged with unprecedented growth rates. America Online, TCI, D.C.M., and Rupert Murdoch's News Corporation all raised the bar in their respective industrial categories. They leapt across to the new continent, without concern for the difficulties of navigating there. And they ushered in an era of voracious growth rates that has not yet sputtered out.

The companies mentioned so far are notable for their growth in revenues and profits; but other Godzilla companies have achieved notoriety without profit. Amazon, eBay, Priceline, and many more have accelerated their share value simply by staking a territory on the new continent, focused around a particular Internet-based service or market, without ever drawing much profit to talk about. One such company, Siebel Systems, was created in 1995 as a spin-off of Oracle, as a producer of sales force automation software. The company's market capitalization at the end of 1999 was $16 billion, and the founder, Tom Siebel, became a billionaire in three years' time after leaving Oracle.

Some observers assume that there is a specious investment bubble at play in the markets today, since so much money is being drawn to companies that cannot possibly earn enough to justify their stock prices. Though one cannot preclude the presence of a bubble, there is good reason to have faith in the market in this case; investors correctly recognize that a claim in the territory of the new continent now, *if it's the right part of the territory and an authentic claim,* could be worth billions in the future.

In Siebel's case, for example, the high share price reflects the investors' expectation that Siebel may become the first company ever to integrate the Web-based customer relationship management (CRM) functions. This means that sales force automation (SFA), call center technologies (computer-telephony integration, or CTI), Web-based marketing, and Web-based sales and service management will all be offered as a coherent set of management tools: a platform on which other companies can build new types of enterprises. This platform will then hook into various well-known software packages to deal with such backroom functions as supply chain management (SCM; packages such as Manugistics and I-2) and enterprise resource planning (ERP; packages such as Oracle, SAP, and BAAN). Siebel's customers are the myriad companies that see they *have* to use the Web, and CTI, to connect their sales force with their vendors and contractors, and with their distributors and customers. By building this platform, Siebel positions itself as a pioneer of that part of the new continent, and qualifies as having the chromosomes of a Godzilla.

Common among the Godzillas is aggressive use of the three "invisible" dimensions of the new continent, described in Chapter 1:

- The cyber dimension: Godzillas use Web- and CTI-based marketing and operations to grow fast without escalating costs and stress in the organization.

- The dimension of high multiples: Through multiples, leverage, arbitrage, and hedging, the size and influence of Godzillas is far larger than their sales or revenues would imply.

- The borderless dimension: most of them reach out to the entire global marketplace right after their birth.

These three factors, in themselves, are not enough to sustain a business, and it is still not clear how many of the apparent Godzillas of the first decade of the new millennium will become extinct. If any given company is operating on high multiples alone, it may well be the result of a stock market bubble, and it will not exist for long. But if it is a true Godzilla company, then it has high multiples as a result of its fundamental characteristics—*but not necessarily the fundamentals to which conventional old-world investors pay attention.* The fundamentals of a Godzilla company represent a proven ability to take advantage of the characteristics of the invisible continent—at least the characteristics that have been discovered so far—and to secure and expand the territory from which they can uniquely harvest their crops.

TRADITIONAL COMPANIES IN A LAND OF GODZILLAS

If the Godzillas seem to have innate advantages in dominating the new continent, where does that leave conventional "excellent" companies? In my mind, I also think of them in terms of old monster movies. They are "titans"—creatures with great power, greater than ordinary humans, but without the ability to contest Godzilla effectively. These companies are inevitably defeated and absorbed by the Godzillas (as AOL has absorbed Time Warner), or driven to occupy smaller niches than they once enjoyed, or else they observe and learn, to become more like Godzillas themselves, as Nokia has demonstrated.

Titans, in our time, are very successful companies. General Electric, IBM, Hewlett-Packard, Lucent Technologies, and Sony (to name just five) are all first-rate blue-chip companies with a great deal of entrepreneurial fervor. They are greater than ordinary companies. They have turned themselves around from past failures, often by extraordinary achievement and attention to performance. They represent the biggest and best actors on the corporate stage today. But they are still operating at human scale, and the needs and values of the new continent are not natural to them. This is probably due to their more traditional (human-scale) chromosomes.

It's tempting to assume that the difference between Godzillas and titans is directly related to the age of the CEO—that younger entrepreneurs, emerging from the various Silicon jungles of the 1980s and 1990s, are naturally more attuned to the needs of the new continent. But it is not that simple. Cisco Systems CEO John Chambers is not that much younger than IBM CEO Lou Gerstner, or Citigroup co-CEO John Reed, or GE CEO Jack Welch. (In fact, Chambers spent eight years at Wang and six at IBM before joining Cisco as senior vice president in 1991.)

The difference has more to do with the organization they inherit. If Jack Welch had started an entirely new company instead of taking the helm of General Electric in 1981, that company would probably be a Godzilla today. Indeed, he spawned a mini-Godzilla in his own small way at GE with the business he headed before becoming CEO: the GE engineering plastics business. This business operated with a far more entrepreneurial and original mind-set than the chemicals industry around it. (Given the dramatic technological breakthroughs in materials and energy since World War II, it's remarkable that there are very few Godzillas in this industry. Had things been different, the chemicals and materials industries might have leapt onto the new continent side-by-side with networks, electronics, and bio-technologies. But they are still poised on the edge, waiting to make the transition, as they have been for the past twenty years.)

It's not the quality of the individual leader that's important; it's the quality of the strategic thinking that they practice and promote in the organization every day. Every Godzilla company CEO can address the issues of business process redesign (BPR) and consequent organizational and personnel changes. Thus every Godzilla business process is constantly redesigned with the latest thinking on customers, supply chain, and customer relationships. Godzilla leaders, from the CEO down through the organization, live and breathe the air of the new continent twenty-four hours a day. They make every decision in the context of the new continent, where a three-month quarter is typically counted as one year.

By contrast, the titans may be well aware of the new continent; but they also have many other things to worry about. They must worry about mainframe legacy software, power generation, and marketing to a mass audience. They must worry about the maintenance of their facilities, the cultivation of overseas sales reps, and the arrangement of international distribution channels. They are much more distracted than the Godzillas, who rely upon platforms and technological advance for the bulk of these details, and leave much of the rest behind.

Thus, Jeff Bezos, the founder of Amazon.com, can proclaim the corporate intention of being the world's largest retailer. This is clearly a Godzilla-like ambition; and the fact that it is obviously possible to realize is remarkable, especially for a company less than five years old. But if Amazon.com is the premier Godzilla of retailing, where does that leave Wal-Mart and Sears? Why are they still building new shopping malls and buying properties, in the face of Amazon's clear statement—that you don't need to be in the property business to be the world's largest retailer?

To be sure, Wal-Mart and Sears are aware of this conundrum, and it represents a genuine puzzle for them. "Yes," their executives will say in conversation. "We know we have to move onto the new continent. It's very important to be there." Then, inevitably, they add the word "but." And they have lost. The "but" boils down to this point: Changing directions represents an awfully large gamble for titans like Wal-Mart and Sears. They cannot just walk away from their investment in land, and from the experience they have developed around it. Similarly, Merrill Lynch cannot walk away from its existing network of brokers, branches, and customers to become an electronic trader. Barnes & Noble cannot turn its back on its existing network of stores, who will feel threatened if the company puts too much emphasis on electronic commerce. Self-denial is one of the hardest things to master for an otherwise very successful resident of the old continent.

The Godzillas have no such gambles at all. They do not need to maintain the same kinds of existing investments that the titans do, and thus they can put a much greater investment in new-continent activities. The titans, despite their experience and capacity, simply do not have the wherewithal to make the same investments on both the new continent and in the old world simultaneously.

Perhaps the titans are correct in not being willing to take the gamble. There is a great deal of money to be made serving people in the old world, and many people will still make purchases from physical stores on real property in the next twenty years. But that population will not be growing at the accelerating pace of the population that purchases products on an ever-more-accessible Internet. In this way, the titans are like the old-style financial titans of Europe, New England, New York, and Chicago during the period from the late 1840s through the 1900s, when the railroad reshaped the American continent. As merchants, farmers, and manufacturers, they invested in railroads because they saw the potential of cheaper freight for increasing their existing businesses. But they could not risk their comfortable status back home, they would not leave the civilization they knew, and they did not grasp the potential of the railroad for creating entirely new businesses and new civilizations. That role fell to a new set of investors. Some were speculative "robber barons," like Jay Gould, who took their profits from manipulating the prices of railroad securities. Others were corporate leaders like Cornelius Vanderbilt, who took a longer view; but both Gould and Vanderbilt (along with others, such as James J. Hill and Leland Stanford) reframed all the prevailing attitudes about business investment and management to see the new railroads move across the continent. Old-style titans, of course, continued to prosper; and they did not suffer the defeats and losses that many of the new "empire builders" faced. But neither did they gain the fantastic fortunes that accrued to Vanderbilt, Gould, Stanford, Hill, and the other pioneers of the West.[1]

Titan companies have continued to prosper in recent years, but not from creating opportunities. They have prospered by downsizing, restructuring, merging with other titans, and practicing tight management. IBM under Gerstner has cut employment from 500,000 to 250,000—to become half its former size. GM and Ford are one-third and one-half of their former sizes, respectively, in numbers of employees. The most heroic CEOs in the old world are those who cut costs; even those who build their companies are only building the companies enough to replace old wasteful activities with new profitable activities. Their businesses do quite well, but they are not creating net job opportunities. They keep the infrastructure that they had around them, and do not allow themselves to move entirely onto a frontier with a completely different infrastructure. In a recent conversation, GE Chairman Jack Welch stressed the importance of creating an "antithesis" to all existing departments, so managers do not take success for granted. He also suggested creating an internal Internet challenger for each of GE's departments, so that cannibalization will come from within rather than from without. Jack Welch's recognition that even the best-managed company might fall without formal and head-on recognition of the arrival of the invisible continent makes him an undisputed CEO of turbulent times.

A third class of company is also trying to establish itself on the new continent. These companies, unlike the titans, do not find themselves cast in the role of competitors to the Godzillas. They too have long-standing pasts, they too must work out relationships with unions, governments, bylaws, and other constraints. But they do not have the leverage of the titans. They are like the human bystanders in the old monster movies, the ones who must run to avoid being crushed. Ninety percent of the actors on the economic stage find themselves in this position. These bystanders also want to be web-shaped, and established in e-commerce, if for no other reason than getting a better multiple in their price/earnings ratio.

They too need a strategy. For the bystanders may actually have a better chance to move into the Godzillean leagues than the titans do (as was the case with Cisco before Chambers). On the new continent, after all, there is no inherent advantage to great size. Nor is there inherent disadvantage to niche markets, and many of the bystander companies already have niche markets. They need to learn how to take advantage of platforms and arbitrage, and how to turn the constraints that limit them into sources of competitive advantage. Their main advantage over the titans, if they are willing to recognize it, is simple: In the world of the invisible continent, they have less to lose.

A STRATEGY FOR THE NEW CONTINENT

The most fundamental thing that titans and bystanders need to lose, to compete at a Godzilla level, is old ways of thinking. Specifically, these companies are hampered by the established ways of thinking about corporate strategy—including some of the methods and ideas about strategy that I championed in my own writing twenty-five years ago. In 1975, in my Japanese book, *The Corporate Strategist*—and then in 1982 in an American adaptation called *The Mind of the Strategist*—I suggested that strategy could be defined as "the way in which a *corporation* endeavors to differentiate itself positively from its *competitors,* using its relative corporate strengths to better satisfy *customer* needs."[2] This approach was not unique to me; most of the established and groundbreaking strategic writers held out a similar kind of definition. All roads thus led to the same basic strategic process. Corporate leaders had to think carefully about their own capabilities and limits (corporation), using competitive research to figure out how they could match or overcome their rivals (competitors), while getting as sophisticated as possible an understanding of the needs and desires of their market (customers).

This kind of thinking spawned industries of strategic practitioners and consultants, all working for incumbent industries (and an incumbent political society), trying to come up with the most provocative and effective answers to the key business questions of the 1970s and 1980s:

- Who are our customers?

- Who are our competitors?

- What are our own corporations' unique capabilities (or core competencies)?

The same questions were tackled at a product level for product strategies, and in-house for staff functions like human resources. Remarkably explicit and elaborate answers were developed, often with remarkable insights, by such strategic visionaries as Michael Porter and Gary Hamel. Until the advent of the new continent, this represented a viable way to set strategic direction. But conventional corporate strategies are useless in a rapidly changeable, fast-moving frontier. We strategy writers could have written with much more prescience back in 1975, had we better foreseen the ways in which the new continent would change the strategy game.

Competition

Competition is no longer definable in any predictable way. For example, consider the coming war over television access. As I noted earlier, most people do not have the patience or the skills to grapple with a complex personal computer software environment, even under a graphic interface like Windows or the Macintosh. If you are accustomed enough to television, you expect images and sound to pop up within split seconds; you don't have the patience for keyboards, mice, and "clicking" through endless windows, even if the transmission time is instantaneous. If the television set evolves into a tool for access to network services, then people on the PC side of the business could find themselves on the weaker side in a fierce war. And that may already be happening, with computer games as the key missing link. As recently as mid-1998, Microsoft seemed the obvious permanent winner of the competition for computer operating systems and software. Its $500-plus billion of valuation led inescapably to that conclusion. Who would have thought that Sony would threaten that hegemony? Yet, within a startlingly short time span, the Sony PlayStation has emerged as a computer operating system on television.

The PlayStation does not resemble a typical computer operating system; it seems at first glance to simply be a TV control device to play interactive games on a CD-ROM. But its hardware and software are as sophisticated as those of most personal computers.

Released in early 2000, the Sony PlayStation 2 unit had Internet access built in with a DVD player as its platform. This $350 unit stored up to 4.8 gigabits of memory locally, more than enough to contain the entire display of a supermarket in three dimensions. And it had a large built-in audience. The previous PlayStation 1, which did not connect to the Internet, had sold 70 million units worldwide, equivalent to one-quarter the number of personal computers and workstations combined.

With its operating system, Aperios, which was licensed by other hardware manufacturers even before the PlayStation 2 release, Sony's Internet machine, via cable modem, became a personal computer platform with a non–Microsoft Windows operating system.[3] It was thus Sony, with a bunch of DVD software producers, not Netscape or America Online, that rendered the U.S. Justice Department antitrust suit against Microsoft irrelevant.

Just as Microsoft was surprised by Sony, Sony will be surprised by new competitors coming from outside their industry—not just Sega and Nintendo, but DoCoMo, US West/Qwest, and Nokia, along with service companies like Starbuck's and 7-Eleven (Southland). These companies do not regard themselves as bound by the norms of any particular industry. They go wherever their interests and capabilities take them.

Neither Microsoft nor Sony—nor the U.S. Justice Department, for that matter—can decide who wins this game; nor can anyone dictate who will end up competing with whom. Such concepts as "business battlefields" are obsolete because competition will occur in manifold, ever-shifting fashion, across the entire universe of the visible world and invisible continent.

The term "unfair competition" should also be relegated to museums of the twentieth century. In the next century, competition will be inherently fair. Consumers will choose winners and losers in a purer way than ever before. Consumers will decide, for example, whether they want their Internet access through a telephone connection, a personal computer with a fiber-optic cable, optical fiber with access to homes via wireless local loop (WLL), globally compatible CDMA cellular phones, a coaxial digital cable TV system, or a kiosk at the local 7-Eleven convenience store. (If they choose the latter, then a 7-Eleven or local gas station will become the winning platform for receiving tickets and parcels on items ordered at home.)

Or consumers may split their votes, in effect, by choosing a combination of all these media, each for a different aspect of life. Using 7-Eleven regularly for computer access might seem odd to people who now cherish their personal computers at home; but if files and electronic mail are stored on the network, it may turn out much more convenient to travel from location to location, using whatever terminal happens to be handy in an increasingly wired world, than to carry one's computer along. Likewise, the public telephone booths, connected with high-speed fiber-optic lines, might become kiosks for such transactions.

None of the roles for competing on the new continent will be static. If the PlayStation suddenly takes the worldwide Internet-portal-device market by storm—which is likely to happen, at least in Japan—that won't represent a one-time reversal of the market. It would be one of many sudden shifts in the market, which would be rife with reversals and continually beset by new "storms." That's why it would be futile, in any book, to try to describe the specific technological landscape of the new continent. One might predict that Microsoft would have control over one part of the market (such as the desktop computer) and Sony over another (such as the living room home entertainment center), and that might be true for a six-month period until the mobile phone sweeps across the invisible continent—but then in the following six months, those positions might reverse. Unix might rebound, Linux might make inroads, or Java might have a chance with the new high-speed digital cable modems. It will be less important, in the future, to know the makeup of the players, and more important to understand the forces that move players forward and back. Even in relatively slow-moving businesses, such as consumer packaged goods, the pace and uncertainty of competition will accelerate. A competitor will emerge from nowhere, dominate the terrain very quickly, and then perhaps disappear just as quickly. The business environment will be much like the Japanese game of Go, where you might feel that you're winning as you march your black stones across the table—but the pattern suddenly shifts and you see that you actually are surrounded by white stones.

Customers

Competitiveness on the invisible continent, in short, cannot be gained by focusing on competitors. Instead, successful competitors will carve out a strategic domain that they can occupy, that they believe has a ready market—and that they can hold amidst unpredictable and unknowable changes. But if this strategic domain is so critical, you may wonder, why then can't strategy simply consist of defining a potential customer base? That would, in turn, shape the boundaries of this strategic domain.

Unfortunately, customer-manufacturer relationships have been shifting during the past twenty years, so that they are now almost unrecognizable in traditional "brand management" terms. If you are a consumer electronics manufacturer, for example, your customer is not the end user, but the wholesaler. If you somehow offend, say, Circuit City, they can retaliate simply by taking your product off the shelf. You can't define your end-users as customers because they're not *your* customers. They belong to Circuit City, and the retailer is the decision-maker. Your ability to win or lose in the marketplace depends on the amount of attention and emphasis that they give to you, as opposed to the attention they give to, say, Sony, Panasonic, Ricoh, Apple, or Dell.

On the invisible continent, the situation is even more extreme: the retail platform leaders, those with the ability to draw customers directly, have far more control over the market than even a powerhouse retailer like Wal-Mart has in the old world. Hence the incentive for companies like Dell, Apple, IBM, and Gateway to sell direct. They are not just bypassing the "middlemen," or the traditional customers. They are redefining their customer relationships.

The more that retail on the invisible continent influences retail in the old world, the more that old boundaries between manufacturer/producers and distributors/suppliers break down. Microsoft is Intel's best customer. But Intel is also Microsoft's best customer. Who is the supplier to whom of these two proud companies? No one can say. You could argue that in any given circumstance, one side or the other exercises more control, but none of the aspects of their relationship is predetermined to last more than a year. Who, then, is the customer in that relationship?

Finally, the customer population on the invisible continent continually changes, just as the competitor population changes. For example, with the advent of Microsoft's CE operating system for smaller, handheld devices, the number of chip suppliers could increase almost exponentially. ComputerLand's platform position to sell PCs could also change at any moment, as sales gravitate toward less traditional retail channels. The biggest customer of an electronics manufacturer, five years hence, might be Amazon.com, Qwest, Priceline.com, or AOL giving away a free PC in exchange for their service contracts. Or it may end up being individual customers, as it is for Gateway and Dell already.

Core Competence

If competitors and customers are so difficult to define, then perhaps a strategic "fast track" would depend on being able to define your company's capabilities, so that you know which customers you can reach. However, defining the boundaries of corporations is no longer viable. The General Electrics of the world build as many capabilities as possible in-house: R&D, engineering, manufacturing, distribution, repair, and service. Then they innovate by selling their internal capabilities to outsiders. For example, many of the internal management training and development services at GE's Crotonville campus are made available to GE suppliers and customers. But the Godzilla companies do the opposite; they outsource almost everything. The core competence may be defined as the ability to manage a company that is almost a noncompany.

Cisco Systems sells its products through a complex, interwoven network of more than 120 companies. I have called this web-shaped and Web-linked *keiretsu* a "value group," to contrast it with the traditional concept of "value chain," but Richard Normann and Rafael Ramirez call it a "value constellation," which is a more romantic and semantically exciting terminology. Cisco has more than 120 partners in its Internet equipment production. They are directly involved in procurement, production, shipment, and the supply of repair parts, as if they were all acting together as a virtual single company (VSC). As shown in Figure 3, customers place orders directly into an "Electronic Retrieval Process" system on the Web—a series of menus and choice screens that allows for highly tailored configurations from a dizzying and ever-changing array of specifications, computer hardware, and software selections. When the order is confirmed, the system selects suppliers for each component, and arranges for one of Cisco's partners to manage subassembly. An integrated engineering function helps adapt the product to the customer's specs, and Cisco's own design department can tap into a database of customer-developed specifications as well.

Cisco Supply Chain Process and System

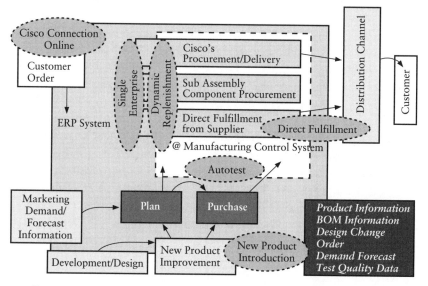

Figure 3. The Cisco supply chain process and system shows how orders proceed from the Web-based connection (at upper left) through a series of processes divided among more than 120 corporate partners. Each oval is handled by the interactive, interrelated computer system; each rectangle represents the activities of a company designated to take part in that particular order. (Reprinted courtesy of Cisco Systems, Inc. Copyright © 1999 Cisco Systems Inc. All rights reserved.)

Companies that join Cisco's partnership become, in effect, part of the corporate nervous system simply by using this platform. There are no secrets among the companies—each of them is aware of the others' capabilities and capacities and of the designs of the system as a whole. But there is no incentive to "steal" this information, for it is worth much less in isolation than the value of continued access to the platform.

To the customer, the platform is seamless; they do not know whether the router is made at a plant owned by Cisco or one owned by a partner such as Solectron. Nor is it certain, until the customer places the order, which company will manufacture which parts of the product. The only certainty is that, no matter where the product is made, it will be run through a series of automatic tests, using the Internet to link it to Cisco's testing computers (shown in the diagram as a circle labeled "Autotest"). On that basis, Cisco can feel confident about each product sold under its brand name. Since Cisco's brand name is such a critical, long-lasting, and stable part of the product—especially when every part of the technology is expected to change rapidly—the maintenance of a high-quality corporate reputation is critical.

John Chambers, Cisco's revolutionary chairman since the company started to change its corporate chromosome around 1995, claims that this system has saved the company $450 million per year, money that provides capital for R&D. But that is not the main benefit, in my view. Cisco Systems doesn't have to predict demand for routers. They make equipment to order. This means that they do not need to invest capital in materials or products that they cannot sell. Nor do they need to keep an expensive field service force.

This type of management system represents one of the primary differences between the invisible continent and the old world. When companies behave like Cisco Systems, there is no need to fear inflation. The production and distribution marketplace is too efficient to generate inflation.

Such arrangements (whether you call them *kieretsu* groups, value constellations, or something else) play a crucial role in logistics and delivery, collection of bills and production, engineering, repair and maintenance operations, and the management of critical internal functions like computer systems and personnel. Orders may come in through browsers via America Online. Assembly and delivery may take place on platforms maintained by FedEx and UPS. All of these external companies are no longer "allies" or "suppliers"; they have become an integral part of the corporate structure. Oracle, for example, has built a global business providing database software; its products are often incorporated as raw material within the consultation sold by value-added retailers such as Andersen Consulting. In Japan, Toshiba, NEC, and Fujitsu act as Oracle's partners, actively improving and interlinking the databases that Oracle maintains for them. This "partnership" has given Oracle an enviable status as a full-fledged member of the Japanese business community. When its subsidiary in (otherwise depressed) Japan went public in 1998, its market capitalization (for Japan alone) reached $9 billion; by early 2000, it was $30 billion, despite 1999 sales in Japan of only $700 million.

Nike (a sports and fitness company with many Godzilla-like qualities) contracts out its shoe manufacturing to about fifty high-class, high-quality producers throughout Asia. Their workstations are all interconnected, and thus they can produce to specified quality and number, in time for shipment. In every way but one, Nike treats these companies as if they were internal subsidiaries. Does it matter that they are actually controlled not through equity, wages, and a command-and-control hierarchy, but through a contract-based supply chain management system?

A company that outsources as much as Cisco, Nike, Gateway, Dell, or Keyence (Japan) cannot be defined by its roles and tasks. Nor are its boundaries determined by the limits of employment, equity, or by the structure of its hierarchy. After all, in a web-shaped company, financially independent entities may be linked to the central decision-making process much more closely than the subsidiaries are linked in a conventional conglomerate. Finally, if people are working twenty-four hours per day, in offices around the world, then the company can no longer be defined by the location of headquarters or by the number of people who clock in at eight-thirty and leave at five. The notion of outsourcing critical functions while sticking to core competence is rapidly fading. We no longer know the boundaries of a corporation when functions and jobs are interwoven and interconnected through networks and database. Literally dozens, and sometimes hundreds, of companies collectively perform a function of delivering the best and cheapest products and services from anywhere in the world in the shortest possible time, as if these products and services came from a single company.

BECOMING A GODZILLA COMPANY

Each Godzilla is different, so one can come up with many different theories about the most critical factors behind its success. But there are a few fundamental features that seem to be most critical, and all (if not most) of these companies have the following features in common. Other companies, if they hope to thrive, must learn to emulate the capabilities and qualities that these Godzilla companies seem to acquire by instinct, as if they were destined at birth to be different.

Clarity of Focus

Nearly all the Godzilla companies are single-product companies, or at least, single-focus companies. Oracle makes database software. Cisco makes Internet routers. CNN is focused on global news. Dell and Gateway are primarily personal computer producers. Sun Micro is a Unix server company. Intel is predominantly microprocessors. AOL is an Internet service provider (at least before its merger with Time Warner/CNN), and Yahoo is a search engine. Microsoft is a three-product company: It produces operating systems, the Microsoft Office suite of application programs, and MSN—an Internet service provider. These products continually influence each other's evolution. None of the Godzilla companies, not even Microsoft, is a full-fledged, full-standing "general production" company along the lines of the prevailing twentieth-century old-world model. They are giant-sized, but you will not find a *General* Motors, *General* Electric, or *General* Foods among them. There is no company called "General Internet." Nor will there be.

Clarity of focus is important precisely because the business environment of the invisible continent is so diverse and free of boundaries. Scott McNealy sees one specific trail for settling the new continent: focusing on providing server hardware, operated in Unix or Java systems. Bill Gates stakes out a different trail, looking to control (as industry observer Mark Anderson points out) the desktop space wherever files are created and stored.[4] This leaves room for Sony to come in and occupy the gateway between the living room and the outside world, the gateway of home audiovisual entertainment. John Chambers of Cisco Systems, meanwhile, focuses on Internet protocol (IP) infrastructure. Each company strives to excel at its particular domain. Yet, all of these companies could, at some point in the near future, end up competing with each other, just as America Online, Microsoft, and AT&T have found themselves to be competitors.

Pursuing a broad corporate purpose is not just dangerous and expensive on the invisible continent; it is unnecessary. As the new continent is so vast, one can get lost, or exhausted, if one spreads resources all over the space. That is why investors flock to narrowly focused companies; they know that no company, not even Microsoft, could take on all the roles needed on the invisible continent, from hardware to software to transactions to financial and information systems. (When Amazon.com's focus shifted from books and CDs to general merchandising, like Sears, Roebuck, that was a danger signal to investors.) And because the new continent is so potentially huge, being the perceived winner in one category is enough to rake in investment capital from investors all over the world. Finally, in an age where technology shifts so quickly, Godzilla companies need the agility that comes from being focused.

There is, of course, a trade-off. Companies traditionally have felt vulnerable when they control only one part of a value chain; that was the reason for seeking to control the full value chain in the first place. And that vulnerability will continue. But unlike the wisdom of the twentieth-century corporate strategists, controlling an entire value chain is not viable in the new continent. Godzilla company leaders recognize this. They know that this limitation will lead to casualties, fights, and divorces; many companies will be swallowed by other Godzilla companies. But in the Godzilla merger and acquisition environment, that may not be a bad fate, as shown by the AOL absorption of Time Warner/CNN.

Territories Based on Customer Primacy

In a business environment without industry-specific constraints, companies must impose their own constraints. Hence, on the new continent, only the self-constrained can grow. They grow by carving out a territory that they alone can dominate. Microsoft excels at this; it carved out the territory of the desktop computer environment, beginning with its work on MS-DOS in 1980. Then it voraciously eliminated or internalized all competitors. It overwhelmed CP/M, the previously dominant operating system; it internalized the graphic user interface of Apple's Macintosh into its operating system, the functionality of Lotus 1-2-3 into Excel, and Netscape's browser into its Explorer. It is now internalizing the hardware-independent software platform, Java, avoiding a head-on crash with the Sun-Hewlett-Packard (Unix) alliance.

One company that Microsoft failed to internalize was Intuit, the makers of Quicken financial software—in part because of the way Intuit has carved out its territory. More than ten million Americans have installed Quicken in their home or home office, which means that every bank that offers home banking must make it Quicken-compatible. Many banks and financial institutions now license the Quicken platform to give away with their services. Even the Internal Revenue Service accepts reports through the Internet from Quicken via conversion software like Tax-Link. For players in the financial industries, the name of the game has shifted, from competing with Quicken to collaborating with it—because Quicken's financial instruments have a lock on the attention of customers. Developing this platform has made Intuit the core of a large American virtual community; Quicken is not just software, but a social phenomenon in which all the financial information of medium- to high-net-worth individuals is stored. Microsoft, with its Money software, did not have the level of trust needed, in the end, to assimilate this community.

The idea of consumer primacy is not new; management theorists have preached attention to customers for decades. But since 1995 there has been an amazing shift in the degree to which technology enables businesses to be attentive to customers, in ways that were not possible before. This does not just mean *serving* customer wants, but developing a customer interface that recognizes and rewards customers for the demands they make upon you, and that anticipates the demands they are likely to make next.

Most old-world companies do not understand their customers, except in the most broad, aggregated fashion. This is a function of the value chain relationships with which they are familiar. The manufacturing department produces products that go to the sales/marketing department. Marketing places products with wholesaling. Wholesalers sell to retailers. Retailers sell to customers, with whom they communicate largely through surveys and statistics about sell-through, shelf space, and customer satisfaction. None of this gives a producer any clue about what the customer is looking for next. The producer hears only complaints—either from wholesalers, or occasionally from customers who break through the customer service barrier. That is not an effective interface.

On the other hand, the new call center and Web-based technologies represent highly effective, human-oriented customer interfaces. They are far more responsive than the artificial intelligence (AI) systems of the 1970s and 1980s. They not only survey customer patterns of buying habits and service requirements, but they update this information continuously, and interactively tailor-make the products or services eventually to each customer.

Using these tools, a company like Cisco Systems gets about 70 percent of its inquiries and orders directly from customers. Even if their number of customers expands to more than a million, they can still keep directly in touch with all of them, using information technology not to aggregate requests but to group requests and respond to them individually. They can also handle most software repairs and upgrades through the Web, using information technology to build rapport with its knowledgeable customers at this critical stage. Gateway, similarly, is one step from its customers, and Intuit is equally aware of what its customers want. These companies continually monitor changes in customer demand, analyzing the trends of what customers are looking for, trying to spot the direction in which customer needs are moving, and trying to avoid being hobbled by their own preconceptions about their customers.

Zero-Based Organization

In conventional manufacturing corporations, "greenfield" is often a term of derision. It refers to a company whose existing plants are so overrun with legacy problems—bad working environments, labor practices, government and community conflicts, and difficult marketing and sales issues—that there is no viable choice except to start from scratch, in a "green field" location. This is seen as a sign of weakness; the management couldn't turn around the existing plant, so they had to start from scratch. It is also seen as an unnecessary expense; starting up new sites is costly.

But Godzilla companies see the benefit of greenfield values. They know that a newly built plant often outperforms the old ones. Konosuke Matsushita, founder of Matsushita Electric Industrial, used to say, "Scrap the old plant, and build a new one based on the latest thinking and technology." He did not like to modify existing plants. If old systems seem not to work, then it's much better to start fresh, and discard the old approaches entirely. Work rules, dress codes, hours of operation, telecommuting policies, stock options, managerial controls, accounting methods—all are up for grabs.

This helps explain why the U.S., then the "new continent," was the primary beneficiary of the Industrial Revolution—which was born in England, an old country with plenty of ingrained dos and don't's. Being unconstrained is a key factor for success whenever we enter a new world.

The same is true for external commitments, including legal and regulatory commitments. Bill Gates once told me in an interview for Japanese television that during the first seventeen years of Microsoft's existence he had never been to Washington, D.C. The 1998 antitrust lawsuit took Microsoft by surprise precisely because, for its first seventeen years, the company had assumed that it was different from conventional companies. For ordinary companies, managing the relationship with government is a paramount priority. But Godzilla companies have neither respect nor much use for the practices and values, or for the goals and strategic methods, of conventional corporations and government agencies.

This is not to say that Godzilla companies can or should ignore the rule of law. But conventional laws will always seem off-base from the vantage point of Godzilla company leaders, who are blithely unconcerned with the established practices of the old world. They have started their companies on a zero-baseline, grounded in new technologies, avoiding as many legacy elements of the corporate system as possible. They assume that legacy aspects of business do not apply to them unless proven otherwise. This allows them to focus on leverage wherever they may find it, including arbitrage opportunities that others don't recognize. It helps them buy the best and cheapest components, subassemblies, and services from all over the world, including places that other companies won't touch. This willingness to break free of old habits lets them feel comfortable with high-multiples transactions and thus take advantage of three of the four dimensions of the invisible continent.

Location

One symptom of the zero-based attitude in Godzilla companies is the locales of their headquarters. Few of them hail from large industrial-age metropolises such as New York, Tokyo, London, Paris, or Los Angeles.

Almost none come from the urban manufacturing centers like Chicago, Detroit, Manchester, or Osaka. Instead, they come from Seattle (Microsoft), Austin (Dell), the Dakota plains (Gateway), Denver (Qwest), the Caribbean (Soros), San Jose (Cisco), or Atlanta (CNN).

This is one of the most intriguing features of the Godzilla syndrome. It partly stems from the use of networks—from toll-free (1-800) telephones to call centers and the (location-independent) Internet. But I think the change goes a bit deeper than mere technology. If our entire society is moving toward the invisible continent, then we are at the early stages of a revolution in economic and social practices. Revolutions tend to bloom in social fabrics that inherit less constraints, bondage, and taboos. In Japan in 1868, for example, the Meiji Restoration was carried out by samurais of three peripheral and coastal provinces. More established centers of power, such as Tokyo (formerly called Edo and home of the shogunate) and Kyoto (the capital until 1868), could not respond to the demand of the West to open the country. Today large cities are, by definition, governed by the establishments and conservative people of our society. India (Bangalore, Hyderabad, and Pune), Ireland, Finland, Singapore, and Malaysia may have a good chance to succeed in the invisible continent precisely because of their status as "backwaters" in the view of the traditional leaders of the old world.

From Broadcast to Pointcast

If consumer use of e-commerce grows as expected, then a far greater number of consumer purchases could follow the business-to-business model of Cisco Systems—dealing with customers as unique individuals. Chances are, the move to tailor-made marketing will take place slowly, but by the year 2005 or so, consumers will be accustomed to choices that, in effect, allow them to co-design many of the things they buy.

Much has been written about tailor-made marketing; yet it is often misunderstood, particularly by managers schooled in the old world. They correctly recognize that the old "broadcast" model of marketing is becoming outmoded. Broadcast marketing proclaims, to a mass audience, that a wonderful product exists—anything from a Toyota car to a can of Green Giant peas—and invites them to purchase it. Since only a small portion of the audience is interested, broadcasting has a very low hit rate. Typically, only one-tenth of one percent of the people targeted by a mass-marketing message buy the product.

Marketing schools today teach that the future is in customer segmentation, or narrowcasting to a "cluster" of customers. This means identifying (through statistical analysis) a subset of customers likely to be interested in

a particular product or service. Supermarket coupons are increasingly narrowcast; printed in different arrangements for people living in different
neighborhoods. Most magazine advertising is, essentially, narrowcast—an
ad in *Ladies Home Journal* will not run in *Fly Fisherman* magazine—and
television, especially on cable, has already followed the same model.
Direct mail (DM) is sent out to a chosen segment of customers who might
be more relevant to the product in question. But narrowcasting at best has
a 2 to 3 percent hit rate. Statistical aggregates are reliable predictors of
purchasing only up to a point.

Pointcasting, or true tailor-made marketing, often has a better than 50
percent hit rate. It represents a vast democratization of the traditional privilege of aristocracy—to be served and catered to on an individual basis.
Under this model, marketers seek only customers who have already indi-
cated they want the precise kind of product described here. As often as
not, customers make the first contact, drawn by the marketer's ability to
match their most precise desires.

The carpet in my office was pointcast. A salesman from the Duskin
corporation visited me and took a digital photograph of a poster from my
campaign for the Tokyo mayoralty several years ago. A computer-generated
proposal showed me how a carpet woven in the likeness of that image
might look in two or three different formats, and I *chose* one of them. (By
this time, I was already "sold" beyond the point of no return.) Had I
wished, I could have suggested a variation in the format. Many of the customers have carpets made from their children's drawings. Then, because
they hate to step on the drawings, they put the carpet on the wall and
select another design for the floor (buying both carpets from Duskin).
Whatever they choose, they know that no one else in the world owns that
carpet. Other companies in Japan provide the same kind of design for
sweaters—knit within an hour from the template of a digital photograph,
often copied from a design that famous movie stars are wearing or a
landscape from one's hometown. The cost is comparable to the cost of a
conventional machine-made sweater. The key is to make the product or
service to order without raising the cost or prolonging the delivery time.

Dell and Gateway computers are well known for their pointcast products, in which people ask them to assemble the computer from specs. But
consumers have only begun to learn the potential of pointcasting. The
time is not far away when purchasers will design cars on computer
screens, choosing not just from a predetermined list of options, but from
the options provided by a variety of manufacturers: a Honda engine in a
Toyota body, perhaps, or vice versa, with Ford seats and interiors. You
might be able to watch the car being assembled—by an OEM supplier—
on a computer screen hooked on to an Autobytel Web site, where you

would also have insurance and car payment terms tailored to your particular situation. No longer would it be primarily a Honda, a Toyota, or a Ford car. It would be primarily *your* car. The same might be true of a wide range of products, from appliances to investment packages to take-out food.

Pointcasting could provide marketers with a response rate better than 50 percent. It is thus far less costly than either broadcasting or narrowcasting. It builds ingrained relationships with consumers, in part because it establishes an ever-growing knowledge base about them. One of the keys to Amazon.com's success is its knowledge of customers; any customer who signs in receives a list of potentially desirable books or music or video, based on past purchases. Its banner advertisements (on the portal page) specifically apply to the individual customer whose past relationships and behaviors are stored on Amazon's database. The sophisticated "response" technology, called "data mining" technology, can profile the customer enough to create a tailor-made message.

Another pointcast service known as Bluemountain.com creates and sends greeting cards, maintaining a database of addresses and important dates such as wedding anniversaries, as well as preferences in card style and message, for each of its customers. After accumulating this kind of information for three years, this company was sold for $780 million to Excite@Home in 1999. A better pointcasting technology than data-mining-and-guessing is the listing of "wanted" gifts. Consumers, mostly children, post in sites such as Della.com and Ashford.com the gifts they would like to receive from parents, friends, and relatives. By the time their wish list is completed, it is already half-bought. The list could be hundreds of items long, with full information of product/models, price, and the home-page links. The same approach is used by Wedding411, where bride and groom record their wish list for a possible wedding shower. This kind of "prompt" or "push" technique represents a perfect marketing strategy for the Internet; it establishes a platform on which friends and relatives can exchange information about purchasing priorities that otherwise would take hours to gather and sort out.

As a generic marketing practice, pointcasting could conceivably take place offline, but it is only really practical through media like the Internet, which allow people to interact in real time with a computer that helps them make complex choices. Thus, it takes place only on the invisible continent. And it helps explain some of the otherwise mysterious aspects of Internet content. Yahoo, for instance, is not primarily a directory of Web sites, or even a portal. It is an index for narrowcasting; a way for narrowcasting marketers and customers to find each other most easily. A long stay in a sticky site like Yahoo makes you subject to pointcasting because you leave enough "footprints" for the merchant to generalize the products you are really looking for.

Web-Shaped Organizations

In Chapter 2, I suggested that companies make sure their CEO can play the role of chief information officer, so that they can intuitively take advantage of (and create) platforms in the invisible continent. Godzillas do this automatically; but they go one step further. Their entire organization is attuned to the demands of the cyber dimension. This leads to "web-shaped" organizations. Instead of creating pyramid-like hierarchies in which each person has a precisely delineated task, they organize amorphously around platforms. The platforms are distinct, and the people do whatever is necessary to develop and use the network effectively as knowledge, management, sharing, and synthesizing platforms grow around the world and around the clock.

Consider the role played by a "telephone service representative," as they are called, at the Gateway 2000 call center in Ireland. When a call comes in, it is routed according to language: Swedish speakers get one rep, while speakers of Italian get another. These two reps might sit next to each other, and they both have been trained to fulfill a variety of functions. First, they are operators; they can route calls to specialists as needed. But specialists are rarely needed, because the reps are also salespeople, suggesting computer options that a caller might buy, and closing and fulfilling the sale. Third, the reps are design engineers. They set up the software and hardware configuration according to the specs they have received.

Fourth, the rep plays an internal role as a driver of the production process. He or she fills in a diagram of required components (such as memory chips) and software, held by the central computer. This in turn directs United Parcel Service—working on Gateway's platform (or vice versa, as often is the case)—to procure the appropriate components (software, display, CPU, keyboard, and so on) and ship them to the assembly depot nearest the customer. The assembled computer arrives at the customer's doorstep as one parcel. The rep controls and checks that whole process.

Finally, if a customer calls with a problem—whether it involves delivery, demand for a new feature, or technical support—the call comes back to the same rep. Each rep, in fact, is given a unique first name. If there are two "Kenichi's" among the 3,500 Gateway telephone service representatives in South Sioux Falls, then one of them will take a different name.

Every customer knows his or her rep by first name, asks for them by name, and feels assured that the company knows his or her needs. The technical support is facilitated by technology; a device is installed in a Gateway computer that allows the rep to investigate some of the computer's problems directly, although more difficult problems are directed to the technical staff.

Dell and FedEx, for all but the largest corporate accounts, operate in a similar fashion to Gateway and UPS. This approach, known as computer-telephony integration (CTI), turns out to be a more effective way to organize a company for customer satisfaction, as well as a better way to drive the entire supply chain. There is no need to worry about the "chimneys and stovepipes" between marketing, engineering, operations, manufacturing assembly, and customer service. They are all handled by the same person who swims across the labyrinth of corporate functions on behalf of a customer, with help from one common database and ERP system. Most of the jobs at Godzilla companies are similarly organized—not around specialization of tasks and functions, but around the relationships with customers and the tasks that need to be handled to make customers feel at home.

Simultaneous Global Reach

In my 1985 book, *Triad Power: The Coming Shape of Global Competition,* I suggested semi-facetiously that corporations relocate their headquarters to Anchorage, Alaska—the city most equidistant by air from Tokyo, New York, and Dusseldorf.[5] Godzilla companies have gone the Anchorage perspective one better. They locate their headquarters in virtual space, equidistant to everywhere. And they expand to all markets, not one at a time, but simultaneously. This "sprinkler" model of globalization—selling everywhere at once, instead of sequentially penetrating one country after another—is keenly attuned to the borderless dimension of the invisible continent.

Cable News Network was a trailblazer in this regard. CNN reaches 240 countries and territories; they entered all of these markets almost simultaneously, piggybacking on the existing platforms of cable television and satellite broadcasting, instead of inventing their own infrastructure. As a result, they are the world's largest and most far-reaching broadcasting station.

The Internet makes it much easier to become simultaneously global and newly born. Most publishing companies are still national by nature; this book, for instance, is published by HarperCollins in the U.S. and by Nicholas Brealey in the British Commonwealth. This arrangement is based on traditions and "home literature preservation" laws going back to the American Revolution. But Amazon.com puts them under enormous pressure by making it easy, quick, and convenient for citizens of both nations to order each other's books. The power of this borderless approach to book buying became clear in mid-1999, when Scholastic books was forced to push forward the publication date of its popular Harry Potter children's book series; tens of thousands of readers were ordering the book from Amazon's United Kingdom Web site, rather than waiting for the American edition.[6] While Godzillas naturally develop global reach, titans and bystanders feel the pressure to do so. The result is a scramble for mergers across "triad" boundaries; thus we see the mergers of British Petroleum and Amoco; Vodaphone and AirTouch; Daimler-Benz and Chrysler; Nissan and Renault; Sumitomo-Dunlop-Goodyear, Firestone, and Bridgestone; and Michelin and Uniroyal-Goodrich. There will be many more such mergers, because even in the old industries, only companies that can simultaneously serve these major markets of the world will survive.

Acquisitions Through Relationships

As we have seen in the acquisition of Time Warner by AOL, the advantage of Godzillas' multiples over titans' has been widely noted. Companies like Cisco Systems, Global Crossing, and Qwest can use their high multiples to acquire companies of substance. For example, Cisco acquires companies with good technologies in Internet routing. Global Crossing is now taking over regional telephone companies (Regional Bell Operating Companies, or RBOC's),[7] evolving rapidly from its original business of crossing the Atlantic and Pacific oceans with fiber-optic cables. Likewise, a three-year-old company, Qwest, has acquired the RBOC, US West. In five or ten years' time, these Godzillas may look like the huge multinationals of today—except for their smart, invisible-continent-savvy use of systems and platforms.

To be sure, the paperwork of a merger is no guarantee that the surviving entity will actually adopt better business practices. The enormous pain of integrating any new acquisition into the policies and processes of the corporate parent must be dealt with first. This is particularly true during a hostile or neutral takeover—an acquisition, essentially, by force. But Godzilla companies have not typically had those kinds of growth pains during acquisitions. As shown in Figure 4, Cisco Systems has purchased many companies, but on the day after the acquisition, the people in the new part of the company act (and seem to feel) as if they'd been working for Cisco Systems for decades.

Acquisitions and Minority Investments

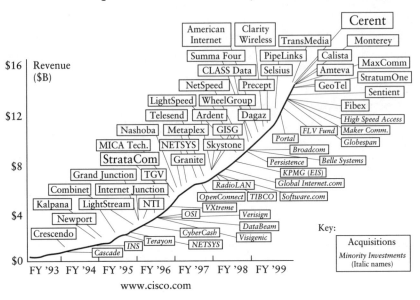

Figure 4. This chart shows the acquisitions and minority investments that Cisco Systems has made since 1993, using the high multiples available through its stock options. (Reprinted courtesy of Cisco Systems. Inc. Copyright © 1999 Cisco Systems Inc. All rights reserved.)

I asked Cisco CEO John Chambers what the most important element was when he made the decision to acquire another company. "It's not what the company does, or their technology per se," he said. "It's the chemistry between our people and their people." When there is a common vision of the company's long-term future, the integration can be very smooth. The Godzilla-style growth pattern also makes a difference; if people on both sides have stock options in the newly merged entity, then they all have incentive to make it work. Because they are looking for chemistry, the Godzilla leaders are more effective shoppers; they know how to find better M&A prospects. And since they are organized in a more networked form, they grow without the distortions and internal rivalries of the traditional pyramid structure, in which available positions, by definition, are limited as you go up. In a web-shaped company, you can keep adding leadership positions both inside and outside the company as you grow.

Moving Slow in the Fast Markets

It's tempting, amidst the booming American stock market, to assume that American corporations know how to manage effectively on the new continent, or how to balance it against the old. But the stock market boom is misleading. Seventy-five percent of American companies have gone down in their stock prices since April 1998. Only one-quarter of American companies are riding the bull market. The market sees this, which is why there are so few bargains. The market is bipolar; it has divided itself into winners and losers. The winners are more expensive every day; the losers are feeling the pinch.

This too is a new-continent phenomenon. It does not mean that technology stocks will necessarily trump older industrials; some of the biggest winners are blue chips like General Electric, Texaco, or Procter & Gamble. It means that every company is under increasing pressure.

Because it is so easy for vast quantities of money to move on the new continent, the markets are unreliable predictors of real wealth. Hedge fund managers, in particular, behave like panicked schools of fish. When one of them moves in a particular direction, the rest of them move the same way. Then, when they feel they've gone too far, the whole school swarms in the other direction. The result is extreme oscillation in currency and stock markets. Over the past decade, in a typical month, the value of dollars per yen might fluctuate by 10 percent or more. In some years, such as 1994, it fluctuated by more than 40 percent. But the growth of Japan's economy might move between plus 2 percent and minus 2 percent per year, and America's economy at zero to 4 percent per year. In other words, there is no basis in the economic fundamentals for this kind of volatile change in exchange rates. The fluctuations are caused by the collective psychology of traders.

Corporate people who wish to survive this buffeting would benefit to think about five- to ten-year time frames. It does not make sense to be moved by the tangents of capital and currency flow, because those flows can switch overnight. Nor will economic theory help in understanding these fluctuations, because despite their large scale, they are not statistically significant; they are merely oscillations at the surface of the economy.

Over and over again, on business news stations, the economic "voice"—the agglomerated voice of the financial/economic community— makes pronouncements after the fact of these oscillations. The yen goes up 1 percent, and they say, "This means that the fundamentals of America are weak, and Japan is recovering." Then the yen drops 2 percent the following week, and the same economic "voice" says, "Japan still has severe problems." Hikes or falls in the Dow Jones index or the ruble (or a dozen other indicators) lead to similar pronouncements. These types of misstatements are inevitable if economists try to explain events in terms of the "fundamentals" and macroeconomic parameters, such as interest rates and unemployment figures, of an old-world Keynesian interpretation.

For nothing is fundamental in the multiples-driven, hedged, and leveraged markets of the invisible continent. The currents and waves of money movement are created by a scared group of people—about five hundred key traders around the world looking at their screens, and trying to clear their position or keep their position, guessing each other's motives and moves. That is the reality of the marketplace. Do not read too much meaning into the resulting oscillations. As a corporation, you need to survive despite these currency and stock price fluctuations, by finding stable holding patterns that will render you immune to their short-term shifts.

Godzilla companies have an innate feel for this. They tend to bet less on financial markets but more on customers. And that is, ironically, the reason the market gives them high PEs. They adapt quickly to changes in customer needs and they design and redesign their organizational channels. But they keep a clear view on their intended direction, and they try to make sure that everyone in their companies is moving in a reasonably aligned fashion. The key is to react to customers quickly, but not to the market so quickly.

Simultaneous Value Destruction

Amazon.com may have destroyed the value of the traditional retail for books. But the game is not over yet on the new continent. Eventually one has to ask what kind of book retail is desirable, be it online or off the shelf. If an author like me can meet with the readers directly in cyberspace, there is no need for publishers or even for Amazon. A low-cost publisher in India can be contracted online to put together a book that I drafted, and the first fifty serious online readers can make a recommendation, instead of the "authorities" chosen by the *New York Times*; then the purchase order for the bound version can be processed by DHL or FedEx. In the end, so long as Amazon.com is simply selling ready-made and published books, rather than being involved in the process of content creation, they are still exposed to the potential for competition coming afresh from those who conduct arbitrage on branded publishers.

Yahoo and other search engines are also exposed. They are today recognized as powerful portal sites. But few customers are willing to leave the traces of their footsteps and visits. They are also weary of providing name, address, phone number, and payment method each time they visit a new site. Citigroup's "electronic wallet" concept, described in Chapter 2, could undermine the hold of portals. Credit and debit card companies are exposed as well, through the kind of "personal micropayments" system that I also described in Chapter 2.

In short, there is a constant challenge coming from the new entrants to the invisible continent. They are vulnerable to new platforms that might altogether replace the platforms they have established. The only rule here is that anybody who wants to set laurels on themselves will be displaced by someone else who can conceive of the more fundamental needs and fabrics of the networked society.

MAKING THE TRANSITION

Can an established company actually follow these prescriptions? I have never seen one do it. Taking this path means, in effect, reshaping a dog to create a cat. As I noted earlier in this chapter, previous category winners like Barnes & Noble or Merrill Lynch know very well what they must do to compete with upstarts like Amazon.com or E*Trade. But they cannot deny the pull of their existing businesses. They have too much to lose.

The Heisenbergian dilemma for the old-world companies has to do, most of all, with time frames. On the invisible continent, events take place quickly, adaptations are needed rapidly, and actions move swiftly toward goals. The stock market urges companies to act even more quickly, and the attractive multiples that the investors give to nimble, outward-focused "upstarts" enable the small to eat the big. In the old world, actions require approval from (or compromises with) people with vested interests in old parts of the system. Of course, old-world companies move more slowly; that is their nature. As the old cliché notes, big ships turn slowly.

If the transition can be made, it will happen counterintuitively. The best analogy comes from skiing. When novices first learn to turn, they must be trained to shift their weight to one side—effectively throwing themselves overboard into the valley (or so it feels). That takes some getting used to, but eventually it adds a dimension of flexibility to the sport, and the fear goes away.

Similarly, the only companies that can make this shift are those that can adopt an attitude of self-denial about their successes in the past. Past successes may have to be sidelined or even put aside for good. Casualties must be expected, as well. The head of Microsoft Japan says that Bill Gates has a deep-seated belief that Microsoft could fall if the company makes one careless mistake. Every night is a sleepless night out there in the Wild West. I respect Gates because, although he is the richest man in the world, he still feels that he could fail. Many industrial companies whose lives are far more endangered do not have CEOs with the same sensibility.

The People of a Godzilla Company

In all of this analysis of Godzilla companies and their strategies, little has been said so far about the people who are involved. But the people, their capabilities, and their aspirations are enormously important. Godzillas avoid failure by involving all their people in the fate of the company. These highly technically advanced companies are also the companies that tend to treat their people best.

It is traditional, in management books, to consider the development of people as a staff function—a management practice, as if the people in a company were isolated from the political and social spheres around them. Perhaps that was possible with the rigid boundaries of the old world. But in the new continent, it is not.

Therefore, before we can look at the future of individuals on the new continent, we must shift gears to consider their economic and political contexts *in addition* to the context of their companies. We must look at the evolution of nation-states and other political entities, which have an enormous influence on the demands that people make from their employers, their platforms, and their providers of goods and services.

In the next chapter, we look at the political evolution of nation-states to date. In Chapter 6, we consider the prerequisites for any country that wants to move full-bore into the prosperity of the invisible continent. And then, in Chapter 7, we return to the question of how governments, societies, and companies can most effectively develop their people—and in the process, avoid the dangers of the "new cold war."

REGIONAL WINNERS AND NATIONAL LOSERS

If I had to pick one country as a harbinger of the coming shift in national economies, it would be Ireland.[1] Only a hundred years ago, Ireland suffered from one of the most consistent, virulent cases of chronic poverty in Europe. Regular famines drove people en masse off the island in search of work. Only 3.5 million people live in the Irish Republic, but there are 70 million Irish people around the world. This statistic, in itself, shows how severe the living conditions there had been.

In the 1960s and 1970s, the Irish economic strategy changed. Instead of, in effect, exporting people to places with jobs, the Irish Development Agency (IDA) tried to draw jobs into the Emerald Isle. They offered grants and preferential taxes to industrial companies, inviting them to migrate to Shannon or Dublin. It seemed like a sensible strategy, but it did not succeed. American and Japanese firms preferred to locate their European operations in Glasgow, Wales, or somewhere on the European continent— closer to the market, with easier physical distribution. It looked for a while as if Ireland would continue to lose economic ground, straight into the new century.

Then in the early 1990s, the Irish changed their strategy. Rather than courting manufacturers, they targeted the service sector. They recognized that they had an enormous asset in their hardworking, intelligent, *English-speaking* people—people already conversant with one of the critical platforms of the new continent. In part by joining the European union, and in part on their own, they removed restrictions on trade, immigration, and commercial activity; they also invested in communications networks and telecommunications infrastructure, without dictating how that infrastructure should be used. American insurance companies soon set up claims-processing operations in Ireland, taking advantage of the time zone difference between the U.S. and Dublin. The Americans shipped over their claims at the end of their working day; the Irish processed those claims while the Americans slept. This type of service became so popular that by now, 2,500 American companies have shifted part of their operations to Dublin. They have created 250,000 jobs; one job for every fourteen residents of Dublin. At the same time, there are more than six hundred Irish-owned software companies, with fifty to sixty new startups every year. Some companies grow at a rate reminiscent of Silicon Valley: Baltimore Technologies, an encryption software company based in Dublin, expanded from $150,000 in sales to more than $10 million in just two years. Baltimore and other companies have exhausted Ireland's labor force, so they are now importing developers and salespeople from Wales, the United States, Australia, and India.

Many people think that this remarkable shift is the result of tax breaks and other incentives. Actually, it was achieved through a single-minded approach to reconceiving Irish industry to take advantage of the invisible continent. The roots of the Irish reconception date back to 1982, when Ireland's government hired Ira Magaziner to recommend a policy to them, and it took shape in the following years, when the government refined and implemented the ideas. As Europe reconstituted itself into a single region with a single currency, the euro, Ireland would become the electronic hub of the new "euroland."[2,3]

The electronic hub (or "e-hub," as Public Enterprise Minister Mary O'Rourke calls it) is perhaps best exemplified by the Financial Services Center of Dublin, located in a redeveloped complex in the old "dockland" area of the harbor. This is not a center for banking, like the City of London. It is a center for backroom operations and *receiving* calls. Gateway, Dell, IBM, Intel, and many other American companies, as well as a large number of European companies, maintain multilingual call centers here— or in Shannon, Cork, Navan, or Claremorris. Europeans of all national origins live and work here, answering calls in German, French, Italian, Spanish, Swedish, Czech, and a dozen other languages. Computer companies, such as Gateway 2000, can integrate telephone, satellite communication, and Internet service to provide a highly integrated customer relationship management (CRM) center, with one location that serves the entire European continent. The growth rate of the Irish economy moved first to 6 to 7 percent in the mid-1990s—equivalent to New Zealand, and one of the highest in the world—and then to an unprecedented 10.5 percent in

1998. In a single decade, Ireland managed to leapfrog 150 years of industrial development and move into the networked society without the conventional industrial development problems of pollution and labor unrest.

To best understand the single-minded approach to realize the e-hub, consider these steps that the Irish government's Industrial Development Agency has recently taken:

- Purchasing state-of-the-art, high-speed Internet connections to twenty-four European cities, the U.S., and Asia, thereby gaining speed and reducing the cost for e-commerce activities;

- The development of a hundred-acre "National Digital Park," an e-commerce campus at City West with a high-speed telecommunications backbone;

- Introducing a maximum 12.5 percent corporate tax rate for all business activities, including e-commerce, signaling a future of stable, acceptable tax rates;

- Introducing legislation to ensure the validity of electronic signatures.[4]

The Irish e-hub concept is possible because of the deregulation that has taken place as a result of the European Union. Since citizens of one European Union member can migrate easily to another European Union country without complex paperwork, it's easy for Dublin to attract speakers of all of the European languages. Now they no longer export their people. Nor do they need to try to import companies. They can import only the jobs, which travel across the telephone line or satellite. This means that the 70 million Irish people scattered around the world no longer need to send money home or look for jobs elsewhere. They can return and contribute to their home country.

There are great implications for countries elsewhere around the globe. Singapore, Malaysia, Hong Kong, Taiwan, Finland, New Zealand, and portions of India have attempted similar strategies, and it has paid off, to greater or lesser degrees, for all of them. The Super Corridor of Malaysia has attracted expressions of interest from more than 900 companies. About 150 of those companies have been granted special waivers on working visas and corporate tax to help make the Super Corridor concept viable. In all of these cases, success has come not by emulating traditional industrial strategy, but by leapfrogging the industrial revolution. Every developing country that wants to escape chronic poverty will have to find a similar way to leapfrog itself onto the new, cyber-enabled, invisible global continent.

SETTING THE STAGE FOR NEW RELATIONSHIPS BETWEEN CORPORATIONS AND GOVERNMENT

In 1995, in my book *The End of the Nation-State,* I proposed that "so long as nation-states continue to view themselves as the essential prime movers in economic affairs, so long as they resist—in the name of national interest—any erosion of central control as a threat to sovereignty, neither they nor their people will be able to harness the full resources of the global economy."[5] I was thinking at the time of such nations as the United States, Russia, China, the United Kingdom, France, Germany, and Japan— nations that had already established themselves as critical players on the international scene. In the nineteenth and most of the twentieth centuries, I noted, corporations that wanted to take part in the international economy had traded their way in, as French or Japanese or American or Russian "corporate citizens." They operated as representatives of their countries, because the global economy was dominated by nation-states, and a national passport was the ticket of admission to trade. But that is no longer true. The world's nation-states no longer dominate the global economy—they do not even give good multiples in the invisible continent.

The decline of the nation-state is a shocking idea to many people, who, after all, still think of it as an eternal verity, dating back to the dawn of human history. But in actuality, the notion of the nation-state—a sovereign entity, dominant over a territory's economy and politics without an explicit link to a religion or group of families—is only about four hundred years old. It is generally credited, in concept and in some early laws that enabled it, to the sixteenth-century philosopher/lawyer Jean Bodin. For three hundred years, the nation-states of Europe were largely governed by monarchs; they only took their current, legislature-dominated form in the late 1800s. And now they are losing their mercantile power as well. The economy of the invisible continent no longer needs to mediate through a national government apparatus, and national leaders can no longer compel economic fealty from their citizens, let alone from their companies.

In Chapters 2 through 4 of this book, I have shown how the values of the invisible continent clash with those of the established blue-chip company. In the next two chapters, I am going to consider the disconnection between the imperatives of the invisible continent and the values and practices of the nation-state. I hope to show how platforms make access to the global economy feasible for anyone, no matter what their national borders dictate; and how efforts to shield nations from the impact of the global economy inevitably will be arbitraged.

Nor am I the only one to say such things these days. In his book *The Lexus and the Olive Tree,* *New York Times* columnist Thomas Friedman suggests that Congressman Tip O'Neill's famous remark about politics was wrong. Friedman writes, "All politics isn't local—not anymore. All politics is now global. Not every country may feel itself part of the globalization system, but every country is directly or indirectly being globalized and shaped by this system."[6] In his book *Jihad vs. McWorld,* Rutgers professor Benjamin Barber goes further, arguing that "[national] sovereignty is indeed in a twilight, condemned to a shadow world by government's myriad postmodern detractors."[7]

But it is not enough to recognize the pressures driving apart the old-world nation-state, without finding something to replace it. Individuals cannot take part in a global economy on their own; as economic actors, they have too little reach. They inevitably will group into larger economic units, and those (with many exceptions) will be formed around the vehicles that people have always found most effective for community: language, geographic proximity, and cultural resonance. As such, what we are witnessing now in the likes of Ireland and Bangalore is a new type of prosperity, a coherent "region-state" that uses cyber-technology to take advantage of its people's creativity and draw prosperity from the rest of the world.

Indeed, in *The End of the Nation-State,* I used the term "region-states" to describe the geographical units that would best thrive in the new economy. These region-states would not be political units per se, and would not always be linked by ethnic or cultural unity. Instead, as they intersected with the global economy, they would prompt cross-border migration of capital, information, corporations, and consumers with unprecedented freedom. Ireland is a clear example of the tensions and capabilities involved in this shift. It has suffered one of the fiercest political civil wars in human history; the bitterness of the enmity between Catholic and Protestant Irish cannot be overstated. But as an *economic* unit, Ireland is an open system in which the old political barriers hold little sway. This will become increasingly clear as the Northern Ireland autonomy is achieved and the concept of a borderless European community (and the use of a single currency, the euro) sinks in; it has already begun to override the traditional boundary of enmity between the Republic of Ireland and the United Kingdom.

THE AMERICAN ZEBRA

A converse example is the United States. In terms of its internal politics, it is one of the most peaceful countries in the world. A war has not been fought on American soil, except for the bombing of Pearl Harbor, since 1865. It has digested the harmonization and integration of California and Texas (from Mexico), Louisiana (from France), Alaska (from Russia), and Hawaii—all far more smoothly than Canada has managed its relationship with the province of Quebec. But economically, the United States is far less unified than Ireland. As writer Joel Garreau noted in his book *The Nine Nations of North America,* the culture and economic capabilities of different parts of the United States have less in common with each other than they do with other parts of the world.[8] Since that book was published in 1987, this situation has not diminished; indeed, it has intensified.

America's economy is like the stripes of a zebra. From a distance, the animal appears gray; but when you move closer, you see that the apparent uniformity is actually produced by a pattern of bright and dark areas. Each "stripe" of the American zebra is an autonomous economic unit. Some, like the areas around Chicago, New Orleans, and Cleveland, are struggling to escape their industrial-era identity and haven't succeeded. Others, like parts of Maine and the Great Plains states, are mired in a moribund fishing- or agriculture-based economy. These areas have declining per-capita gross domestic product. Yet, other parts of the U.S. have economic growth of 20 percent per year: Colorado Springs/Denver/Boulder; Austin; San Antonio; Phoenix/Scottsdale; Seattle; San Jose (Silicon Valley); Boston/Cambridge; parts of the New York City area; and recently the outskirts of Washington, D.C., known as the "dot.com belt."

I came to understand the "zebra economy" during the 1970s and 1980s, when I worked with Japanese companies that were trying to target markets in America. We recognized that there were pockets of intense interest with great numbers of potential customers, but that there were also pockets of "white space," where it would be fruitless to invest much marketing money. The automobile companies, for example, started with California, then went to the Northeast, and then to the Pacific Northwest—avoiding Detroit for fear of anti-Japanese feelings. With this sequential approach, it took fifteen years to cover the entire United States. We also understood that different "stripes" would exist for different products: Northern and Southern Californians might purchase consumer electronics similarly, but have very different tastes in automobiles.

It was clear then, and remains clear now, that (unlike Japan) the idea of an average economic growth rate for the United States is thoroughly misleading. The country as a whole, on average, grows at a 4 to 6 percent annual rate, but the economy is polarized. Some cities grow rapidly; others decline. Some rural areas grow at phenomenal rates; urbanites are eagerly recruited to mountainous regions where they can sit at home and work at a desk overlooking dramatic scenery. Other rural areas have growth as flat as their terrain, or prospects as remote as they are. Some regions are divided into fractal mini-regions; Orange County has high growth, while other parts of the Greater Los Angeles area are stagnant. The bright stripes are not just growth regions; they are the regions that lead the world economically and will continue to do so through the next ten to fifteen years.

Some of the bright regions show remarkable creativity. Nevada, for example, was once so poor that it was used as a nuclear test bomb site; that was the only service it had to offer. Then the area around Las Vegas became a haven for gambling, divorce, and prostitution—"shameful" activities for which only the "shameless" people of Nevada were willing to provide a legal home. But over time, those ceased to be the sole linchpin of the Las Vegas economy; it is increasingly a family-oriented and high-end tourist destination, with 1.2 million permanent residents and 30 million visitors annually. It is also a preferred site for international conventions such as COMDEX, hosting people from around the world. This business generates a net revenue of $30 billion to the city. And the Las Vegas area has become a favorite place for retirees, who have lots of entertainment to offer their visiting families.

Orlando, similarly, was a marshland when Walt Disney, in the last years of his life, bought twenty-three square miles of land there with an eye toward building an East Coast amusement park and an "experiential prototype community of tomorrow" (EPCOT), to use his own terminology. Today Orlando's economy supports 2 million residents, only a fraction of whom work for the Disney company. Like Las Vegas, as a natural outgrowth of its business in theme parks, Orlando has become a major convention center. Forty million people visit Orlando annually from all over the world, staying on average four nights. I arrived once on a flight from Gatwick, London's second airport; the flight was jam-packed. Indeed, nearly every flight from Europe to Orlando is full. There is not even a natural beach in Orlando; it is landlocked. But there are many beaches, all designed and maintained as tourist attractions, together drawing far more people than most natural beach sites (such as Daytona, which is only one hour's drive from Orlando). There are fireworks every night, and boardwalks everywhere. Orlando is comparable in population to the third-largest city in Japan, Nagoya, and is eight times greater than Iceland, a member of the UN and OECD.

The success of Orlando and Las Vegas is particularly remarkable when you consider that tourists travel there from places with a much more genuine sense of historic presence—an authenticity that Las Vegas and Orlando's Disney World cannot even copy. The historical sites of Florence, Heidelberg, Barcelona, Stratford-on-Avon, and Paris are still compelling, but the tourist attractions there have existed for centuries. Orlando and Las Vegas (and Baltimore, Long Beach, Phoenix/Scottsdale, and the San Francisco Bay Area) continually reinvent and redevelop their old areas, and reinvent their economies in the process. Often they outperform the places they mimic: There are "Animal Kingdom" theme parks in Florida that draw far more people, and make far more money, than their genuine safari equivalents in Africa, and not just because they are more convenient.

I do not claim that living in Orlando, Palm Springs, Fort Lauderdale, or Las Vegas is preferable to living in Paris or Tokyo (although many people have made that claim, in effect, by migrating to these newer cities or to others in resort settings). Nor are the beaches of Orlando better than their equivalents elsewhere. Nor do Orlando and Las Vegas have access to a unique pool of creativity. In fact, there is probably a much larger pool of creative people from which to draw in France, Italy, and Japan than in Florida and Nevada.

Why, then, is it so easy for local economies to put their creativity to work? The answer lies in their degree of autonomy. Japan is a large nation, with 130 million people, renowned for their arts and unique insights. But not one of the country's 3,300 municipalities could accomplish what Orlando or Las Vegas has accomplished, because their economic fate depends on the whim of a handful of bureaucrats in Tokyo. The average Japanese businessman travels an average of once a week to Tokyo to seek permission—to build a new plant, to change the shape of a dock, or to arrange a shift in transportation patterns. It could take a century, and discussions with hundreds of people, to arrange the necessary issues for a new Orlando to emerge.

For example, Orlando required an international airport, so that people could fly directly there from European cities and Latin America. But in Japan, the Ministry of Transportation decides which airport can permit flights of which airlines from which cities. This is regulated so that existing Japanese airlines will not lose out. No Japanese airports except those in Narita and Kansai are allowed flights to London or New York, because that ensures that the airlines already flying to Narita will thrive. Similarly, the national government could not approve the construction of a Disney World–style park in one prefecture without approving a similar construction in forty-seven other prefectures, just to guarantee fairness—and all would have to be 70 percent financed by the government, with lots of red tape attached to the grants. As a result of this, there are theme parks in every corner of Japan, featuring Holland (Haus ten Vos), Denmark (Tivoli), Spain (Porto), Russia, Korea, Mongolia, Oceania (Sea Gyer), and you-name-it. There is only one common feature among them: They are all financially troubled. The Japanese prefer to fly around the world to see the originals. Unlike Orlando or Las Vegas, the Japanese theme parks cannot compete through continual reinvention; their faithful re-creations become, instead, an increasingly valueless commodity.

Bureaucrats in Paris, Beijing, Moscow, Berlin, Ottawa, Seoul, Mexico City, and even London make decisions according to similar tacit criteria. They plan for the coherence of the nation as a whole at the expense of local sources of economic autonomy and creativity. They foster tourism around the country, but only for "historic" attractions that already exist and that seem "appropriate." They do not let local individuals decide for themselves how to create new types of attractions or other new types of industries. Their national economies grow not in regional "zebra stripes," but across the board. And then their economies go down across the board.

The United States, by contrast, has an autonomous economy. While it may seem highly regulated, it is comparatively free of central regulation. Fifty states compete economically against one another. This fortunate state of affairs, from the point of view of the new continent, is an accident of history. It goes back to the Treaty of Paris that settled the U.S. War of Independence from Great Britain, and to the Articles of Confederation. America's founding fathers could not have foreseen the rise of the digitally enabled networked community; but nonetheless, they established forevermore the idea that the United States would be a confederation of states, and not a state in itself.

I have already noted that in the U.S., Bill Gates did not have to deal with Washington, D.C., for the first seventeen years that he ran Microsoft. In Japan he would have had to come to Tokyo to wine and dine MITI officials, so that he could be buffered against lobbyists from established businesses who would otherwise sabotage his sweeping new efforts. Only in the United States, thanks to its founding fathers, could two out of the three main branches of the federal government be engaged for a year with the sexual peccadilloes of the president and an intern, with the economy still thriving. In Japan, France, Germany, or Russia, if the media were preoccupied with a Monica Lewinsky–style story—or for that matter, an O. J. Simpson–style story—the whole country would be paralyzed. Instead, there was little or no impact on the real business of America—the thriving amalgamations of regions, each striving in its own way to gain an economic foothold on the world.

Thanks to the historical "dumb luck" of the Treaty of Paris and Articles

of Confederation, the states of the U.S. have a reasonable level of autonomy on many internal affairs: taxation, regulation, transportation, zon-
ing, and even divorce and gambling. The U.S., uniquely among modern
nations, thus has an innate latitude for creativity built into its governance
structure, particularly apt for the invisible continent. Canada, a similar
nation in many respects, does not have the same latitude. This makes an
enormous difference to the two nations' relative prosperity—today, and
for some time in the future. In Canada, there is still a "Nova Scotia versus
British Columbia" syndrome; provincial forces battle over who gets
awarded what privileges. The province of Quebec is still soul-searching as
to where it belongs.

These are typical dilemmas of the nineteenth-century nation-state
model. The implicit assumption is that there is a limited slice of the pie,
and politics consists of battles over how to slice the pie. The new regions
aligned with the new continent have graduated from this model in two
ways. First, their leaders now see that there is no limit to the slice of the
pie, so long as they allow the region to interact with the global economy.
Corporations and capital can come from outside. (In fact, the successful
regions or city-states—be they the City of London or Orlando or Las
Vegas—all make sure to call in the global economy. Instead of begging the
central government for subsidies, they demand enough autonomy to deal
with the global economy.) Second, these regions have learned to expand
the horizon into cyberspace. Like Dublin and Bangalore, they've learned
that jobs and money can easily migrate over telephone lines and satellite
transmission.

For the European Union to succeed, the most important step for Brussels to take is to free the regions—geographic areas smaller than countries—to become competitive in the global economy. These regions could
be the size of Catalonia, Lombardy, Wales, or Scotland. They could even
be smaller. Their potential success depends upon the clarity of each
region's strategy and its ability to market concepts such as e-hubs to the
world.

THE RISE OF THE REGION-STATE

Ireland is one of the rare cases where the bright stripe of the zebra—in this
case, the zebra of a newly unifying Europe—is contiguous with a national
government. The United States and Germany are more typical: the prosperous and nonprosperous regions do not fit neatly within national borders. Economic boundaries drift and change far more rapidly than

national boundaries. In recent years, for example, Seattle and Vancouver together have come to constitute one prosperous stripe, while the North American Free Trade Agreement (NAFTA) helped create a single "stripe" out of parts of southern Texas and northern Mexico. It would be fruitless to try to reconfigure national boundaries to match the stripes of any particular zebra.

In my 1995 book *The End of the Nation-State,* I hypothesized that the optimal size for such a "global business unit" in the borderless world economy was between 5 and 20 million people. This was, as I put it then, "small enough for their citizens to share interests as consumers, but still of sufficient size to justify economies of . . . service—that is, the infrastructure of communications, transportation, and professional services essential to participation in the global economy."[9] In other words, the region-state would be defined not through its production, but through its consumption and its capacity for interaction with the global economy. A prosperous region-state would need a large educated class capable of providing some service to the global community. It would need an international airport and capacity for international freight-handling. And although I didn't state this clearly in *The End of the Nation-State,* it would need a highly developed cybernetic infrastructure. It would need not just computer, telephone, satellite, and digital transmission links, but the ability and will to use them to reinvent old industries or develop new ones. In other words, the "people factor"—the know-how to best take advantage of the shift to an information-intensive society—has become critically important.

At the time, Singapore was a good example I could point to of an emerging region-state. Now I could name dozens. Some, like Ireland (call centers), Finland (telecom), Trinidad-Tobago (chemicals and fertilizer), and New Zealand, are countries in themselves. Some, like the "bright stripes" of the United States, like Bangalore of India, MSC of Malaysia, and Dalian of China, are semi-autonomous parts of larger countries. Only a few, like Ireland, base their economy on becoming an e-hub. Others look to tourism, to programming, to finance, to petroleum refining, to multimedia development, or to new innovative economic bases that no one else has noticed yet.

There is Penang, an island off the shore of the Malay Peninsula. It is a booming center of exports. Even during the depressed health of the Malaysian economy during the so-called Asian crisis, this island was short of workers. In 1998, they asked the government to relax the immigration restrictions on Indonesian workers coming to the island.

There are Bangalore, Hyderabad, and Pune, three cities in India with between 3 and 6 million people each. India's average per capita GNP is one of the lowest on earth—about $500. India used to export engineers.

For several generations, Indians earning money in Europe and the U.S. sent money back home to their families, who had to remain in India. But in Bangalore, software engineers earn as much as they would in Australia. They are hooked up to the rest of the world through satellite-based telecommunications. They bypass the conventional land-based phone system, which requires waiting hours on end before an operator will put them through to Tokyo or New York. (Even those rare Indian exchanges with automatic switching have a successful completion rate of only 85 percent—meaning that almost one-sixth of the calls don't get through!) Satellites carry Bangalore's voice and data signals to Singapore and out to the rest of the world.

Living in an impoverished country, with the salary of an industrialized-world professional, the software engineers of Bangalore, Hyderabad, and Pune live like nobility. When InfoSys, one of the three joint-venture partners that I have developed with Indian software developers, went public on NASDAQ in the spring of 1999, more than 100 out of the 3,000 members of the company's employee stock option program literally became millionaires. Another 800 InfoSys engineers, after only several years of employment, achieved overnight a nationwide household goal: to save $35,000 in a lifetime. By the end of 1999, a half year after its IPO, the company's stock reached $402 a share, and its market capitalization climbed to $21 billion, or six times its initial value. Opportunities like these are more egalitarian than they might seem at first glance; they give some hope to the new world. Even if you are born in a poor family (or lower class in the caste system), poor region, or poor country, the invisible continent can bring you wealth so long as you can add intellectual value on the network.

The region of Catalonia, centered around Barcelona, is another such region-state. It is so eager to dissociate itself from the far less wealthy Spain that some people refer to their province there as the "Autonomous Republic of Catalonia." Another is Hong Kong—whose prosperity depends, in part, on handling the money that Chinese officials have smuggled out from mainland China to invest outside and thus enter the global economy. This represents a dramatic shift in the direction of money through Hong Kong; the global economy no longer uses it as a "port of entry" for investing in China. Privileged Chinese people now see it as their window to the free world.

Arbitrage favors regions over nation-states. Regions are defined by consumers, who can use their power to choose alternatives to draw wealth away from the producers of their nation-states. The nation-state paradigm suggests that everything and everyone within a particular territory owes allegiance, first and foremost, to the government of that territory. If outsiders invade that territorial line, even one inch, the country will fight back. Citizens who live within that territory belong to the nation. If the nation becomes poor, the citizens become poor. If the nation becomes wealthy, the citizens become wealthy.

These political beliefs are espoused by most governments (and held by most citizens), but they are relatively recent in terms of human history, and they have been outpaced by events for more than a century. The globalization of the economy turns around the logic on which their economic power is based. The poorer India gets, the more prosperity the citizens of Bangalore enjoy, because the standard of living around them is lower. Other citizens elsewhere in India cannot improve their lot by making India stronger, but only by finding a way to develop a regional identity and link to the global economy. Similarly, Penang booms in inverse relation to the national fortunes of its national parent, Malaysia; as the Malaysian ringgit goes down in value, the desirability of Penang's consumer electronics exports goes up. Support for Malaysian government policies will not necessarily do anything to improve Penang's lot; it might even make matters worse there.

It is also no longer possible to compare one country to another economically—to say, for example, that Japan is stronger than Germany—using the established macroeconomic metrics of the old world. The gross domestic product of Japan, Germany, the United States, or any other nation (even Ireland) does not measure any significant economic factor—any factor at a level of aggregation where it can tell you how to become wealthier or more competitive, let alone how to live a good life. If you really want to compare nations, you must do it industry by industry, region by region, and even *company by company.*

DEER HUNTERS

In July 1999, there was an unprecedented phenomenon: the surge of stock markets around the world. In the past, the global markets were seen as a zero-sum game; if the American stock exchanges went up, Japan's or Europe's went down. Occasionally, there were simultaneous plunges (Black Mondays) around the world. But never before had we seen all major stock markets go up together. What had happened: Internet trading had promoted trading without regard for national borders. Few investors who watch the screen flicker with the price of Nokia, Softbank, or Fujitsu seem to care that these stocks have headquarters in different countries, ranging from Japan to Finland.

Instead of countries vying for capital and investment a priori, companies around the world are competing for global investors. So it is entirely possible for the NYSE, NASDAQ, TSE, FTSC, and CAC to go up simultaneously, assisted by the best performers in the respective markets, while the majority of member companies post declines in their prices. (For example, during the stock market boom of the U.S. in 1998 and 1999, only about one-quarter of the listed companies increased their market prices, while the majority of share prices declined.) This phenomenon, which I call "deer hunting," is relatively new. The day-traders watch for movement on the screen, and "shoot" (i.e., buy the stocks of) anything that jumps. They will not hesitate to cross national borders; in fact, they probably don't know that Vodafone is British, that AirTouch is American, that both are now merged, and that they are trying together to take over Mannesmann of Germany, which is 10 percent owned by Li Ka Ching of Hong Kong! The market selects its winners and losers, similarly, without regard for any national and/or macroeconomic considerations.

Unfortunately, the national economies are still crafted by macroeconomists fiddling with the levers they can handle—prime rate and money supply. The result is a habitual disconnect between a government and its national economy. For example, during the economic recession of 1992–1999, Japan kept its export competitiveness with a constant $5 to 10 billion trade surplus every month. But global capital escaped out of Japan, because there were too few Japanese companies with attractive upsides (i.e., multiples). Some of our industries, such as chemicals and pharmaceuticals, were basket cases, by and large. Japan's biggest enemy was the Japanese government, which tried to protect globally weak industries and banks, and tried to keep the economy going at any cost. As we shall see in the next chapter, this protective attitude of the Japanese government was the single biggest reason for the prolonged and severe damage it received in the 1990s.

In the end, we must leave behind the traditional view that wealth is created only by governments operating within national borders. If you follow this traditional mercantile model out to its natural conclusion, you will come to the belief that wealth must be created through exploitation—conquering other countries for their labor and markets, or colonizing them for their natural resources. If this were true, then countries with large land mass, large markets, or natural resources would prosper. But that does not happen in practice. Over the past twenty-five years, the country with the largest land mass in the world has ceased to exist. Meanwhile, a group of nations with overwhelming natural resources tried to conquer the world. They were the OPEC nations. They had a monopoly on the largest, least expensive energy source in the world, the one source of energy that no nation could ostensibly do without. Their monopoly control lasted sixteen years—from 1973 to 1986—and then dissolved. This type of economic empire-building cannot be managed in a way that sustains itself, either now or in the future, because it is too easy to arbitrage anything, even a nonrenewable resource like oil.

If the nation-state is no longer meaningful in economic terms, then what is the meaning of the economic statements made by politicians? What do we make of the proclamations that promise "prosperity" or "jobs," either by shutting out the rest of the world, financing public works projects, or by creating more government jobs? We can only conclude that they are the equivalent of show trials: pieces of theater designed to assuage people who are still mired in the psychology of the nineteenth-century nation-state. Jobs are no longer created by national politicians. Wealth is created by the agility and creativity of people in regions. Even when national politicians play a role, as they did in Ireland, they do so by letting go of the governmental grips on the economy.

Instead, wealth will accrue to nation-state governments only when they learn to let go. Wealth will accrue to Malaysia, for instance, when internal regions such as Penang (and its sister regions Selangor and Johore) grow wealthy enough to share their prosperity with the rest of the nation. Malaysia would then become enough of a consuming nation, as opposed to a producing nation, to be able to compete in the intellectual value-added game of the cyber-society. It will still compete as regions, not as a "Malaysian unit"; but with the rest of the world relying on Malaysian intellect rather than the sweat of factory work, the networked regions of this nation could prosper across the board. The same would be true for most other nations—they will develop into region-states.

PRESCRIPTIONS FOR A NATIONAL LEADER

These changes, of course, stem from the presence of the invisible continent and its influence on national affairs. As a result, the governance strategy for a national leader elected in, say, 2001 should be very different from the strategy that the same leader might have followed in 1951 or even 1971.

First, a paradigm shift needs to be made, from national sovereignty to people sovereignty. This means deregulating those industries that allow consumers to thrive and build better lives for themselves, so that they have access to the best and cheapest products and services in the world. This translates into reducing tariffs on imports, removing restrictions on shipping and communication, and allowing as much flexibility as possible in travel and finance. In particular, it means eliminating favoritism toward "homegrown" industries, because in an economy driven by consumers, it is counterproductive for countries to try to favor any particular home-grown industry or company to succeed. National success is no longer linked directly to the success of home producers—who after all can move from one country to another—but to the success and viability of con-sumers and employees, and investors from home and abroad.

If a government creates a comfortable bed for global corporations to come in and sell products or services, then the resultant prosperity is much better than the home country superficially prospering at the expense of tax-payers' subsidies. If Toyota, with headquarters in Japan, sells to the benefit of consumers in the U.S., returns investment to the benefit of investors in the U.S., and employs to the benefit of workers in the U.S., then the U.S. has gained more than Japan has from the activities of this company.

But deregulation is not enough in itself; a company that focuses on its people must invest in the infrastructure that links each nation to the new continent. Transportation, communications, and finance infrastructure are all needed for a country to become cyber-enabled. You can understand the importance of this by comparing Ireland to another island country with a similarly sized population (3.5 million) and many similar advan-tages: New Zealand. New Zealand has deregulated its industries just as much as Ireland, and it also has the advantage of being an English-speaking nation. Both countries entered the global economy in the 1980s. By the early 1990s, both countries had recovered from the recession of the 1980s. But there was a difference between the two countries: New Zealand did not build a financial services center, nor did it enable cyber-access; it has no equivalent to Ireland's e-hub concept. It has settled on being a very efficient country with a deregulated economy, that remains basically based on producing and selling commodities. Perhaps eco-tourism would be a good vehicle for New Zealand; but it would require someone to innovate and market an ecotourism equivalent to the power and reach of Disney World. Given the current conservative political and economic leadership, if there is a young Walt Disney in New Zealand, he or she has a much more narrow platform on which to test his or her cre-ativity. Deregulation is a prerequisite for sustained economic growth, but in itself it is not enough to call in the global economy. The region also must be fully committed, in its legal framework, its sociopolitical predisposi-tion, and its human training, to migrate into the new continent.

In the mid-1990s (as Figure 5 shows), New Zealand's economy as a commodity exporter faltered along with that of Asia. Ireland continued to thrive because by the early 1990s, it had become the European home for the American Godzillas, e.g., Dell, Gateway, and Intel.

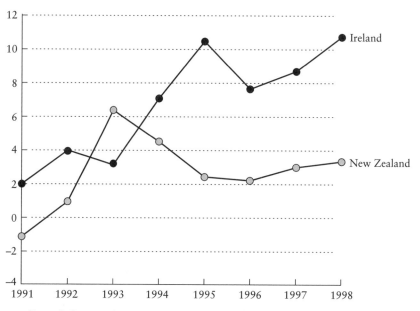

GDP Growth Rate (% per annum)

Figure 5. Comparative growth rates through the 1990s for two countries with many similar advantages, including a laissez-faire government and a large English-speaking population. Ireland, which invested in cyber-infrastructure, far outpaced the growth of New Zealand.

Many Latin American countries—Brazil, Argentina, Peru, and Chile, for example—have gone through the same sort of deregulation, often at the instigation of the IMF and the World Bank. But like New Zealand, they have done nothing to ensure that their people can work in the new continent's economy—the global economy—and thus their people are trapped in a national rat race, always limited to the income they can make in homegrown commodities. It's no wonder that they always find themselves in the same dilemma: Short-term prosperity makes their currencies expensive and their economy inflationary. That brings down their competitiveness and short-circuits their prosperity. The lack of financial and telecommunications infrastructure investment literally defines them as incapable of sustaining their competitiveness in the new continent.

The wrong types of government investment can also hurt a nation's ability to join the global economy. Japanese farmers, who used to represent more than 50 percent of the working population of the country, once suffered greatly from the natural disasters of their island country during the years before World War II. Many of them traveled overseas to escape from hunger, to Brazil, California, and Hawaii. There are now more than 1 million ethnically Japanese nisei and sansei in Brazil. Their descendants have carved out a significant presence in the economies of the Amazon and the American West Coast.

But today, when they have a problem, Japanese rice growers need only visit Tokyo and ask for a subsidy. They have received almost $500 billion in subsidies over the past decade, in part for modernization and in part to mollify rice growers (and construction companies) in the face of recession and world trade agreements. During the past fifty years, not a single farmer has had to leave Japan because of hunger. And this has been the worst possible thing for Japanese farmers. It has kept them from establishing a presence in the global economy. With the money spent on subsidies, the Japanese government could have bought Cargill, ConAgra, or other global agriculture companies; or it could have invested in competitive farm lands in Australia, the Ukraine, and Argentina. This would have been far more effective in establishing Japan's "food security," a phrase the government always uses as an excuse to subsidize its domestic agriculture.

THE ROLE OF REGIONAL GOVERNMENT

Nation-states as they exist today are both too large and too small to truly represent their constituents in the global economy. For example, in Japan the dominance of Tokyo's central government over 3,300 separate municipalities and forty-seven prefectures is ridiculous. Japan should devolve into eleven different self-propelled engines of growth, each with its own autonomous government, each with between 5 and 20 million residents.

One such region would be Kansai, which includes Osaka, Kyoto, and Kobe—22 million people in a territory about the size of Connecticut. Overshadowed internationally by Tokyo, its economy is bigger than that of Canada, a member of the G-7. To marketers, it is one of the most attractive regions in Japan; it is densely populated and affluent. Yet, not many companies, even Japanese companies, are organized to tackle this region with the attention it deserves.

Every one of the eleven Japanese regions should be free to establish its own identity vis-à-vis the global economy. Some might continue the traditional industrial direction of Japan. Others might strike out to emulate Ireland, Switzerland, Las Vegas, Singapore, Hong Kong, or Orlando. And some, no doubt, will reinvent themselves in new ways that make a new kind of contribution to the world's economy.

But local regions are most effective when they are attuned with large-scale supranational regions, such as those defined by the NAFTA, European Union, ASEAN, and MERCOSUR agreements. Ireland's success, for example, depends on the role it plays as the business center for all of Europe. Without the promise of the euro and the EU's equalization subsidies, Ireland never could have achieved that position.

The movement toward large-scale regions began forty years ago with the Treaty of Rome, which first established the European Common Market. Then in 1992, the movement was boosted when the European Union was formed. Now, since January 1999, the euro has emerged as the first regional currency. The euro may take time to develop a base of investors and traders, but as we saw in Chapter 2, it could well become as stable and critical as the dollar. That would create another platform for investors.

(Parenthetically, while the euro is sometimes criticized for its weak exchange rates to date, it has worked well to start the euro as a relatively weak currency, particularly against the U.S. dollar. If it were stronger, there would be too much competitive pressure from the U.S. The ECB and eleven member countries would have to fight against the much more experienced and coherent American financial vanguards.)

Regardless of the position of the euro, most of the world will soon be able to adopt my personal investment strategy: one-third in dollars, one-third in euros, and one-third in a currency related to the investor's home country—settling accounts and making payments at the end of the month with whichever currency is strongest.

If the investor's home country is in Asia, then the currency may be the "asea"—a pan-Asian currency that could link Asian economies in the near future as the euro does in Europe now. This would be a natural emergence from ASEAN, the Association of Southeast Asian Nations, which includes Indonesia, Malaysia, the Philippines, Singapore, Thailand, Brunei, Vietnam, and Myanmar. Unless they develop a single currency, these nations will not be able to accomplish their global goals—with or without an end to the Asian economic crisis. The Japanese yen may play a critical role in the formation of the asea, although most of the ASEAN countries today tend to use U.S. dollars for settlement of their external trades.

Other global regions will also grow more prominent during the next decade or two. NAFTA, which took full force in January 1999, will make the United States, Canada, and Mexico into a single market. MERCOSUR (Mercado Comun del Sur), the union of four South American nations—Brazil, Paraguay, Uruguay, and Argentina—will soon be joined by Chile, the most stable economy in South America. This will create an economic entity that spans the continent from the Atlantic to the Pacific, with a strong and growing consumer presence.

Ironically, the primary force driving such macroregional growth is the continued triumph of global speculation—the derivative and leverage multiplying forces of the invisible continent. National currencies have little defense against speculators, but pooled currencies, if accompanied by reasonable political harmony and commitment by their national leaders to innovation and productivity improvement, are much stronger. Speculators thrive because they create the response to their own machinations in a relatively small market; they drive a currency price down by short-selling a large amount (through multiples) of the target currency, prompting the national government to try to prop it up. They then profit from the reaction they have provoked. This leads to obscene profits, drawn at the expense of the governments involved, as we have seen in the case of Tiger Funds in Thailand in June 1997. And it leads to an oscillation of wealth, decoupled from the productive capability of the economy, which nonetheless makes it very difficult for the economy to sustain its growth in the short term.

In general, if multiples are used against a relatively small and undeveloped market, then the currency exchange rate and the stock market can be pushed to go up or down so sharply that the market becomes a paradise for arbitrageurs. As happened repeatedly in Russia during the 1990s, the people inside such economies suffer from the unstable environment. Any serious attempts to improve productivity and competitiveness are erased by the wild inroads and exodus of capital across the national borders.

But it is very difficult for speculators to make these profits when governments don't play along—and they *can't* play along when their currencies are closed for exchange (as in Malaysia in September 1988), or tied to the currencies of larger-scale regional entities, like the euro. Some countries, such as Brazil, Argentina, and Hong Kong, have tried to peg their currency against the dollar, arguably the most enviable currency in the world. But this peg does not last long unless the other countries' economies move in sync with the U.S. The pressure that builds up in these economies is always a source of speculation; it leads to more instability than in the economies with the natural float, as we have seen in Brazil during the 1998–1999 crisis. The experience of the past two decades suggests that a better approach is a regionally pooled currency, if the sociopolitical chemistry of the region is compatible. If all of the major regional blocs had their own currencies like the euro, speculators would be left with only a few currencies in countries like Russia and Ghana, which might oscillate dramatically but would still be too small to provide the profits that speculators need.

These changes, of course, would require the voluntary devolution of power and control from central nation-state authorities. Can governments actually take these steps? Many political leaders, in Japan and elsewhere, have talked with me at length about the need for reform. They agree in principle with the two basic changes needed: to put the domestic economic system in line with the global economy, and to move toward a greater regional structure. They often say that they understand the importance of those changes, and they occasionally show signs of moving in the right direction. But in the end, they do not act. Instead, they retreat; they argue that once they have fixed some pending domestic problem—like the Japanese financial institutions' bad debt problems, for instance—from the top down, they finally will be in a position for reform. But there is always some other feature of the system that needs fixing. I have come to believe that asking a government official to change in this way is like asking a cat to bark; it requires a genetic makeup that simply isn't present.

Yet, as we shall see in the next chapter, taking the necessary steps is feasible. The United States has already done it. Unfortunately, as we shall also see in the next chapter, the U.S. experience represents a direct contradiction of the path that America is recommending to the rest of the world.

In summary, the world economy today represents a simultaneous shift of power from the traditional national government down to region-states, and up to super-national economic blocs. Governments in tune with this change will seek economic stability through the latter, and prosperity by means of the former.

6

THE LONG TUNNEL

Throughout the late 1990s, economists have tried to single out the most critical answers to the "American paradox"—the ongoing conundrum about why America has enjoyed low inflation and high employment. According to conventional economic theory, that combination *should* be impossible; so what factors have proven conventional theory wrong? By 1999, a number of prominent economists had finally given in to an argument that they had formerly resisted: The productivity gains from new computer-based technologies, they admitted, were revitalizing the American economy.

But they still haven't explained why these productivity gains have had such a dramatic effect without creating unemployment. One new theory has proposed that under the "new economy," fueled by the creativity of people in cyberspace, the old restraints have been released. Since there is no inherit limit to human creativity, there is no limit to productivity gains. Incidentally, they say, this explains the surge in market capitalizations for some American corporations.

Economists define productivity as price minus cost divided by the number of people employed, or value added per capita. If you use this definition, Evian water (part of the French/Swiss/Spanish Danone Group) may have the highest productivity. But it doesn't have the highest market capitalization. Something else is needed to explain the "American paradox."

In Chapter 2, I alluded to this paradox, and suggested that there was a reason for it—a unique characteristic that America shared with few, if any, other countries. This characteristic is much less dramatic and romantic than the innate creativity posited by economists—but it is also more realistic. America succeeded because former President Ronald Reagan did the best job of any politician in history to prepare a country for the arrival of the invisible continent. I don't know if Reagan understood what he was doing; neither he nor anyone else in the 1980s could have articulated the forces of the time in the same way that we can articulate them now, in hindsight. But whether explicitly reasoned, arrived at through intuitive foresight, or simply the result of a string of dumb luck, his policies on labor and trade worked as if they had been designed intentionally to bring America to prominence in the future.

Ronald Reagan's legacy is this special status for his country. This triumph had little to do with his party affiliation, or with his political conservatism. The two American presidents since Reagan—Bush and Clinton—have continued his most critical policies, even when their political constituents differed. These policies were highly controversial at the outset of the Reagan era—indeed, they were hotly debated—but in retrospect there has been little criticism of them, because they worked. There were costs associated with them; the United States is still struggling with some of those costs. But no one would seriously argue that the country should be changed back to the way it was during the Nixon/ Carter days.

Reagan spoke of building a "strong America," but underneath that rhetoric his most fundamental change was to create a more *open* America. He deregulated the three industries that had to be freed up to bring the American economy to a leadership position in a borderless world: finance, transportation, and telecommunications. When Reagan took office in 1980, these were among the most regulated industries in the nation—regulated not just on a national level, but on a state-by-state level.

Telecommunications, for example, was dominated by a single monopoly: American Telephone and Telegraph (AT&T), then the largest single company, in both revenues and number of employees, on the planet. AT&T's deal with the U.S. federal government went back to 1913 when, to avoid being broken apart on antitrust grounds, the company had agreed to be closely regulated by the government. All calling charges were approved by state public utilities commissions, meaning that there were, in effect, fifty different state-government-controlled telephone rates, often varying according to local jurisdictions. Long-distance telephone service competition was prohibited, and those rates were approved by the U.S. Federal Communications Commission. Long-distance and business phone charges were kept high, so they might subsidize more inexpensive local and residential calls. International calls were particularly high. Innovation was so frowned upon that actress/comedienne Lily Tomlin could build her career by satirizing "Ernestine from the telephone company," the smug factotum who brooked no nonsense from her customers. In short, AT&T resembled the highly regulated, often government-operated telephone companies of most other nations today. Cable television, meanwhile, was regulated on a municipal basis; few people imagined that it might be a competitor to telephones. The Internet existed, but it was entirely bound up in government monopoly—run by the National Science Foundation and the Defense Department, and used primarily by government-funded administrators and university scientists.

Transportation industries were similarly fettered by labyrinthine, all-controlling regulations. Trucking licenses were commissioned on a state-by-state basis. Airline schedules, destinations, and fares were set by the Civil Aeronautics Board, a branch of the federal government that micro-managed such details as how many planes airline companies could buy, what kinds of refunds they could offer, and even whether two affiliated airlines could clothe their staffs in similar uniforms.

Similarly, financial industries were kept local, for fear that if they grew too powerful, they might trigger another depression. Banking licenses were awarded primarily within states; California had Bank of America while New York had Citibank, and never the twain should meet. The only nationwide travel, communications, or finance organization was the U.S. Postal Service.

Yet, all of these were, and are, fundamentally borderless industries. Wires, satellite transmission, and all communications channels cross national borders naturally. Airlines, oceangoing ships, and trucks can also easily cross borders; moreover, without a deregulated transportation system, a deregulated communications system cannot move into electronic commerce. Thus, a vibrant transportation system is crucial if an information system is to flourish. Finally, financial traffic also flows across borders instantaneously. These are the three most influential industries for any country's economy—and they are fundamentally impossible to contain within the boundaries of that country.

Reform, when it reached the United States, seemed to take place overnight. It seemed impossible one day; the next day it was everywhere. The transportation industries were first; airline deregulation had begun under Ronald Reagan's predecessor, Jimmy Carter. Reagan made the new atmosphere of transportation deregulation real in 1981 when he broke the strike of the Professional Air Traffic Controllers Organization (PATCO), one of the unions that had fought bitterly against deregulation on the grounds that it had led to poorer working conditions. By 1984, both PATCO and the Civil Aeronautics Board had been dissolved. By 1987, when the U.S. government sold its interest in the freight railroad company

Conrail, the privatization and deregulation of American transportation was nearly complete.

Similarly, in 1982, the U.S. Department of Justice reached an agreement with AT&T for the sake of permitting new technologically advanced companies to link into the public network and to open up long-distance service from its current monopoly status. On January 1, 1984, seven new "Baby Bell" companies (officially called "Regional Bell Operating Companies") were created to oversee the former national "Bell System"; and over the next decade, the companies in the industry became more and more deregulated. (The breaking up of the Bell System was not necessarily a prudent action for the companies involved, given the inherent nature of telecommunications as a "networked" business. In fact, the Baby Bells are now merging, as in SBC's acquisition of Pacific Telesis, and moving back into a role as national and global carriers. But the breakup was the right thing at the right time for the industry; it created many new common carriers, and the subsequent competition prepared the U.S. telecom industry for mega-competition among the global telecommunications companies.)

Finally, beginning in the late 1970s, the American financial system was also deregulated. This arguably began in 1978 with a tax cut on capital gains, specifically aimed at channeling investment to high-tech entrepreneurs. This tax cut, and the 1981 Reagan tax cut that followed, have been credited with breathing life into the venture capital business (which in turn financed much of the cyber and multiples dimensions of the invisible continent). At the same time, the banking industry was gradually deregulated. In 1980, Congress passed a number of measures designed to help the dying industry of savings banks, which could not compete for customers against commercial banks. Price controls were lifted on the interest that banks could pay for savings deposits; the types of investments that all banks could make were expanded; and in 1982, Congress allowed banks to pay unlimited interest rates. Banks essentially became unregulated in their options for making investments (opening up their inroads into securities business and derivatives), although one facet of their regulation remained: the commitment of the federal government to assume responsibility for depositors' losses that the banks couldn't meet, up to $100,000. This would later become the source of the U.S. Savings and Loan crisis.

But that crisis, in the long run, was largely inconsequential compared to the overall change in regulation. Regulated businesses are always protected businesses; the government keeps competitors away by dictating whom companies can deal with, how they can operate, or what they can charge. In 1976, 45 percent of the GDP transactions had this kind of government protection. By 1990, only 5 percent of American businesses had it.[1] In other words, the United States had a 95 percent free-market economy by 1990. By contrast, in Japan, about 45 percent of all businesses are highly regulated even today.

The 1980s and early 1990s were difficult transition years for the U.S. economy. According to all the macroeconomic indicators, the U.S. economy was continuing to get worse. Unemployment rose almost to a two-digit rate. This was the era in which the large corporate "titans," as noted in Chapter 4, cut most of their workforce. GM went to one-third of its former size; GE continually laid off 15 percent of its population per year. Corporate profits also shrank—at least during the first years, before the effects of restructuring showed up in balance sheets. Three thousand banks were effectively removed from the system through mergers or closings. All of these indicators were indeed signs, but not of economic malaise. They were signs that the United States was going through the difficult work of restructuring itself, to realign itself with the emerging economy of the new continent. As shown in Figure 6, the American stock markets behaved very conservatively until after a dozen years of Reagan revolution.

GDP, Unemployment, and the Stock Market Index (USA)

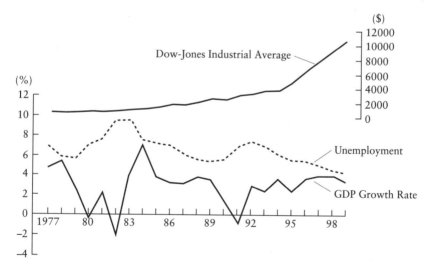

Source: "World Economic Outlook," IMF, "Labor Force Statistics," OECD 1998, Yahoo Finance.

Figure 6. Leading economic trends for the United States during its trip through the "long tunnel" of the Reagan revolution. Note in particular that the stock market did not begin to boom dramatically until 1993, twelve years after Reagan took office; and that the unemployment rate fell thereafter as the economy grew.

During this stressful time, the high rate of unemployment was not as inherently destructive as it might seem. The United States has rather extensive unemployment insurance laws and generous severance packages, particularly for people laid off from the blue-chip companies. This gave people more of a chance to start home-based businesses, striking out on their own. Unemployment insurance also gave people time to retrain themselves, which meant that the American workforce, particularly in the 1980s, was much more flexible and capable than it was usually given credit for being. There was also a growing pool of young, emerging companies (including the nascent but voracious "Godzilla" companies) looking for people. High unemployment in an economy under reconstruction may have been painful for individuals, but for the country as a whole, it turned out to be a blessing, because it forced those individuals to reinvent themselves and it led the working population to shift to more promising industries and regions.

Similarly, downsizing and cutting back expenses were not just matters of "leanness and meanness." They were signs that the privileges that the business establishment had long taken for granted were finally being eroded. As former *Wall Street Journal* editor Robert Bartley, one of the strongest boosters of the Reagan economic policies, would later point out, Reagan's policies were not necessarily beloved by the largest corporations. For example, General Motors resisted the end of wage and price controls. Like other big companies, said Bartley, GM had used these controls as a means to "browbeat its suppliers into charging GM lower prices." Indeed, throughout the world, whenever large companies are tightly regulated, they are also protected. Tax breaks and wage/price regulations foster stability at the expense of innovation; they keep new entrants from competing. The early resistance to Reagan's policies by large corporations, noted Bartley, "shows a lot about the attitudes of the business community, especially the schism between big business and businesses that want to become big. . . . For the economy will slog if big business gets government help to keep little business from expanding."[2]

Government found itself similarly hobbled during the transition—by itself. The Gramm-Rudman bill, sponsored by Senators Phil Gramm and Warren Rudman, limited the extent of government spending. This reversed a trend that had continued since the 1930s—that government would lead the way in innovating new activities for the country. Suddenly there was no longer money to lead with. The government would have to follow the market. For anyone in government, at either the federal or state level, this was a profoundly dispiriting time. Just two decades before, in the 1960s, there seemingly had been no limit on what government could do. The best and brightest people, from the greatest American universities, had gone into government to reshape the world. Now they were lucky if they could get approval to forestall a staff cutback.

All of this legislative change took seven years, from 1978 through 1985. Then it took another fifteen years for the effects to fully take hold. Bad industries, such as the moribund American steel industry, had to diminish and die before such good industries as the emerging, innovative American steel mini-mill industry could emerge. The government and economy had to collapse, at least in part, so that the influence of existing special interest groups could be diminished. Cities had to decline so that they could be rebuilt. Most important of all, the three industries at the center of deregulation—the telecommunications, transportation, and financial institutions industries—had to endure periods of chaos and devaluation before they could be re-created, and take their host country ahead to the new continent with them. All of this inevitably was slated to happen after the Reagan-era innovations took shape.

Some might challenge the amount of credit I have given here to Reagan's policies, on the grounds that the Reagan revolution created the 401K-ites: American pension-fund investors who are driven by greed, and who could care less about the poor and what is happening in the world so long as the Dow is up. To a large extent, I agree with that criticism. It is true that this has created a rather dangerous vulnerability in both the U.S. and the global economies, as we shall see later in this chapter and in Chapter 7. But President Reagan deserves credit for the benefits of his policies; he prepared America for the invisible continent's economy when few other people saw it. The long-term negative consequences will have to be addressed and resolved by his heirs.

Across the Atlantic, Margaret Thatcher was accomplishing much the same thing, and going one step further. The United States was atypical because its communications, transportation, and financial institutions were largely private, except for the U.S. Postal Service. But in the United Kingdom, as in most countries, these services were often managed by centralized, government-owned agencies: British Rail, a state telephone system, the BBC, and government-owned companies controlling airports, ports, and oil. All of these were privatized; the most critical early step came in 1984, with what Daniel Yergin and Joseph Stanislaw called "the hiving off of the state telecom system into British Telecom. This, more than any other [event], shifted the balance from the producer to the 'consumer.'"[3] In New Zealand, a similar form of deregulation was reshaping the economy during the 1980s under Labor Party leaders David Longe and Roger Douglas. In all of these cases, economic indicators got much worse before they got better; yet, after five to ten years, each of these countries showed signs of unprecedented revitalization. New Zealand, for example, changed from a country that was all but bankrupt in 1984 to one in the mid-1990s with public debt at less than 30 percent of GDP, an unemployment rate of less than 6 percent, and economic growth rates between 4 percent and 7 percent per year.

A recovery based on deregulation and privatization is not sufficient in itself to thrive on the invisible continent. But it is a necessary prerequisite. Many countries, including Japan and continental Europe, will have to go through a similar experience. Many of them will face a dilemma that the U.S. did *not* face, but that Britain (and New Zealand) did: As the economy grew, the unemployment rate went up (shown in Figure 7).

GDP, Unemployment, and the Stock Market Index (UK)

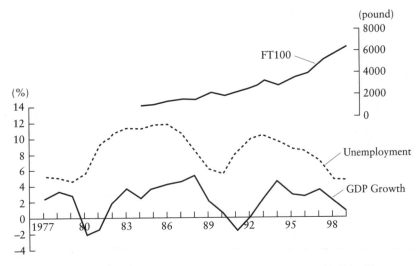

Source: "World Economic Outlook," IMF, "Labor Force Statistics," OECD 1998, Yahoo Finance.

Figure 7. Leading economic trends for the United Kingdom during the Thatcher years and beyond. Note in particular that the stock market began its rise in the 1990s, but the unemployment rate continued to oscillate.

This happened because in the UK, uncompetitive industries had been held back under protectionist governments. Government rules restrained economic growth, so profitability could be increased only by allowing the companies to lay off workers. The UK government had to deal with the employment issue in tandem with other economic and competitiveness problems. It is probably for this reason that Mrs. Thatcher, despite her contribution to the UK economy, was not liked by a large number of British workers.

Compare this with Figure 6 (page 145), the American situation. In the "hire-and-fire" U.S., as the economy grew the unemployment rate went down. In that happy circumstance, the government can concentrate on the economic growth in order to solve the unemployment issue as well—a polar opposite of the UK.

FOLLOWING THE AMERICAN EXAMPLE

I've argued that Reagan's deregulation of the three critical global industries—telecommunications, finance, and transportation—made the critical difference to America. But why should that change in policy have such a great effect? The answer isn't simple. There are three characteristics of the American economy, all reinforcing each other, upon which the American success depends. All three factors may well be vital for any government that wants to thrive on the invisible continent. All of them stem naturally from the deregulation of telecommunications, finance, and transportation. In Chapter 2, the chapter on platforms, we discussed factors unique to America that give it an almost unassailable advantage: e.g., economic prosperity without the fear of inflation. But the three factors I am about to describe can be emulated by any country—if it is willing to take the appropriate steps. Moreover, if these factors are not sustained in the United States, the American economy could run into storms.

A Stable, Attractive Currency for Investment

As I noted in Chapter 2, the dollar itself is an international platform. This platform status insulates America from the vagaries of other economies and makes it much easier for Americans to buy products from other countries. Another country with such huge trade and current account deficits would not be able to continue to buy foreign goods. The dollar's platform status gives the United States government an enormous political weapon, which it continues to use to bolster the dollar's position as a common currency for settlement. In addition, the dollar's platform status removes the negative impact of the American foreign debt. The American government does not need to borrow directly from banks (or from the IMF or World Bank) to raise money. The government can simply issue new notes and bonds, which investors worldwide flock to buy, and which do not require the same stringent payback rules that a loan would require. The irony is that the rest of the world is so dependent on the dollar that the freefall of its value, if it happened, would be a blow to everyone. So when the Chinese leaders talk about keeping up the RMB (RenMinBi, or yuan), they are talking also about keeping their dollar-based assets (both official and private) intact.

At the moment, the dollar is the predominant platform currency; but it is not the only one. The yen and the euro are also platform currency candidates that continue to attract investors. It is conceivable that either of these, or both, could be more attractive in the future—especially if, one, they hit bottom (investors always want to come in at the bottom), and two, investors recognize the dangers of American complacency. If the euro, yen, or any other currencies gained more confidence as savings and settlement instruments, then the dollar would lose some of its value. That might threaten some of the economic balance that Americans have enjoyed. This situation is much like the emperor's new clothes. If someone with significant influence were to point out the dollar's naked vulnerability aloud, or if there were better-clad emperors around, the situation could turn sour overnight. In this context, the euro after 2002 might be a major challenge to the dollar. So might the yen be, after cleaning up the debris of Japan's property bubbles of the late '80s. We will return in Chapter 7 to consider the potential impact of this scenario.

Meanwhile, any nation could follow America's example, and adapt its currency into a safe, stable haven for investors. This would take time, for safety and stability are matters of perception. The first step is to create a deregulated financial infrastructure, an infrastructure free of government-established friction, in which it is as easy as possible for investors—inside and outside the country—to buy and sell financial instruments, or to use it as a settlement currency for trade. America's lead in deregulation, particularly in the financial institutions market, was the secret of its success in making the otherwise troublesome dollar the only commonly accepted currency in the world.

A Stable, Attractive, and Open Marketplace for Products

America is the largest and most attractive market in the world for consumer products. This is because of the freedom and liberalism inherent in the American marketplace. Its consumers, while demanding, are free of bias as to where the products they buy are made. Americans themselves deserve a lot of credit for this openness.

To be sure, at the level of production, the United States is a highly regulated and litigious economy. Rules about antitrust practices, occupational safety and health, equal rights, diversity, sexual harassment, intellectual property rights, and insider trading make it very difficult to operate in the U.S. as a manufacturer. Nor is it easy to export industrial products to the

U.S. Producers of building materials, for example, must comply with extremely complex housing codes that vary from municipality to municipality. There are thousands of water districts, irrigation districts, agricultural districts, and regional planning boards, which means that an exporter of, say, irrigation pipe to the San Joaquin Valley must negotiate with a dozen different public agencies. Each district's agency employs a different corps of engineers; each of those has a manual that is a couple of inches think. You must get your product into that manual before anyone in that district will specify your product.

By contrast, if you wish to sell irrigation pipe in Japan or Germany, it is very difficult to get your product into the specifications book. But once you're in the JIS (Japanese Industrial Standard) or the DIN (German Industrial Code) books, you have made your product into a universally accepted specification that reaches 120 and 80 million people, respectively.

All of this, however, is limited to industrial products. Openness to trade in industrial goods is fine, but the more critical openness exists with consumer products and service sectors—where the choices are more varied, and distribution and perception/image take up a large part of the consumer's decision-making. For consumer products, the U.S. is a thoroughly transparent and competitive market. To sell a consumer electronics devices in the U.S., you need only get safety approvals from the Underwriters Laboratory, a privately organized lab in Chicago. The best and cheapest products tend to prevail in America, no matter where they come from. In addition, America is a highly lucrative market: It is large, prosperous, and easily reached through mass merchandisers and mass advertisement.

American consumers reap the benefits of living in a highly arbitraged marketplace, because they *are* the arbitrageurs. Better, cheaper producers always undermine complacent and protected incumbents, thereby curbing inflation. Japanese companies occasionally may be tempted to try to force American customers to pay in yen for their Toyotas or Sonys, especially when the value of the dollar declines. In fact, the dollar has lost two-thirds of its value against the yen since 1972, which would provide ample reason, in any other country, for Japanese companies to show their muscle. But they don't dare alienate their sales in the American market. When the Japanese automobile companies tried to pass the currency appreciation to the American consumers in the 1980s, Koreans undermined them, along with Detroit's Big Three. Thereafter, the Japanese learned the lesson. The only way to make money in the U.S. is to improve product performance and perception (to raise price), and to improve productivity (to lower costs). Consumers' confidence came back by the early 1990s, and most of the Japanese automakers and consumer-electronics makers have survived in the U.S. despite the huge volatility in currency markets.

Most other countries, by contrast, make it as difficult as possible for their consumers to purchase products made elsewhere. Suppose, for example, that you want to remodel a house in Japan. Your choice of building supplies is set not just by the government, but by the requisite industry associations. No insulator board manufactured overseas will meet the stringent Japanese fire protection code—not because that code represents superior specifications, but because it is specifically designed by the Japanese insulator industry to keep out foreign competitors. Even testing methods are specified to favor the Japanese producers, instead of simply specifying physical parameters and criteria that any manufacturer might meet. Similarly, the Japan Water Workers Association approves the plug on each faucet. Japanese consumers thus cannot buy cheaper-priced American Standard or Kohler faucets online, because unless the JWWA has approved it, item by item, the metropolitan Tokyo water utility will not supply water. These American products are available only with exorbitant surcharges imposed through officially sanctioned importers. Even some Japanese products, including some made by Toto and INAX of Japan, are available in Southeast Asia at lower prices, but a supplier cannot import them into Japan. This is one of the reasons housing is so expensive.

It's worth noting that while the Japanese market is heavily biased toward favoritism, not all the favorites are Japanese. Quite a few American companies have very profitable marketing operations in Japan. They have run the gauntlet and become insiders, and once they are inside, they find themselves in paradise. They often join the lobbyist associations to protect the market against "foreign" invaders. The prices are set high, and the system is highly protective of incumbents. The only losers are the consumers and the new entrants into the market. These kinds of visible and invisible barriers exist across a wide range of products and services—ranging from rice and baby carriages to financial products. The world's second-largest economy is not open to the credo of the invisible continent: the "best and cheapest products and services from anywhere in the world."

America's market, driven by consumers, is far more open to newcomers. It may be mercilessly competitive—any producer may find its market taken by a newcomer at any time—but it also inspires producers to excel. It is no coincidence that the companies that have gained the most dominance on the invisible continent, whether they are American in origin or not, have had "American roots"—a great deal of experience marketing and operating in the United States. Sony, for example, is positioned to be an important company in networking consumers during the next decade, if not longer. Sony has earned that position in large part through its energetic and evolving presence in the United States. Every other country that hopes to thrive on the new continent will have to develop some equivalent experience.

To accomplish the same, a government must relax its tariffs and consumer product controls—and deregulate the freight transportation industries (as in Reagan's package). Freight and tariffs represent much of the cost of imported goods. One might argue that lowering the cost of imports weakens the labor force—but by strengthening the consumer force, it gives a country a much stronger position on the invisible continent. Businesses will migrate for consumers these days far more readily than they will migrate for jobs. This is also the single biggest beneficial force at work on American labor. It has shifted the American working population out of low-cost manufacturing into intellectual-value-added services, and made it ready to compete on the new continent.

An Internalized, Institutionalized Cyber-Economy

As we saw in Chapter 5, Ireland has surpassed New Zealand's growth by coupling deregulation with a high degree of strategic investment in cyberspace capability. For any country, this does not just mean wiring critical areas with high-speed, ubiquitous data communication for production companies. It means developing specialties that can be leveraged on the new continent—software development in Bangalore, call centers in Dublin, and Internet production in Austin, Texas, and in Washington, D.C.'s dot.com belt. And it means establishing better and more effective channels for consumer purchases and information-gathering online.

Any country that wishes to thrive should encourage and nurture an economy in which people purchase products online, no matter what the source. That will lead to greater clout on the invisible continent. Building this capability, in turn, requires deregulation of telecommunications channels, financial institutions, and logistics; all three should be unfettered by geography.

This is important because online shopping is inherently smart, and makes an economy inherently smarter. It enables consumers to meet with more products, to screen them with logical criteria, and to find the best and cheapest ways to have them delivered. It takes away the emphasis on façade and surface in brand merchandising and displays. Online shopping incorporates advice from experts, including other shoppers. Such clout exercised by consumers inevitably shapes up producers.

Whether through an accident of history, a fortunate congruence of forces, or an innate capability inherent in its people, Americans were first in the cyber dimension of the invisible continent—first with online access to business opportunity, employment, shopping, and education. But America's position on the new continent is no longer as unique as it once was. The U.S. already has been joined by the United Kingdom, Finland, Ireland, (cyber-enthusiast) Singapore, and India. Japanese animation movies and videogame platforms are not too far behind. Other communities will stake claims on the new continent, gaining the same kinds of returns for themselves, through arbitraging new opportunities, as the prosperous stripes of the American zebra.

DARK MILES AHEAD

Must all countries adopt Ronald Reagan's policies to enter the new continent? Not necessarily. Their path may or may not involve deregulating or privatizing telecommunications, transportation, and financial services (though it is hard to imagine a country where such steps would hurt the economy in the long run). Whatever the details may be, however, a successful national strategy will tend to have the three key elements in common: deregulating currency and financial markets, opening regional markets, and enabling the cyber-economy to take hold. These three elements are essential to invite the global economies to come in and to link the region with the rest of the world.

It takes a great deal of courage to make these moves, because the first impact typically will not be popular. Deregulating these and other key industries, and opening the country to free and open exchange, triggers a crisis in the existing institutions. As we have seen in the U.S., the UK, and New Zealand, it can easily take a country ten to fifteen years to make its way through the crisis out to the other end. Jobs are lost, companies are cut back, industries are restructured, and governments enter periods of austerity. The existing financial infrastructure—the "old guard" banking and financial system—is often the worst hit. And this hit cannot be avoided. The United Kingdom and the United States both went through this period of crisis during the '80s and '90s; the United States amassed its gargantuan national debt during its "long tunnel." Despite the harrowing darkness, entry into the long tunnel should not be postponed. The quicker, and more readily, a country makes the transition, the easier the transition will be.

Life in the long tunnel requires a different attitude toward mainstream economic values. Double-digit unemployment might be the best possible thing for the country, especially in a country with a long history of full employment. If the industrial spectrum needs to shift, then full employment will slow that shift and cause it to stagnate. Unemployment will lead to greater mobility, and that in turn will lead to a shift in the larger picture. To be sure, this will seem very unpleasant to unemployed people, but just as you can't have your cake and eat it too, you can't have perfect employment and still shift the industrial spectrum into the new continent.

Making this shift also takes away the levers and controls that politicians ordinarily use to direct the economy (and guarantee themselves popularity before elections). If politicians make their currency stable by removing tariffs, they remove one of their easiest pieces of leverage for dealing with other nations. If they open up their consumer base by removing regulations, they undo one of their most established mechanisms for controlling economic activity (and justifying their existence). If they institutionalize the reach of communications technology, they risk making many established businesses and consumers uncomfortable, because both products and ideas will suddenly be forced to compete in a much more dynamic atmosphere.

And the long tunnel can be lonely for traditional leaders on a personal—almost a spiritual—level. Politicians see themselves, at the core, as advancing the identity of their country. But a leader can go down this route only if he or she recognizes that the creation of the invisible continent is blithely and cheerfully sacrificing the ego of the individual nation-state. Suddenly political leaders and their constituents will seem to be at the mercy of economic and technological forces beyond their control, beyond the control of any nation-state or any individual company. These forces will strike no matter what any individual tries to do. But will the political leaders meet them halfway and take advantage of their benefits? Or will they fruitlessly resist these forces?

Adapting to the euro has raised this question for a number of national leaders in Europe. Taxation and legislation now need to be "harmonized" with other member nations through the bureaucracy of Brussels. A national government normally controls financial markets (through money supply and interest rates), the military, and diplomacy. The euro takes the first away from the prime minister of Italy, for example, and NATO takes the second away. As for the third, what is left of diplomacy without money and military control? The prime minister of Italy is far more than a figurehead, to be sure, but that role now becomes much more equivalent to a state governor's position in the United States. No longer can the prime minister practice diplomacy using the currency as a weapon; no longer can he or she try to forestall inflation or create jobs by adjusting the money supply. Romano Prodi may have lost his job as prime minister of Italy, but he will have a more significant job ahead as the president of the European Community Commission to foster the euro and other challenging EC agendas.

Two possible situations might trigger a traditional leader into daring the entrance of the new tunnel. The first is a catastrophic event. As a Japanese individual, I am very aware of the power of these events to effect change. My country has been changed by many of them. Commodore Perry's "black ships" demanded that we open our borders in 1853. Atomic bombs landed on two of our cities in 1945. The energy crisis of 1973 reshaped our entire industrial structure. The Japanese nation is very good at responding to these catastrophic situations, because our collective memory is very short. Before the Meiji Restoration, we had maintained a closed country—*sakoku*—for 270 years. But when we decided to open our doors, we no longer remembered the reasons for the closed country.

Similarly, before the A-bombs fell in 1945 and we surrendered unconditionally, we had thought of America and the West as enemies, pigs, and devils. On August 15, 1945, in twenty-four hours' time, they became friends and gods, as if we had completely forgotten about the agonies and hatred. It's as if our memory is a calculator, and we have grown good at pushing the collective "Clear" button. Other countries, such as Brazil, Indonesia, Pakistan, and the Philippines, seem to periodically engineer their own crises, in the form of a coup d'etat. That's their way of changing the mode of government. But it is an expensive, wasteful, and unreliable trigger for change (even when the change moves in the right direction), and not all cultures respond to crisis the way the Japanese did—as the recent tragedies in the Balkans and Indonesia have demonstrated.

The other possible trigger, increasingly prominent since the 1970s, is the growing awareness that the current way of government cannot be sustained—that something significant must change. Thatcher, Reagan, and Longe all realized this in the late 1970s and early 1980s. But in itself, the realization is not enough. It must be coupled with the energy of a charismatic political leader. An unusual individual must become a central figure in the otherwise democratic government and find a way to break the stalemate of the existing political system.

When a leader steps up to take a stand on the global economy, it often comes as a surprise to everyone involved, including perhaps the leader him- or herself. Those who worked with Ronald Reagan when he was governor of California knew his essential conservatism; but few would have guessed that as president he would play a primary role in moving the new continent forward (and in pushing the Soviet Union to dissolution). As many have noted, the most revolutionary aspect of Reagan's revolution was, in fact, his willingness to speak frankly, consistently, and clearly. If he had debated tax cuts and deregulation with Congress, scholars, and bureaucrats, and then adopted the average position stated in the room, he would not have achieved any form of Reaganomics. Instead, he stuck to a set of basic principles, which he encapsulated in two words: "Strong America." He kept repeating the same message every day, even when his policies were increasing unemployment in the short run (again, see Figure 6, page 145).

In New Zealand, David Longe provided an even more surprising example. Elected in a kind of upset, he and his associate, Finance Minister Roger Douglas, focused on a simple, clear message: New Zealand must change to survive. Either they would deregulate and privatize everything, creating a real small government, or the country would go bankrupt. Had anyone predicted before he became prime minister that David Longe, coming from the Labor Party (traditionally opting for large government), would take that stance and carry it out, no one, including Longe himself, would have believed them. But once placed in the role, he and Douglas played it to the hilt, with all of the charisma they could summon. The surprising aspect was not the views that Reagan and Longe held; I don't think either of them changed their opinions after they became national leaders. But they showed a surprising ability to get their views across, and to implement the most crucial changes.

Margaret Thatcher was also unpredictable; no one would have guessed that she would gain stature and authority through the unlikely means of a war with Argentina over the Falkland Islands. Suddenly she showed even the most conservative, masculine men that she could preside over a victory—and send a member of the Royal Family, Prince Andrew, off to war in the bargain. Her success paved the way for leaders in several other countries; after all, if Great Britain, with its history of hidebound social welfare, could engineer an anti-statist revolution, then any country could do it.

The most surprising charismatic figure of the 1980s was probably Mikhail Gorbachev. When he was a minor apparatchik in the Communist Party, no one would have predicted that he would one day destroy the institutions that held the Soviet Union in thrall: the KGB, the Communist Party, and the Soviet military. Had anyone known it in advance, these institutions would probably have eliminated him. But they had to be destroyed, if the Soviet countries would survive, and it took an inordinately charismatic leader to do it. Unfortunately, Gorbachev did not get a chance to lead his country into the long tunnel afterwards.

Most, if not all, of the charismatic leaders are very stubborn people. Margaret Thatcher, Ronald Reagan, David Longe, Lee Kwan Yew of Singapore, and Dr. Mahathir Mohamad of Malaysia did not give in to political pressure, or to argument from within or without their own nation. They stuck to their beliefs. That, in fact, is the only commonality they had. And that is why such leaders often get thrown out or simply become unappreciated in the end, while their political opponents appropriate their approach (as Tony Blair has done to Margaret Thatcher and Bill Clinton to Ronald Reagan). Longe, for example, built a groundswell of support during the first flush of his policies, and then was removed from office in a reactive election in 1990, to be replaced by another party, the National Party, that followed many of the same policies.

"I was a Don Quixote," David Longe told me in 1997. "I did everything I could, and ultimately people threw us out. But today we grow at five to seven percent—a very prosperous New Zealand that nobody had dreamed of before my time. Nobody thinks of me and my colleagues any more today. They think they have won it as individual citizens. Still, I could not go back to government there—in the end, I've done the job—the only way is to leave the scene, go out, and go on."

UNDERSTANDING THE ASIAN "CRASH OF '97"

Before 1997, it was common for Asian government officials to think of themselves as part of a flock of flying geese. They were all moving forward at high speed toward becoming wealthy nations—with Japan at the head of the flock, then Singapore, South Korea, Taiwan, Malaysia, Thailand, and even Indonesia and China. Since all the countries around them were also growing, the leaders of each nation assumed that they could keep growing simply by continuing business as usual—borrowing money, inviting in corporate investment, and contracting for large technological projects. They would not need to pursue fundamental change, either in their government structure or their business environment; they needed only to carve out niches as low-cost producers of goods. If they stayed in line, in V-formation, they too would reach a level of $10,000 per capita gross national product within a few years.

This goal of $10,000 per capita GNP is particularly significant because passing it brought a nation into the OECD "club"—the self-selecting group of "developed nations" with a permanent, prosperous middle class and reliable, widespread industrial infrastructure. Once a country reaches this threshold, the average discretionary income of its citizens rises to about 70 percent of total income after taxes—and then it has a large enough pool of consumer capital to develop a thriving new-continent economy. With an active market of consumers with high discretionary income, wealth is created within the country.

There are 189 countries in the world, but only a relative handful have moved up to this level during the past twenty years. (Figure 8 shows the roster of countries that have reached this level since the 1970s.) Japan hit

$10,000 per capita GNP in 1984; today it is up to $35,000 per capita GNP. New Zealand reached this point in 1987, Israel in 1988, and Singapore in 1989. The Republic of South Korea reached $10,000 per capita GNP in 1995, but in the crisis of 1997 the Korean won was devalued by a factor of two. Its per capita GNP went back to $5,000, and while it is technically a member of the OECD, its average discretionary income is still a long way from the total of 70 percent. As long as any government tries to maintain control over exports and imports, and seeks to influence which companies will succeed versus which will fail, its country will not be wealthy. Wealth accrues to a country and a region when its consumers can exercise their power to decide.

Netherlands (1979)	Singapore (1989)
France (1979)	Ireland (1989)
Belgium (1979)	Spain (1990)
Finland (1980)	Macao (1991)
Canada (1980)	Germany* (1991)
Austria (1980)	Portugal (1995)
Australia (1980)	Korea, Rep (1995)
Japan (1984)	Greece (1995)
Bahamas (1985)	
Italy (1986)	
United Kingdom, (1987)	
New Zealand (1987)	
Israel (1988)	
Hong Kong (1988)	*Adjusted for integration

Figure 8. The year in which nominal per capita gross domestic product (GDP) passed the $10,000 mark in twenty-two countries.

Investors pursued Asian nations before the crash because they recognized the returns they would reap if they could stay with the countries during their transition into wealthy-country status. Then, when the crash struck, the same investors ran for cover. Unlike most Asia observers and global economists, my analysis of Asia during the 1997 "crisis" was that it was a good and healthy reality check against the global economy, or prerequisite to enter the new continent.[4] The Asian crisis, for all the harm people felt from it, was not so much a crisis as a crash. It was never as dire as it was made out to be. In my twenty-seven years as a consultant, I had seen the dollar fall to less than a quarter of its value against the yen—from 360 yen to 80 yen per dollar. I had seen the Indonesian rupiah fall to one-fifth of its former value, the Thai baht to one-third. I had seen the Russian ruble tumble to one two-hundredth its former value, and the Mexican peso to one five-hundredth. By those standards, the Asian crash of 1997 was not abnormal.

In fact, the "crash of '97" represented one surface symptom of a more fundamental transition. It took place because most of the Asian countries refused, in one way or another, to go through the long tunnel. Their government leaders did not see the limits of their national sovereignty. They tried to finesse the necessary changes, and they failed to implement most of the reforms that they needed. They took advantage of global business without recognizing that international investment and trade are two-way streets. They tried to import capital and technology, but did not open up the markets in return. The disclosure of government, banks, and corporations was not enough; they needed to disclose the hidden arrangements that channeled investment in particular directions. The *chaebols,* the prevailing Korean corporate consortia, had borrowed heavily from American banks, but the complex intercompany system of under-the-table capital exchange was not well known to the outside world—nor to the South Korean government. Its central bank had scarcely any reserves against this volatile situation. Thailand was in a similar position. So when they were attacked by a handful of arbitrageurs in 1997, the central banks' reserves were empty in a month.

It was easy for national economies to operate this way during the first stages of their industrial growth phase—which started in the 1950s for Japan, during the 1970s for Korea and Taiwan, in the 1980s for ASEAN, and in the 1990s for China. From the perspective of the old-world, nineteenth-century nation-state model, it looked at first as if they were managing their countries' transitions into the post-industrial era very well. They maintained a positive balance between exports and imports.

But 1997's crisis represented the reality of the invisible continent (particularly the multiples of the hedge funds) knocking at their door. Finally, the gap between their production capacity and their own markets caught up with them. The value of their capital investment, including their real estate, plummeted. Their stocks and currency declined accordingly. Most of them have found themselves forced into the long tunnel, at a pace and rate they didn't choose.

Many of the politicians from these countries blamed international currency traders and speculators for their miseries. But it was not the hedge fund magicians who sank South Korea, Mexico, Brazil, Malaysia, and Russia. It was *their own citizens:* the corporate and high-net-worth individuals who took their money to the U.S. during (or just before) the crisis. Hedge funds might have triggered the tsunami, but the real wave was caused by the arbitrage-seeking residents of the borderless world. It is difficult to comprehend the mechanism of the new global financial system, but when you do, you see that the system of arbitrage is fundamentally fair and symmetrical. If the businesses of the United States do not merit investment capital, then the system of arbitrage will turn with equal severity on America.

Nor was the crash permanent. By mid-1999, most of the Asian economies were back on the road to recovery. Asian currencies were already back up to 70 percent of their overall value against the dollar from just before July 1997, when the Thai baht first fell. More significant still is a shift in attitude among Asian leaders. Instead of talking about the IMF or America as sources of financial investment and stability, they now espouse the idea of creating stable growth from within. Bit by bit, the "air time" of the old autocratic leaders, men like Suharto, Kim Yong Sam, and Lee Kuan Yew, is being reduced; they are gradually being replaced by newer, quieter figures, who keep in constant communication with each other. These new leaders are finding their way, slowly and with more stability, to harmonize with the global economy.

One result is the emergence of the Asian Monetary Fund (AMF) and its loosely defined Asian common settlement device: a currency settlement instrument that is independent of the U.S. dollar, a sort of less formal euro-equivalent. This instrument, and the all-important discussions that led to it, have fostered an atmosphere in which 90 percent of the trade settlement between Asian countries can take place in Asia, without having to go outside—yet can take place without restriction or tariff, with all the wealth-building force of the invisible continent. This would not have been possible with the prima donna national leaders of yesteryear. In embryonic form, a new spirit of trust is developing among the leaders of the new Asia. As they become more attractive to foreign investors, during the next few years, international attention will return to these countries.

We can also now see that the crash did not hit all Asian countries with equal severity. Before 1997, it was often thought that the Asian economy was monolithic; that the Asian tigers were indistinguishable from one another. But the market reacted differently to each nation. Some, like Indonesia, continue to decline; others, like Thailand, South Korea, and Malaysia, are already on the way to recovery. Taiwan, Hong Kong, and Singapore did not sink throughout this period, as their laissez-faire government attitudes did not attract the speculators to begin with. The countries that refused to engage with the borderless, global economy of the new continent were punished most severely. Consider the fate of some of the different nations of the region, caught up in this fundamental correction that masqueraded as a storm.

THE JAPANESE CHOICE: BORROWING FROM OUR GRANDCHILDREN . . . OR OURSELVES

Most Asian countries are poor nations that suffer when they act rich. Japan is a rich nation that suffers because it acts poor. Unless it is stopped from its current practices, it will instill a set of policies that could cause it and its people to suffer unnecessarily for decades.

The first symptom of the Japanese problem was its startling success in the late 1980s. Contrary to popular belief in America at the time, this success was not grounded in the superior nature of Japanese management. It was an investment bubble—a price surge based in large part on a perception, then in fashion, that the Japanese knew something about management that the rest of the world did not know.

Anyone who looked closely at the Japanese corporate efforts to build worldwide markets, however, could see that there were clear long-term weaknesses among many Japanese companies. They were internationally strong in only a narrow range of industries. To be sure, they were visible in manufacturing industries such as automobiles, consumer electronics, and the critical components to assemble them, but they employed only 13 percent of Japan's working population. Japanese management approaches, including team-based management and subcontracting, proved to be difficult to export to companies in other nations, including Japanese overseas subsidiaries, except with an extremely large amount of training—and the Japanese, while highly adept at learning from elsewhere, were not particularly skilled at codifying their own knowledge and imparting it to others. Nor did the Americans and Europeans who managed Japanese subsidiaries seem very interested in learning from their bosses.[5]

All of this suggested that Japanese businesses would have difficulty moving into a global era. In 1987, I wrote a commentary for the *New York Times*,[6] suggesting that when the Japanese bubble burst, the whole world would have a serious problem. It would have enormous repercussions on the United States and the rest of the world. As it happened, this article appeared three days before "Black Monday," the day of the 1987 stock market crash. I was accused by some of having caused the crash.

Then the Japanese bubble burst, and its repercussions were felt around the world, especially in Asia and Latin America. (The United States was not affected, as I once thought it might be, because of the protection from its platforms: the dollar and the English language.) Today the price of property in Tokyo is worth one-fifth of its 1990 value. Anyone could have seen this coming simply by looking at the trends in Tokyo vacancy rates. At its height in 1989, Tokyo real estate was worth more on paper than the value of all the real estate in the United States—but vacancy rates were climbing. Had they paid better attention to that connection, Japanese bankers might have been more careful about overlending to construction and real estate firms. But most of them were not careful enough. Tokyo, like Houston, New York, Los Angeles, London, and Melbourne before it, oversold its potential for rapid business expansion. This was easy to do in recent years because improvements in computer-aided design and manufacturing have made it easier and cheaper to build large office buildings more rapidly. With technological limits removed, office building growth accelerated. Unfortunately, there is no similar quick-fix solution to the problem of finding tenants; they will only emerge at the rate of economic growth.

This bubble, unfortunately, destroyed much of the Japanese banking industry. Japanese financial institutions used to be divided between "good" banks (those with relatively low-risk, stable portfolios) and "bad" banks (those that made riskier investments). Since nearly all of these banks were tightly controlled by the Ministry of Finance, and since they were all tightly connected with cross-ownership and mutual investment, the distinction between "good" and "bad" banks was not very meaningful; essentially, there was one large Japanese bank, regulating investments. This had been a very clever approach during the years after World War II, when Japan was a rapidly developing nation on the old-world industrial model. The government controlled the banks, the banks offered reasonable interest, the people saved, money was recycled back to the industry, which grew rapidly to pay better salaries, and everyone was very happy. This system worked so well that there was hardly any need for a stock market where companies could raise fresh capital directly from investors.

But the system was very vulnerable to the multiples and derivatives of the invisible continent. By 1990, the "bad" banks had overextended themselves in the Tokyo real estate market. The "good" banks, watching their competitors make enormous short-term profits there, learned from their "mistake"; they moved more aggressively to lend money to China, Indonesia, and Thailand. Japanese banks thus exported their naïve lending policies to the rest of Asia (while the Americans followed suit in South Korea, Russia, and Latin America). Then the Japanese bubble broke in 1995, and the Asian currency crisis followed on its heels. To hide these bad debts, the Japanese banks rushed to buy dubious derivatives in the hopes of hiding their crisis, at least for some time. By the end of 1997, they had bought up as much as 36 percent of the $41 trillion extant in global trade in derivatives.[7] These derivatives existed mainly in the form of hedge funds. Ironically, the hedging technology originally had been developed to stabilize the investment against unexpected fluctuations of the market. But the $15 trillion hidden away by the Japanese banks represented the biggest land mines for the global economy throughout the mid-1990s.

Today there is no "good" bank left. All the Japanese banks are confronted with mounting delinquencies and losses—if not from Tokyo real estate, then from Southeast Asian institutions, from currency and derivatives speculation, and from nonperforming loans within Japan. Our banking industry, once so admired that Japan was known as the "world's banker" during the 1980s, became a shambles. According to Moody's balance sheet evaluation, the best bank (Tokyo Mitsubishi Bank) currently has a "D" rating, and all the other money center banks are in the "E+" category!

The crisis was then exacerbated by the Japanese government's efforts to deal with it. As I noted in Chapter 1, the Japanese government printed money and issued bonds frantically to keep the liquidity in the market and artificially stimulate the economy through public works. In 1999, the Obuchi government passed the Financial Institutions Recovery Act, which guaranteed $600 billion in bailout money, simply to save the already dead banks in Japan. The American expression for this type of activity is "corporate welfare," but in Japan it was institutionalized far beyond American levels. And our individual welfare program was also the richest in the world. A retired man or woman today receives 250,000 yen per month, at a minimum, equivalent to more than $2,000 per month in 1999. Japanese pensioners put an average of 30 percent of that income into savings.

In the 1990s, the Japanese government used up *1 trillion dollars* in public works, over and beyond the call of ordinary budgets, in an effort to stimulate the economy. Most if not all of these public works were redundant and useless. There is a new forty-two-kilometer toll road in Hokkaido, right next to an old and empty highway. There are 2,948 fishing harbors— but 2,000 of them make more income from construction and repair than from fishing. There are 1,200 cargo harbors, so fragmented that even the best of them, at Yokohama, is not ranked among the top five ports in Asia, though Japan is the world's largest trading nation and has the world's largest maritime fleet. All of these harbors are considered inefficient and wasteful; they do not have the Web-based tracking and handling systems for customs, forwarding, and stevedoring that have become commonplace at harbors in Singapore, Hong Kong, and Long Beach.

The primary beneficiaries of the public works are the construction industries that produce them—and which thus have no need to become competitive. Bureaucrats, whose performance is measured by the size of their budgets, also love them. Each new project was like opium for both groups, and each new project made it harder to leave behind the system of subsidies and outmoded public works.

Japanese bureaucrats, in justifying all of this, used expressions left over from Franklin Delano Roosevelt's New Deal. They talked about demand creation, market control, "price-keeping operations," and economic stimuli. And in fact, they were re-creating Roosevelt's Tennessee Valley Authority in forty-seven different prefectures every year. It would be hard to imagine a more disastrous national strategy in light of the demands of the invisible continent.

The worst of it is that the current generation of leaders, imposing this terrible price on the nation, will not have to pay it. All of this borrowing has placed an enormous tax burden on future generations in Japan. In 1999, the total outstanding Japanese national and regional bonds reached $6 trillion, surpassing the $2.5 trillion outstanding in U.S. federal bonds, though Japan's GNP is less than one-half that of the United States. Simply stated, this means that a baby born in 1999 in Tokyo or Osaka would have to pay back $75,000 to the government during his or her lifetime *just to cover the loans that were ostensibly saving the country.* In effect, Japan is avoiding the long tunnel by financing a Viagra-like construction boom, an artificially enhanced effort to maintain vitality—and borrowing from its own children (through 30-year bonds) and grandchildren (through 60-year bonds) to do so. Indeed, by 1998, Japan had surpassed Italy to become the "world record holder" in cumulative government debt as a proportion of GNP. If there were a world financial Olympics, we would be the gold-medal record holders in debt.

Japan's Plausible Alternative: the "Big *Batan*"

Borrowing from the future is an American invention; America's debt put an enormous burden on its children in the early 1980s. But the Gramm-Rudman Act of 1985, by placing a ceiling on government spending, put a stop to that. Shortly thereafter, America entered its long tunnel; and after it emerged in the late 1990s, the U.S. government has steadily run surpluses. Bit by bit, America will be able to pay back its huge debt out of this surplus. But the same U.S. government wanted Japan to take this wasteful policy, for fear of the chain reaction of downward spiral caused by the contraction of Japanese markets and economy.

Could not Japan do the same as the Americans—i.e., pay back the debts later? An awareness of the values of the new continent would suggest a very effective alternative. We should go through a "big *batan*"— named after *batan*, the Japanese word for a fall or breakdown. This would involve a fundamental reform of the Japanese economic infrastructure. We should get rid of failing financial institutions; instead of subsidizing them, cut them off and let them go bankrupt. America lost more than 2,000 banks during its long-tunnel phase; Japan, despite its crisis, has lost only a few dozen. As banks collapse, we should rescue their depositors and consumers, up to the 10 million yen covered by nationally mandated deposit insurance. There is a precedent for this; in 1992 and 1993, the Swedish government deliberately allowed its financial institutions to crash, but used a nationally held credit line to guarantee deposits to a certain level. Knowing that the government, through its "emergency room," would sell national assets to return their money to the depositors, people did not panic. All but a few businesses escaped collapse and/or nationalization in Sweden.

In addition, the Japanese government should recognize that it must enter the long tunnel. By deregulating the economy and leaping into the long tunnel, the Japanese government could foster the production of new wealth. It could initiate a wave of entrepreneurialism like that of America during the past fifteen years; but even more focused on revitalizing communities by linking them more closely to the new continent and its global connections. It could invest in the future of Japan: educating our people more effectively, constructing fiber-optic channels (or digital coaxial cable, DSL, or whatever), and helping us learn to get around our worst handicap: the Japanese language.

To make this work, the government would have to accept the prospect of higher unemployment, at a rate of 7 to 8 percent (though it could temporarily overshoot 10 percent), because that means more job mobility. But this should be *planned* unemployment, with the proper infrastructure in place to help people navigate to new opportunities. We need to retrain people and reabsorb them into new-continent forms of work. Frankly, our famous safety net for employees offers too much safety, so nobody wants to move; we need a certain kind of anxiety, so that people are interested in doing something new and better. There is no reason to fear this kind of anxiety; Japanese people are highly capable and resourceful, and there are better ways than full employment guarantees, as we shall see in Chapter 7, of providing the means to a high quality of life.

Similarly, if we were willing to undertake fundamental reform of the banking and government system, then the "Japanese bubble" crisis would represent an opportunity. It has lowered prices, making real estate and goods more accessible to people. Japanese typically save 17 to 18 percent of their income. With real estate prices low, Japanese people have a wonderful opportunity to re-create their lives: to build better homes, to develop small businesses, and to jump-start their communities from the bottom up. It's a chance for Japan to develop an equivalent to America's 1950s and Germany's 1960s: a "golden age" of more universal affluence, centered around housing.

Finally, and what is most important, the Japanese people need to hold open discussions about our country's future. We need to recognize, as a people, that we own the largest pool of private savings in the world. In total, we have $40 trillion socked away somewhere in the private and public sectors, in current and fixed assets. We have financed, more than anybody else, the U.S. government debts of the 1980s and 1990s; for example, we hold $300 billion in U.S. government bonds alone. We are currently just beginning to spend this enormous reserve on trivialities like red wine, bottled water, and cellular phones. About $1 trillion would be enough to cover the cost of paying off the debt and making us ready for the new continent. About $2 trillion, total, would cover the government problems that have been hidden "off the balance sheet." Even paying $2 trillion represents a sacrifice of only 5 percent of most people's assets. It's not too large a sacrifice to make for a genuine re-creation of the country—into a nation that is ready to enter the new continent and is run by the people instead of by the bureaucrats.

This could not be *mandated* through legislation; the Japanese government does not have the moral position, or the economic position, to issue old-world commands to its people. But the government could make a difference indirectly, by providing Japanese investors (and global investors, for that matter) with the kind of equitable openness that would induce the Japanese to bring their money home. Investing that money in our own country would remove the crushing debt burden that threatens to suffocate our children and grandchildren.

For more than a decade, I have been active in a citizen's movement called the "Reform of Heisei," which has proposed this sort of plan publicly, along with proposals for more autonomous local and regional government within Japan. The best driver of reform, we believe, is to give people the political wherewithal to create a good life for themselves. In democratically governed countries, that means making the choice, and the situation facing the country, explicit, so people can talk about their aspirations openly. People understand that if the leadership of the country can talk and listen openly about the country's desired direction, then they can develop their own future and take advantage of opportunities. They can use the millions of tools available to them to find the economic freedom they need. There will be no need for governments to spend taxpayers' money to create wealth. People will create their own wealth.

It would also take a great deal of political will and honesty to explain the nature of the problem to the people, to expose the corruption in the current system, and punish those who have profited illegally. That is a problem, because the Japanese industrial-political system does not have much inherent political will or honesty.

In the long run, Japan's leaders have little choice. They do not have the resources to fix multitrillion-dollar problems. The critical corporate and private resources have migrated to the invisible continent, and left most governments behind.

For example, Japan's SoftBank is the largest investor in Yahoo, E*Trade, and Ziff-Davis (the company that manages COMDEX, the largest annual computer show). While a resident of supposedly depressed Japan, SoftBank CEO Masayoshi Son has demonstrated that he can participate in the dot.com frenzies of Wall Street. (In fact, SoftBank has put money into more than 120 Internet-related companies that have been IPO'ed over the last three years.) Investments like his are the bulwark of the Japanese money that has poured into the U.S., to push the Dow to its current heights, and only Japanese investors like him can bail our country out of its current problems. But it won't happen until the people who manage Japan's large institutions learn how to appeal to those investors in a language that they respect.

The American Block to Japanese Recovery

Perhaps the biggest, and the most egregious, roadblock to this solution is the Americans. U.S. policy-makers, ostensibly the champions of the free market, continue to insist that Japanese leaders rebuild their economy through government investment. Throughout the late 1990s, the Clinton administration consistently demanded that the Japanese government fix Japan's problems with its "own resources," meaning the 60-year bonds that borrow from our children and grandchildren. In 1998 through early 2000, American government representatives openly demanded that Japan lower interest rates (to zero!), reduce income and corporate taxes, increase the money supply and public spending, rescue banks, and come up with more "urgency stimuli" budgets to boost the economy. These solutions would never be accepted in the United States itself. Japan would greatly benefit from its own version of the Gramm-Rudman cap on government spending, but the American government, the IMF, and the OECD have pressured the Japanese government to boost government spending instead.

Whether consciously or not, American politicians are doing everything possible to discourage Japan from following the same course that made America successful. The reason has less to do with any feelings about Japan than with the need that American politicians feel, *no matter what the cost,* to keep the "longest bull market in history" alive and growing. These American leaders understand that the American financial markets have successfully attracted funds from Europe, Asia, and Latin America, and many Asian nations over the past seventeen years. Indeed, fearing the defeat of their own economies, overseas investors have poured $300 billion into U.S. stocks and bonds during 1998 alone—money that otherwise would have been invested at home, but that now provides stability and prosperity to America. The American administrators rightfully fear that if foreigners withdrew their American investments, American investors would follow suit, or even lead the way to rebalance their portfolio allocation, and there would be immediate adjustments of stock market prices and currency exchange rates. This in itself could jeopardize the inflation-free American boom of the past decade. And since the Clinton administration's mandate depends upon economic good times, they feel that a credit crunch must at all costs be avoided.[8]

That is why the U.S. monetary authorities keep pressing for the continuation of low interest rates in Japan and Europe, to ensure that Japanese and European money remains in the U.S., and so that American investors do not seek yen and euro instruments in any sizable way. The same people are demanding that developing countries, either directly or through the IMF, keep their interest rates high to curb the inflation and exercise austerity measures.

This is not Bill Clinton's fault per se. American politics in the Clinton era has been driven, from start to finish, by the 401K-ites: working people who vote on behalf of their retirement nest eggs. These are the people who reelected Bill Clinton as president in 1996, and who pressed to keep him in office even through the adversity and shame of the 1998–1999 impeachment process. They see Clinton and his appointees, particularly the influential Committee of Three (Federal Reserve Chairman Alan Greenspan, former Treasury Secretary Robert Rubin, and current Secretary Lawrence Summers) as the bulwarks of the new continent's prosperity.

There are a lot of 401K-ites. Eighty percent of the American population owns stock, either individually, through mutual funds, or through their employee pension funds. They mistrust the safety nets of the old continent, such as Social Security. Their security is grounded in the safety net of the invisible continent, the perpetually rising stock market. Contrary to the general image of U.S. citizens as pioneering, resourceful, can-do citizens, the 401K-ites take this money for granted; they act as if they believe that they have already earned it, instead of simply benefiting from forces that have created the boom around them. They don't care what happens to other countries, so long as they do not bother American financial markets. The only time they show interest abroad is when any country offers an attractive alternative, albeit partially, to American markets. But they would rather see everyone come to NASDAQ for their IPOs so that the U.S. could ultimately internalize the global economy.

History may judge Americans of this period harshly, not for their ill intentions—they are well intentioned enough—but for their complacency and self-centeredness. President Clinton's second inaugural address in 1997 exemplified the mood: He congratulated the Americans for their accomplishment and hard work, as if the market's rapid rise was due entirely to the innate superiority of American companies and people. Although he didn't mention other countries in comparison, it was easy, listening to him, to feel as if the rest of the world were a basket case; Asia and Latin America were trouble, Russia was in crisis, and Europe was struggling to compete as a unified entity. Whatever was good for Wall Street was clearly good for the country.

Anyone who challenges this point of view draws cries of outrage. Even Alan Greenspan is vulnerable to that kind of reflex calumny. Late in 1996, in a speech at a Washington think tank, he commented that the market was prone to "unfounded euphoria." The market fell more than 100 points almost immediately. It rose back to its former position within days, but Greenspan was excoriated by politicians and the media. A few months later, he made a similar comment during a U.S. Senate question-and-answer session. Once again, the market fell. And the same thing happened in the first few months of 2000. (There is a strange illusion built into the American stock market psychology. Whenever Greenspan hints at raising the interest rate to curb inflation, the stock market tumbles. But the higher the U.S. interest rate, the more money is attracted from low-interest countries like Japan and Europe. So after a while, the U.S. stock market bounces back and keeps renewing its record highs. Nobody seems to catch on to the gimmick.)

To be sure, part of the stock market boom is due to American productivity—just as part of the Japanese boom of the 1980s was due to

Japanese management. But in America, as in Japan (and anywhere), prosperity breeds arrogance and ignorance. American investors are ignoring, at their peril, the fact that part of their market performance stems from the status of the dollar as a platform. International investors keep the market high in America; and should the dollar lose its unique platform status, or should there be another reason for international investors to withdraw their money, the market could quickly fall. And of all the groups of international investors, the Japanese have the most—more than $600 billion overall—invested in American properties, securities, currency, and bonds, excluding the currency holding by the Central Bank. If the Japanese (or the Chinese, Germans, or other major investors) pull their money back to their country and the Dow Jones index drops down by a few thousand points, the Americans will no longer credit themselves for their prosperity. They will blame the nations that withdrew their money, and they will blame their own politicians for letting it happen. The American media, which once worried about the "rising sun" overrunning America with investments, will now complain about Japanese "capital flight."

(It is important to note that if this capital flight took place, the 401K-ites, not the Japanese or European investors, would be the first to put their money into euro and yen. They are after all the best and the brightest, and would not show any hesitation in cross-border investment; they would not be stopped by romantic pleas for "patriotism" or "fundamental confidence in the U.S. economy.")

In effect, America is micromanaging the world's second-largest economy, that of Japan, in fear of the new-continent pressures of the global economic crisis, by promoting old-continent fixes like heavy-duty government investment. This kind of diplomatic bullying, to keep others investing in the U.S., is a dangerous game for America over the long haul. It will be seen throughout the rest of the world as American efforts to monopolize prosperity. Already, by early 1999, one could detect a widespread anti-American sentiment brewing in Japan. Shintaro Ishihara, a former Diet member and the co-author of *The Japan That Can Say No* (to America),[9] was elected governor of Tokyo in a landslide victory. A few months later, in July 1999, the government passed a bill to make the rising sun the official national flag of Japan, and "Kimigayo" the official national anthem. They have always been accepted as such. But a law defining them never existed, nor was it needed. The fact that the government is "officially" defining the national flag and anthem at this point is spookily nationalistic.

The rise of Japanese anti-Americanism is unfortunate because the Japanese people, by and large, basically like Americans. And Japan is highly influenced by America; indeed, the U.S. and Japan are the two strongest consumer economies in the world. They have fifty-five years of amicable, close-knit relationships to draw upon. To be sure, there is a great deal of Japan-bashing in America, and it is very visible to the Japanese—but a startlingly large amount of it has been bombastic play-acting for the benefit of American voters. Some of it has even been insti-gated by the Japanese themselves, as a way of putting pressure on their own government or industry.

But the new anti-American feeling in Japan is no longer playacting. It is more deeply felt and more widespread than it ever has been before; it is based on a solid mistrust of the Japanese government's own policies. In effect, the average person has sent a message to the government: "You shouldn't be spending this money on dams and highways." And the gov-ernment, in effect, has replied, "It's not our choice. It's an American demand. We cannot trigger a worldwide depression by dragging Wall Street down. The U.S. Congress will never tolerate us unless we come up with these tax cuts and public works simultaneously. This means that we have to borrow from the future, and have you all pay more for your own pensions and health care, month in and month out, for the rest of your lives, and those of your children and grandchildren."

People in Japan and in other nations conclude from this that the Ameri-cans are cavalierly draining money away from their country. The Americans are increasingly seen as manipulators, rigging the credit rating system, dic-tating policies imperiously to other nations, telling them to become more consumer-oriented and free-market-oriented while demanding political acts, such as the reckless investment in infrastructure, that would never fly at home.

As we saw in Chapter 1, this perception of bullying represents a major challenge to the United States, and particularly to 401K-ite leaders such as Greenspan, Summers, and President Clinton himself. In a way, this repre-sents a new kind of challenge to democracy, a paradoxical challenge from the invisible continent. Throughout the history of mankind, the majority have always been poor, and have been on the side of demanding fair dis-tribution from the rich and blessed. Yet, for the first time in human his-tory, the majority of people in one country have become the "haves." With their pensions, they are reaping the new-continent benefits of a seventeen-year-long continuous bull market. They demand overwhelmingly to keep going regardless of the means. American politicians (and by extension the rest of the world) are thus pushed around by the majority—passengers on a streetcar named "Desire," one might say—and the right of self-government may be threatened as a result.

Japan thus will be a test case for American good faith and cooperation everywhere. In the long run, having Japanese people reinvest in their own nation is good for Japan, good for America (giving them access to the second-largest market in the world for their own goods and services), and good for the rest of the world. It is even good for the 401K-ites, who benefit more from global prosperity than from prosperity in their own country at the expense of others. Setting Japan free from American dominance will allow Japan to bring itself onto the invisible continent, and give the United States a more powerful partner in both the new continent and the old world. Americans need to learn that they benefit when other nations are economically stronger, and other nations can only become stronger the same way the United States did—through the exercise of freedom. If the U.S. can promote the same kind of freedom in Japan that it promotes for itself, it will signal to Japan, to the rest of the world, and to Americans themselves that it can indeed be trustworthy and worthy of global leadership.

THE CRISIS THROUGHOUT ASIA

As we can see in the U.S.-Japan relationship, the invisible continent is interdependent with all national economies, and makes them interdependent with each other. This results in greater cross-border exchange of information, capital, and goods and services, and that creates political pressures. While the economy might have migrated to the new continent of the twenty-first century, the political world is left in the nineteenth century. The natural instinct for politicians is to praise their own nation's economy and workers, and blame others. Consumers, while they have become partial residents of the new continent, enjoying the benefit of global shopping, do not have the education to comprehend the sources of their prosperity or the lack thereof. So they often believe what the government is saying about the causes of prosperity, without ever thinking that the rest of the world may help or hinder. This tends to create global consumers (and investors) with unwittingly sentimental patriotism that belies their own actions.

In my experience, nobody is looking for conflicts and trouble. What people are looking for, even in troubled areas, is the "good life." They are searching for the ports of entry to the invisible continent, rather than resorting back to sovereignty-seeking war for the nation or even for the tribes. But they are susceptible to political leaders, bureaucrats, journalists, and even some scholars, who focus on the faults of other countries, ethnic populations (or tribes), and regions. As we have seen in the case of Eastern European countries, there is a deep-rooted distrust of their own government behind the seemingly offensive attitude of the peoples against their perceived enemies. This is now turning out to be true for Serbia, Iraq, Russia, North Korea, Pakistan, and even Cuba. Until people understand this point and share a much brighter global vision, there will be many unfortunate disputes.

Let us examine a few countries with this point in mind. It is a pity that these countries could often have arrived at much better solutions than they found, had they recognized that the new continent does not put at stake any particular government, or any specific (tribal) leaders. The invisible continent is indifferent to existing political parties and to most political ideologies. It simply and fundamentally challenges the style and mind-set of political leadership and governance. People can make peace with the new continent from just about any political starting place, so long as they can keep aware of its imperatives.

Malaysia: Overreacting to the Global Economy

Until mid-1997, Malaysia enjoyed the reputation of being the nation that most enthusiastically embraced the principles of the invisible continent. Its "Vision 2020" was one of the most comprehensive national visions, with numerous flagship applications of multimedia technologies. Over eight hundred global companies signed up to invest in the "cyberjaya" (the Malay equivalent of an e-hub) and the Multimedia Super Corridor (MSC), under construction immediately south of Kuala Lumpur.

Then the long tunnel began to seem too onerous. The prime minister, Dr. Mahathir Mohamad, lashed out at international speculators, currency traders, and the "great powers" for bringing down his country by shortselling the Malaysian ringgit. First he disagreed privately with his pro-IMF deputy, Dr. Anwar Ibrahim, on monetary policies. Then he and Anwar broke ranks publicly; and finally, late in 1998, the police force arrested Anwar on charges of sodomy—a charge that had nothing to do with his real offense, the act of publicly protesting the government's policies. Anwar, who had been designated as Mahathir's successor, was not just removed from office, but imprisoned.

This widely publicized event was at heart an overreaction to the reality checks of the new continent. Personally, I found this a tragic event, because I have been an advisor to Dr. Mahathir since 1982. I worked with him on the "Look East" programs and later helped him design the MSC that would have brought Malaysia onto the new continent. We designed, for example, a prototype "cyber-law" that allowed the MSC to flourish without Malaysia's otherwise restrictive bureaucratic laws. It was agonizing to watch this brilliant leader lose sight of his past policy. He was driven, apparently, by the concerns and fears of his own supporters, particularly the residents of the old industries, who were barking at the shadows of international outside speculators. Mahathir's bête noire, George Soros, never even reached the shores of Malaysia; Soros and the Tiger Fund's Julian Robertson short-sold Thai bahts in June of 1997, but Mahathir's open criticism in August 1997 fended off outside speculators rather quickly. In reality, the speculators in Malaysia were Malaysian themselves. These outspoken industrialists were indeed overstretched, and when the property bubble burst, they were illiquid.

When Malaysia's liquidity dried up, and the long tunnel began, this was not necessarily bad news for that country. It accelerated the long-overdue restructuring of the domestic industry, and stopped some of the wasteful investments in the old continent. More important, the devaluation of the ringgit—the ostensible trigger for Mahathir's change of direction—was a boon for Malaysia. It made Malaysian corporations competitive in the short run. That country had been so successful over the last ten years that they were importing labor from other countries, notably from Indonesia. They had an unemployment rate of minus 6 percent, or close to a million foreign workers.

In short, if Mahathir's government had kept calm, the Malaysian economy would have continued to thrive, perhaps with some Indonesian workers going back home. Why, then, did they panic? The panic was clearly psychological. Suddenly the economy was out of control. Speculators like Soros represented the government's loss of ability to direct the economy. This triggered, in my opinion, a deeply seated set of anxieties, not just in Mahathir but in many of his key advisors. These feelings propelled them back into the nineteenth-century nationalistic paradigm, and took them to the extreme step of closing the foreign exchange markets. Underneath the surface was a dawning realization: the ASEAN economies were firmly interlinked. A process of constant arbitrage across the ten or so countries was taking place, and this made the "hydraulics" for steering individual economies very difficult. There was nothing new or breathtaking about this kind of regional epitome. It had struck Nordic countries in 1992, and Latin America several times over the last decade. But it had never taken place in Asia before.

Interestingly, one year after these events took place, Dr. Mahathir visited me in Tokyo. He said that he was still willing to adapt the system to the invisible continent, as long as the rest of the world adapted too. But his country was too vulnerable if it went first. Luckily for him, his country is sound. It should go first, at least in the region, to demonstrate once and for all that a commodity-based economy can prosper as a cyberjaya, or e-hub. And as we shall see in the Chapter 8, the Malaysian experience does have one very significant implication for the rest of the world: It points the way toward finding an effective means of curbing the destruction of unbridled currency speculation.

Indonesia: The Curse of Former Nonaligned Countries

Malaysia may have been temporarily unwilling to accept the global economy, but Indonesia is probably congenitally incapable of doing so. Malaysia will probably bounce back to the new continent, but Indonesia will find the transition much more difficult.

The problem is the country's governance structure. Indonesia is composed of 189 million people living on 13,700 islands (of which 6,000 are inhabited), divided among 300 tribes. These tribes practice a variety of religions; Christianity, Hinduism, Buddhism, and Islam are all prominent. The land mass is as long as the distance from Ireland to Turkey, and the central government is incapable of governing. It is doubtful that this political entity can remain intact; already it has been enmeshed in a bloody civil war in East Timor, with other potential civil wars, wars of independence, and border wars in Sumatra (Aceh), Kalimantan (Borneo), Lombok (Mataram), Maluku (Ambron), and Irian Jaya (Papua).

The fundamental problem is a legacy of the Cold War. Nonaligned countries, such as India, Indonesia, and Yugoslavia, thrived during that period by learning to play one side off against the other. They united themselves, under the formidable leadership of Nehru and Gandhi, and Tito and Sukarno, respectively, who cleverly played against twin threats—the United States and the Soviet Union. Now these nations find themselves thrust toward division. On the new continent, nonalignment no longer conveys much legitimacy, because every nation is now unaligned. Since regional identity offers more leverage, countries that were loose confederations of ethnic groups now feel irresistible pressure to split, and there is deep resistance to splitting by any of the ethnic groups whose leaders seem to feel they should dominate the whole country.

Indonesia's leaders cannot accept the global economy until they resolve their governance issues. This is very unfortunate because there are many conscientious Indonesians who would like to put their economy in harmony with the rest of the world. While they wait for a political resolution, some of them are joining the new continent by divorcing themselves as much as possible from the Indonesian mainstream. The Balinese, for example, are technically part of Indonesia, but they have consistently tried to position their territory as a peaceful tourist destination. They are competitors to Hawaii and Tahiti; they are not part of the Indonesian economy, which is based on either natural resources or low-cost labor. If parts of Indonesia join the new continent early, it probably will take place in Bali first through destination tourism. But will the autocratic central government let a region like Bali determine its own fate on the global map?

South Korea: Trapped in a Developing-World Mind-Set

South Korea has a very hard choice to make, between status and reality. The decision before them—which they will be forced to make, perhaps by the time this book is printed—is interesting precisely because it sets into stark relief the choices that will face many fast-growing nations as they recover from the currency crisis. Developing countries are tested several times as they become "developed" and fully open to the global economy. Even developed countries, such as the UK and Sweden, are exposed to reality checks from time to time by the speculators and arbitrageurs. The best remedy against speculation is to develop an economy based on real competitiveness, as opposed to showing only self-aggrandizing signs of economic growth to the rest of the world. In other words, instability creeps in when countries try to pretend to be full-fledged members of the global economy.

During the late 1990s, South Korea gained entry into the OECD by reaching a per capita GNP of $10,000. Then their currency was devalued, which was appropriate—it had been overvalued before. Per capita GNP fell to half its former international level, to $5,000. Hence their choice. If they hold to the $10,000 figure on paper, and remain in the OECD, they will keep their status as a member of a wealthy nations club. They will keep their pride. But they will lose the help they need to achieve real wealth, and they will risk losing their hold on economic growth and their entry into the invisible continent.

On the other hand, if they accept the $5,000 status, they must follow the programs imposed on them by the International Monetary Fund. This will rankle, because it means being perceived as dominated, once again, by America. Very few Koreans know that the American public doesn't support the IMF at all, and doesn't want to put money into it. They perceive the IMF as an occupation army and a puppet of America's expansionist agenda. The South Korean public is anti-foreign and anti-America in its mood.

The government's leader, Kim Dae Jung, is not doing a good job in coming to grips with this choice. As a longtime opposition leader only recently come into power, he is predisposed to listen to American investment bankers and the IMF. As with Japan, they are giving him exactly the wrong advice. They tell him to practice and preach austerity, to promote savings. They suggest he freeze wages to avoid inflation and to keep the currency from falling further. He has agreed to keep interest rates high, at least initially, and to dismantle the *chaebols*, the South Korean corporate consortia that have dominated the country's economy. Each *chaebol* will be allowed to keep only three core businesses.

This IMF package represents, in effect, a rescue plan for American banking. (The Japanese and Europeans were not involved much in South Korean lending.) When South Korea was caught by the Asian currency crisis, the U.S. authorities had panicked. The $55 billion IMF package ensures that South Korea will return the money to the Americans, and pay for it through austerity and the sacrifice of future growth. American investment bankers get nearly all the subsequent merger and acquisition deals, and America's big accounting firms are blessed with due-diligence and evaluation assignments in restructuring the economy.

But South Korea's situation is exactly the opposite of Japan's. It must convert itself into a consuming economy or it will not attract foreign trade. It needs to become a global player. Currently, South Koreans buy only goods made by Koreans, though they import raw materials and key components. Despite the fact that they have deregulated much of their trade in accordance with the IMF, this makes them an unattractive market, as there is not a real consuming public at large. No Japanese company has succeeded in South Korea—not because of the traditional antagonism between Koreans and Japanese, but because it is difficult to succeed in South Korea. Even Korean companies sometimes have difficulty, unless they are given special privileges to dominate the market.

South Korean labor unions are also some of the toughest around. This is one of the reasons even the large *chaebols* have tried to exit South Korea to establish production bases in China, Vietnam, Europe, India, and Latin America. The money the *chaebols* had borrowed from the American banks was largely used to finance "operation exodus" from South Korea. In other words, the *chaebols* were trying to repeat their success overseas, as they found it difficult to keep wages down and get increased productivity from their own workers.

Instinctively, the South Korean people and government want to conserve resources and save, but that means they have already, in their minds, gone back to being a developing country. If they want to act as a developed country, they must learn to do the opposite of what their instinct tells them. They must give more money to their people, to encourage them to build better lives for themselves, and thus to spend more. They must develop their people to be much more globally oriented and more accepting of non-Korean psychologies and products and services. Only then will they be able to return to "real" OECD levels, to the $10,000 GNP level, but this time with a consuming market of 40 million people that is far more attractive for anyone—for the global economy to come in, and for themselves from within. Their biggest enemy is themselves: their own nationalism, and their narrow focus on the export success of their country during the growth spurt of the last thirty years.

Singapore and Taiwan: Quietly Escaping Failure

The world was shocked by the catastrophic earthquakes that hit Taiwan in September of 1999, not because of the magnitude of the disaster (the quake in Turkey, just before, was more severe), but because of the magnitude of the shock wave it sent to the personal computer industries around the world. Few had recognized the industry's heavy reliance on Taiwan as a source for chips and other critical components for high-tech products. This is just one example of the ways that Taiwan and Singapore are making a rather smooth (and calculated) transition to the invisible continent. And their financial markets have provided further evidence.

In all of the Asian nations, the more avidly the government tries to exercise control and the more willfulness its leaders show in keeping their currency high, the more punishment they receive from speculators. Singapore and Taiwan make the case for this argument effectively, because they did the opposite. They let the market dictate currency levels, and the Asian crisis had the least effect on them.

It turns out that speculators are not interested in countries where the government accepts the market's valuation of their currencies and equity stocks. There is no room with such currencies for speculators to make a killing. Only governments with willpower, trying to forestall speculation, fall prey to speculators, who then have the opportunity to outmaneuver and arbitrage the government's efforts at control. This has been the pattern with every country that has lost currency value to speculation: Russia, Brazil, the United Kingdom, Mexico, Malaysia, Indonesia, Thailand, and many more.

Not long ago I was in Melbourne, staying next to the Crown casino—a favorite locale of Asian gamblers in better days. Most of the Asian gamblers are gone, but the national flag of Taiwan was still hanging there. The Singaporeans go to Perth for the casino and the game of golf, and they did not slow down their weekend stints there even in the midst of the so-called Asian crisis.

Of course, Singapore and Taiwan did not escape the Asian crisis completely unscathed. They merely responded effectively and promptly, with an aikido-like willingness to bend to the market and then bend back. Their currencies are worth 90 percent of what they were worth before, and they will rebuild their value more quickly than any of the other Asian nations.

China: Too Large for the Global Economy

It is fashionable to think of China as the world's largest potential consumer market, but few people understand the changes that this shift would require. To be a large player on the new continent, they would need to rise to the $10,000 per capita GNP level established by the OECD. That is simply not possible for China as a whole.

There are five reasons for this. First, the government, with its legacy of Communism, is still too intent on central control. But the country is too large and too diverse to manage effectively from the center. Some major cities are very prosperous and open to the world, while other regions, particularly in the western plains and mountains, are very poor. The contrast between the nouveau riche and the poor is distorting the sense of equity of Chinese society.

Second, the government's ability to collect taxes is shrinking. The poor don't pay taxes, but the rich are finding more and more ways to arbitrage themselves out of the tax rolls. And as shown in late 1999 in the Province of Fujian, corruption and smuggling at the highest levels of government (rumored to amount to $10 billion) discourages any honesty in the disclosure of income or the payment of taxes. For a while, the Chinese government financed its operations through "red-chip" stocks—dummy companies floated in the Shanghai and Hong Kong stock markets. But now investors are wise to the parentage of these stocks, and are no longer interested in investing in them. While there are quite a few private enterprises rising to power, they are not enough in number and size to make a dent.

Third, the cavalier Chinese attitude toward outside investment is coming home to roost. Few will lend money to China, because the Chinese do not honor their debts or contracts. In a country accustomed to centralized control, it is not uncommon for an official to come in and refuse to live up to past commitments: "Sorry, the rules have changed now." But foreign businesspeople will not accept that. As a result, China is losing not just investment, but technology and partnership from abroad. The first symptom of this emerged in 1998, when Chinese banks, which are known as "international trust companies," fell into a liquidity crisis; twelve out of 240 of these trust companies, notably the ones in Guangdong and Dalien, were declared insolvent, defaulting on nearly all their overseas loans. With such a low level of trustworthiness, there is little possibility of getting investment from overseas, even from the overseas Chinese.

Fourth, the Chinese currency is inherently unstable. The RMB (yuan) is pegged to the Hong Kong dollar, which in turn is pegged to the United

States dollar, as spelled out in a bilateral agreement between the United Kingdom and Beijing. Every time Hong Kong mints 7.8 Hong Kong dollars, it must deposit $1 (or equivalent hard currency) in one of the three banks: the Bank of China, Hong Kong Bank, or Standard Chartered Bank. On the surface, it seems like a clear system, but it is polluted by the fact that a large part of the money that comes into Hong Kong is illegally obtained income from China, invested by Chinese politicians, bureaucrats, and lucrative merchants. That's why Chinese leaders insist on keeping intact the link between the Hong Kong dollar and the United States dollar. But suppose that they learn how to deal directly with Swiss banks, hedge funds, and other off-shore investments, and thus become less dependent on Hong Kong as their safe haven. Then they might pull Hong Kong loose from the American dollar. The result would be a series of financial oscillations overtaking China; no one knows the depth to which the Chinese currency might sink.

Fifth, and most important, is the decline of Chinese competitiveness. Joining the world economy has meant inviting foreign companies to enter China. These companies are more competitive than domestic Chinese companies, which are owned by the state or provinces. The domestic companies, instead of making money for the Chinese government, are becoming a net cash drain. Seventy percent of the state-owned institutions are now losing money. There is no hope, once the "China fever" subsides, that these companies will make money.

The size of the potential market and the avidity of corporations seeking to enter China has kept the country's economy afloat so far. But "China business fevers" tend to run in cycles. Japan has taken part in the last three of these cycles, while the West has only taken part in the last one. They all tend to follow the same pattern. Outsiders look longingly at the Chinese market. "If every Chinese person bought a pair of shoes," they think, "or a television, we would have it made." Then they struggle to find a solid footing for their business. After five or ten years, the outsiders give up, and China begins to decline.

In 1999, there were already signs that the country was poised for a Brazil- or Russia-style slide down the steep slope of depression. If it continues, this could have devastating effects on the rest of the world, in part because of China's access to nuclear weapons, and in part because the Chinese have large holdings in American government bonds. Their liquidity crisis could lead them to dump these bonds, which could trigger, in turn, a rush of capital out of the United States. Considering the way the Chinese handled the "trust banking" liquidity crisis, it's possible that the reserve banks in China may not have the reserve holdings that they should have saved up from the trade surplus. Key players have already taken money out to safer havens elsewhere. Should that fact come to be known, the Chinese market will become a paradise for hedge fund arbitrageurs.

The pressure that this would place on China would be very difficult for any central government to manage. There is a very plausible future in which China thus devolves into ten or twelve separate region-states. This would not be as outlandish as it sounds in the West—China has been divided into separate countries many times during its four-thousand-year history. It has also been governed by foreign forces, such as the Mongols and Manchurians, for over three hundred years (though the conquerers were later naturalized to Chinese). In fact, there has been only a brief period during the Qing Dynasty (1616–1912) when the country was unified into anything like its current borders.

If China devolved, its new regions might not have the kind of stable governance structures that we associate with nations; they might remain confederated as China, or even "Chung Hua," a prosperous Chinese federation. But economically, the regions would be completely separate entities, and life among them would vary considerably from region to region. Some, like the Dalien region, would be worthy of foreign investment, with an excellent industrial infrastructure and very capable administrators; others might still be risky and need to compete with other regions for global recognition. Taiwan may choose to be part of such a federation, so long as it is organized like the British Commonwealth, allowing each region autonomy or even independence. Devolving in this way might be the only viable strategy for a country of China's (and for that matter, India's) size as the new continent emerges.

Which brings us to Russia . . .

The End of the Russian Nation

In the 1980s, I predicted the end of the Union of Soviet Socialist Republics.[10] This prediction was not oracular; it was based on an analysis of the forces that were making the governance of such an organization increasingly difficult. Nor was I alone in making this prediction: Warren Bennis and Philip Slater, Peter Schwartz, Herman Kahn, and Peter Drucker all went on record with similar statements. But many other people overestimated the USSR's staying power. And they are doing the same with Russia. I thus make a prediction here that *very* few others are willing to make today: the Republic of Russia, as a single political entity, is just as ungovernable as the USSR was. Russia, as a nation, will devolve.

Those like Jeffrey Sachs of Harvard (and the Harvard Institute for International Development), who advocated reforming the Russian economy (and Indonesia) on the American model, have overlooked the organizational and governance issues. They have thus contributed to destroying Russia.[11] Based on their advice, the presiding officials reformed the basis of economic activity around the free market, but they provided no organizational reform in the government to counterbalance this. The central controls of the Moscow establishment were kept intact. The regions were not freed to act as separate political and economic entities. As a result, a small set of privileged groups were able to take over the country. The country is now controlled by a Russian/Azeri "mafia" with no allegiance to the people of Russia at large. This is not a problem of leadership per se (although former President Yeltsin contributed to it through both his leadership style and corruption among his associates); it is a problem of political structure. Regions do not compete for excellence in Russia, as they do in Germany and the U.S. And a country organized around a mafia-like model will fail on the invisible continent.

Unified politically but lacking a coherent social and economic fabric, Russia has been particularly vulnerable to currency speculators. They push the market up by buying rubles, and then short-sell so the ruble falls. The government, which doesn't understand the difference between these oscillations and the real economy of goods and services, plays along and tries to boost the currency. Such government measures—propping the currency back up and drawing away productive investment from the country—take place at the expense of the businesspeople who are trying to create new enterprises.

The solution for Russia would be to decentralize—to give as much power as possible to regional/city-state entities. Moscow could become a region-state unto itself, and the coordinating leader of the federation. St. Petersburg could become a highly cosmopolitan cyber-region, like Singapore, Ireland, or Finland. Siberia itself could become a federation of four autonomous region-states, respectively encompassing Irkutsk, Vladivostok, Sakhalin/Kurils, and Kamchatka. Once Moscow loosens its control over these regions, investment will flock from literally all over the Asia/Pacific regions and from the overseas Chinese entrepreneurs. A group of long-range planners, similar to the Jefferson-Washington-Adams team for the U.S. two hundred years ago, could design such a federation.

But there is little hope of any of this, given Russia's incumbent politicians and political system. Without dumb luck, Russia will become an organized-crime-dominated police state, with any law and order upheld by temporary force. The most tragic aspect of this is the lost opportunity. The Russian people are very smart, thoroughly well educated, and ingenious. They held their own in the space race; they managed to survive forty years of Cold War against a power that was wealthier and better equipped. And they are fully capable of managing the high-tech aspects of an information economy. But they have been sleeping, since Gorbachev, in an intensely anxiety-ridden dream state, and they have not shown any signs of waking up. If they did, we would see Russian city-states deliberately spun off as experiments in adaptation.

The key is for them to understand that the challenge is not whether to adopt a market mechanism as opposed to the Communist planned economy. The key is how to work with the global economy and the economy of the invisible continent, and to design a governance structure accordingly. Russia today is still centrally controlled and functionally organized. Unless it breaks up into manageable units autonomous without losing the overall coordination, there is little hope that regions will be able to establish enough credibility so that investors will come in and stay to work with the local corporations and consumers for their long-term benefits.

Beyond the Asian Crash

Like the "Year 2000" computer crisis, the Asian currency crash will ultimately be remembered as a catastrophic one-time event—an event that left its mark on the world, but didn't linger. For most Asian nations, like most European and Latin American nations, will eventually make their way through the long tunnel.

Every country is different. Yet, all of them have one thing in common: They cannot succeed as producer nations alone. If you want to bring your country to a higher standard of living and a better quality of life, you must learn not just how to produce goods that the rest of the world will want, but also how to consume goods that the rest of the world makes better and more cheaply. Only if your people can obtain products and services more cheaply than you can make them at home, will your nation's real standard of living (its quality of life) improve. To succeed, people must be able to add intellectual value on the invisible continent's networks of information. To build up their consumer base, the nations of the new continent must present their people with a vision for a better life. Indeed, this may turn out to be the most valued function of government during the decades ahead—not fixing the problems of today, but presenting clear images of what type of world might be built tomorrow, and what kind of individuals will succeed in such a society. The biggest remaining job for any government is to develop a vision for the country, to prompt and catalyze such a change, and to create a legal framework within which people can enjoy life in the new continent.

I know of no nations, including the United States and the United Kingdom, that have successfully created such a vision. Even the most acknowledged political visionaries of the past twenty years have focused their attention only on fixing problems at hand. Mikhail Gorbachev, for example, talked clearly about the problems facing the Soviet Union. His solutions—glasnost and perestroika—clearly represented the right solutions for those problems. But he had nothing to say about the kind of society that he wanted to lead the Russians into *after* glasnost and perestroika took hold. All he said was, "We'll let the free market come in." He might as well have tried to teach a school of fish to fly; instead of leading the Soviets to a new world, he opened them up to the theft of a nation by Russian organized crime.[12] The British Broadcasting Corporation (BBC), in one documentary on the effects of the mafia economy, reported that there are 6,000 active mafia-style organizations today in Russia, with 80,000 active "executives." These people divert 40 percent of the overseas investment in Russia, or $114 billion, to overseas banks and havens. One cannot build a country with this kind of leakage.

Ireland, with its image of being an e-hub nation, may be the closest nation in the world today to having a clear and shared vision of the future it wants to create. That is why Ireland led off this chapter. But the Irish e-hub is only a first step. To see what kinds of visions are possible, we need to look more closely at the activity within nations, the activity that will be galvanized to create new kinds of wealth. First, let's consider the economic engines of the new continent—the new forms of corporate endeavor. Then we will return to look more closely at the people whose temperament is changing, and whose ideas about citizenship are adjusting, as they get used to straddling two types of worlds.

THE NEW COLD WAR

Imagine that the year is 2015. The population of the planet has stabilized at 100 billion people, but the proportion of poor people is growing more rapidly than ever. To have access to wealth and to a high-quality life depends on being born under the right government—a difficult trick for many people, because much of the political landscape exists as terrain without a formal government or country. Many parts of the world have, in effect, become "company towns," plugged in to the Internet but communicating only with the sanctioned city-states and regions that have complementary corporate interests at heart.

Trillions of dollars flow into and out of all of these states and regions every day, but very little of it is translated into new investments in productive activities. In any case, the number of people who live at a means above subsistence is growing smaller and smaller. Thus, the market for both goods and services has become smaller as well, and competition grows fiercer. Companies and nations both compete to lure the fewer and fewer winning customers their way. Everyone recognizes the problems this causes, but feels powerless to stop it; after all, if any one city, region, nation, or company breaks the pattern of continual strife, it will lose both power and economic market share to its competitors.

How did we get here? The interplay of the four dimensions of the invisible continent—and in particular, our misunderstandings of them—has led us here. The invisible continent has its own imperatives, and if we meet its demands with old-world solutions, the results could be very dangerous.

For example, most people have aspirations for peace and prosperity that contradict the borderless dimension. It is tempting to imagine, as John Lennon sang in the 1970s, that a world with no rigid national boundaries, with no political reason to kill or die, would be a peaceful world. But when national borders dissolve, to be replaced by economic borders, then nationalist wars can be replaced by economic wars.

In our time, that may be happening. The world war of the next century could be a war without bloodshed; no bullets might be fired. Much of it would be fought on the invisible continent, using the weapons of the dimension of high multiples. The consequences might be just as devastating for civilians caught in the "cross-fire" as for those caught up in the carnage of the Cold War and its isolated battles around the world. This would be a new cold war, and possibly an enduring one, with worldwide presence and continually shifting alliances, rife with betrayal and double-agentry.

Conventional descriptions of the next cold war assume that it would take place between the United States and China, aligning themselves against each other just as the U.S. and the Soviet Union did during the years after World War II. But that was an old-world war, a war fought by nineteenth-century rules. During the Cold War years, in fact, business was often compared to the military, precisely because old-line businesses were as bureaucratic and staid as military institutions. Such military jargon as "line and staff," "span of control," and "pyramid structure" were imported to the businesses of the old world without hesitation. On the invisible continent, the influence will move in the other direction. The new cold war could be fought on the battleground of business, and military institutions will be as rapacious and fast-changing as the Godzilla companies that they emulate.

The players in such a war would be not just the remnants of countries, but the superarching blocs that countries belong to and the companies that operate within and outside them. Potential casualties include the assets and livelihoods of civilians around the world, especially their opportunities for making wealth and the pensions that would protect them as they age. The weapons of the new cold war would be economic, but they would be deployed with as much viciousness and damage as an AK-47.

Such a war is not predetermined or inevitable—but it is all too plausible. Indeed, chances are that it will take place unless something deliberate is done to avoid it. Worse still, it could easily happen with such subtlety and ambiguity that most people would not realize the danger until they were already immersed in it.

ANATOMY OF A NEW COLD WAR

Consider the tendencies and forces that exist in our world today, which could lead in such a direction. In this section, I make a series of predictions—not because I expect them to come true in literal detail, but because they illustrate the forces of the invisible continent and the way those forces are moving the world.

High Financial Risks

In 1998, the collapse of the hedge fund operator Long-Term Capital Management (LTCM) brought into focus the potential for danger from the invisible continent. While the average multiple of LTCM (the money it could trade with) was only 45 times the amount of assets (cash and stocks) that it held, the extreme transactions apparently went up to 250 times assets. This meant that for every dollar in LTCM's coffers, investors were willing to bet $250 on its success. The lenders of money were all first-class global banks. Yet, they were risking their existence on the survival of LTCM and other such hedge funds.

As it happens, in America during the 1920s stock market boom, there were funds with a similar reputation for high-risk, high-yield, daring experimentation, and uncanny savvy. They were known as "brokers' funds." The brokers' funds were available only for up to five times the money put down, or for multiples of 5; but they were seen later as one of the factors leading to the stock market crash of 1929 and the Great Depression. Much later, during the "go-go years" of the 1980s, the American stock market averaged multiples (defined as share price divided by earnings) of 25. During the high point of the Japanese bubble, Japan had multiples of 75. All of these multiples, at that time, were accused of being wildly out of control. Now, even after the example of LTCM, international hedge funds work with multiples two orders of magnitude higher than their 1929 counterparts, and some of the NASDAQ heroes have multiples approaching 1,000.

On the invisible continent, the sheer magnitude of money involved and the frequent use of the large multiples and options, all cross-border and cross-currency in nature, make the global financial market into a different beast than it has ever been before, a beast too nimble and slippery for governments (who, by the way, do not use multiples to combat the speculators)—and the whole world, for that matter—to deal with. Knowing this danger, nobody in the world would have the wisdom (and courage) to challenge NASDAQ, as everyone, every company, every bank, and every country is involved in the bonanza in one way or another.

Playing with leveraged multiples this way is a dangerous game, but the new companies seem to be willing and able, at least in the short run, to do it. The danger comes in part from short-selling, which is why the failure of hedge funds has been so visible. In short-selling, you sell at an agreed-upon price and settle a certain number of days later. If you go bankrupt, it happens not at the time of the sale, but at the time you settle, if you don't have enough money. This practice destroys companies and countries. A number of Japanese companies learned this in their efforts to come out of losses through derivatives, working with an American hedge fund called the Princeton Bond—which went bankrupt in 1999 before it could deliver some $4 billion.

The hedging technologies that made Long-Term Capital Management so bold were impeccable in logic. Their theory was advanced. But the theory backfired because the people at LTCM did not include human psychology in it. The theory had predicted that investors who found themselves confronted with unexpected risk (as American speculators in Russian currency were) would go next to the next-lower level of risk (which would have been securitized housing loans). But the investors in Russian derivatives panicked, and put their money immediately into the safest instruments they could find: U.S. government bonds. The LTCM hedgers were poised, waiting for their mythical "rational Americans" to buy the next-safest investment. But the rational Americans never came.

In such cases, the problem is not with the equations, but with the boundary conditions in place when people apply the equations. This is analogous to most accidents involving airplanes, nuclear reactors, computers, and cars—which come not from technological design in itself, but from stretching a technology beyond its expected boundary conditions. (Anyone who has a personal computer knows this. Add a new "init" to your "autoexecute" files, and you've changed the boundary conditions. The same is true of finance.) Hedge funds work perfectly well when they are exercised in the right conditions. But the presence of the right conditions is not guaranteed.

A Regulatory Structure with Rules But No Protection

The old-world policies set in place by many governments and financial regulatory bodies, seeking to protect against abuse or risk, have often backfired—precisely because the regulators of the old world don't understand the mathematical dimension of the invisible continent. For example, BIS (International Settlement Bank) regulations dictate that a bank must keep equity reserves on hand (including both currency and owned stocks) of 8 percent of all money that it lends out. This means that banks can lend

12.5 times as much money as they hold, and still be judged as safe.

But suppose that there is a temporary oscillation in the market—a surge and decline, as might easily happen in the fungible economy of the new continent. The bank's holdings would first be inflated to a huge amount, driven by multiples, and then would fall equally far. The same accounting regulations created to enforce old-world-style fiduciary responsibility would require the bank to adjust the book value of its assets—first up, and then down. On paper, if it follows this rule, the bank loses much more than the real value of its assets; it could suffer the far more extreme losses that it temporarily incurred. If it is forced, by the laws, (now it is required to do so by the International Accounting Standard, or IAS) to write off these losses during a particular accounting period, the bank may be artificially driven to collapse, simply because the accounting regulations do not recognize the volatile, transient nature of wealth on the new continent.

In effect, the bank that straddles the line between the old-world economy and the new-continent economy is at a disadvantage. It must book the appreciation gains in good time and cut its losses much faster in bad times than the rest of its old-world peers, but it does not get to retain the leverage of its new-continent counterparts. The laws, in short, treat the new-continent world of finance as if it were the old world of dry goods.

Keynesian Economic Decisions

The mismatch between the imperatives of the invisible continent and the Keynesian, old-world mind-set of many decision-makers helps explain some of the more counterproductive political and regulatory moves of the past decade. For example, the international financial market continually lends money to Russia and then, in times of contraction, pulls back the money faster than Russia would ordinarily be required to pay it back. Then the financiers accuse Russia of default. Russia is thus caught in a double bind, and struggles to emerge through the same measures that have put it in a bind in the first place. The Keynesian assumptions of conventional economics—that new borrowing and spending will create more jobs, and that new jobs will translate into tax revenues that allow Russia to pay back its debts—ensures that the problem conditions will keep getting worse, as lenders drown Russia, Brazil, and many other developing economies with capital and then contract, again and again and again.

The Keynesians seem to implicitly assume that a country could move through the entire economic cycle—borrowing, spending, jobs, taxes, revenues, and debt payback—in a year or two. It would be more realistic to assume an order of decades. For example, China experimented with the new market economy in Shenzen and Shanghai for ten years before Deng Xiaoping decided that the approach could be expanded to an additional dozen or so regions. The resultant surge of direct investment after 1992 indicates a favorable response to this cautious step-by-step approach. However, even with this slow an approach, the Chinese had difficulty maintaining their balance. By 1997, the Chinese market was drawing capital from literally all over the world, only to collapse in late 1998 with the symbolic fiasco of GITIC (Guandong International Trust and Investment Corp.), one of 240 such entities to take in foreign capital into China. Today the Chinese investment situation is like a sauna bath. It's going between hot and cold and does not seem to have a steady middle ground.

This does not mean that we should blame the high-multiples nature of the invisible continent wholesale for the troubles of Russia or China—or Malaysia, Thailand, the UK, Japan, or any other nation. On the contrary, the new continent offers unprecedented ways to create wealth across national borders and to distribute it from nation to nation. But the redistributive fast capability of the new continent will succeed only if the political institutions that are rooted in the old world learn how to work more effectively with it.

The American Cash Drain

Historians may someday agree that the starting point of the new cold war occurred in January 1999. That was the month when the United States, coasting on its laurels as the "victor" of the previous Cold War, entered a period of unsustainable economic activity. American consumers had always maintained a low savings rate: They saved 5 to 7 percent of their income on average, compared with 17 to 18 percent in Japan. But starting in 1999, Americans have actually had a negative savings rate. They spend more, on average per capita, than they earn in salary. In other words, enough Americans have prospered from the stock market boom that they spend beyond their means as a nation. This statistic reflects the fact that some people are putting their savings into higher-risk investments (which don't count as savings in the metrics), or actually borrowing from their expected stock gains to pay for their consumption.

This means, of course, that Americans are borrowing from the rest of the world, since about one-third of the Dow Jones boom has been supported by the net influx of capital from non-U.S. investors. And they are also borrowing from taxes they don't expect to pay in the future, since both the Republicans in Congress and Democratic President Bill Clinton have announced that they will use their surplus to pay back government debt. As a nation that pioneered economic activity in cyberspace and steadfastly maintains open borders to free trade, America deserves its prosperity to some extent. But if Americans, caught up in the wave of soaring stock prices, have become this complacent about by their fortune, they may no longer act with the same kind of good judgment that had brought them to the heights in the first place. For no one, no matter how strong and well intentioned, can spend beyond their means for very long.

The Propensity of the American Military and Diplomatic Establishment for Enemies

A pattern has been established since the 1970s: First Khadafi's Libya, then Iran, then Noriega's Panama, then Haiti, then Saddam Hussein's Iraq, then North Korea, and finally Slobodan Milosevic's Serbia have become demonized as countries that had to be stopped, as potential threats to America. To be sure, some of these countries were truly horrific, but none of them had picked a fight with America directly. The U.S. government made enemies out of each of them precisely because America seems to need enemies as a pressure valve for its aggressive instincts and an excuse to maintain military spending.

In truth, America has no real military enemies of any consequence. It is difficult to have military enemies *and* a significant presence on the invisible continent, with its strong borderless dimension. No one could seriously believe that Panama, Haiti, Iraq, North Korea, or even Serbia could actually threaten the United States in any significant way.

The Influence of the 401K-ites on American Political Decisions

In Chapter 6, I described how the needs of America's new class of pension-conscious workers has dominated U.S. policy toward Japan. In fact, it has come to dominate all U.S. policies, both international and local. To stay in office, American politicians depend on the continued optimism of its newly wealthy people. That in turn requires the stock market to stay high, to defy the heretofore immutable law of the business cycle: that all stocks must rise and fall.

This leads to an ever more narrow focus on day-by-day fluctuations. Securities analysts and the researchers who advise them react to minute movements of the GDP growth rate, interest rate, unemployment statistics, consumer price index (CPI), wholesale price index (WPI), trade balance data, and wage hikes. Instead of seeking to understand the long-term viability of the economy and its institutions (such as corporations), they buy and sell retroactively, constantly trying to catch up with these indices of the past. The stock price of a given company should reflect the net present value of the company moving forward, but it often is derived from a reactive view of the past, comparing last quarter's results to analysts' expectations, even though the analysts often have no basis on which to expect anything. Some cable channels broadcast around the clock these expectations and reconciliations, so much so that the vast majority of 401K-ites are becoming convinced that they truly understand the economy and the market.

With this confidence, the money once assembled in the U.S. has started to spread all over the world, with inherent naivete and commensurate boldness. With the help of the invisible continent's cyber dimension and dimension of high multiples, American investors have spread around the world.

To make this "globalization" happen smoothly, American politicians—some consciously, some naively—have begun to play a desperate political game. They have tried to corner the global market on opportunities to create wealth. In particular, they are trying to monopolize the new continent, and to become, in effect, a colonial power over it, by dominating (for example) decisions about Internet protocols, sales tax, copyright and trademark laws, local subscriber access charges, and telecommunications governance.

There is no malice intended toward the rest of the world, no hatred of enemies. Indeed, American diplomats tend to appreciate the rest of the world. But they are not about to risk losing their status as global economic leaders. In January 2000, for example, the U.S. Trade Representative (USTR) declared that Japan should halve the tariff on local access. They added that they would stick to this "demand."

In other words, while the U.S. military is increasingly involved in "peacekeeping" missions, the U.S. Commerce Department and USTR are increasingly sent to wage the new cold war. Or, at least, their activities are consistent with the nature of war. War is very rarely fought for ideological or political reasons alone; wars are rarely triggered by simple hate. They take place because of unresolved conflicts of interest: conflicts in which two or more countries believe that another country's presence will block their opportunities to create wealth. Wealth—its creation and distribution—are the primary drivers of war. Even the most deeply rooted conflicts, such as the war in Northern Ireland, is not purely ideological or religious. Its root cause is the belief, held by Catholics and Protestants, that either group in power will block the other's opportunities, will control patronage positions, will slant tax rates, or their implementation, and will indenture the other side as laborers and servants. After several decades of bitter opposition, these types of presentiments become self-fulfilling prophecies.

There is a real danger that the United States—the richest country in earth's history—may train itself to fear the rest of the world. This could happen if Americans believe that, from any nation, a rogue like Milosevic or Saddam Hussein might spring up and threaten the U.S.'s easy prosperity. Worse still, an ally might figure out how to duplicate America's success; and then America would lose its "rightful" inheritance of a perpetually rising Dow Jones.

Smaller Regions of Wealth and Poverty

It is reasonable to think that the most prosperous economic entities on the invisible continent would have somewhere between 3 and 5 million people. They might be part of larger nations or regional entities, but they can only thrive economically, as we saw in Chapter 5, if they can act autonomously and creatively. Larger entities will survive, to be sure, but only if they can provide a coherent and harmonious context for regions, with good infrastructure. They will need to maintain open markets, to privatize industries, and to deregulate their infrastructure and critical industries (finance, telecommunications, and transportation).

Countries on the "short list" of prosperity probably include Singapore, New Zealand, Finland, Ireland, Israel—and few others. Some autonomous regions, such as Catalonia, Dubai, Lombardia, and Cascadia, will continue to thrive.

Other areas in the world will face gruesome poverty, with almost no control at the national level. Even countries that contain prosperous regions, such as India with its cyber-cities, will not be able to build upon that prosperity. The Bangaloreans are Indians in name only; they seem to have no interest in subsidizing reform for the rest of India, and may well vote to secede to a new state. In desperation, countries like India may merge with other countries, devolve into a series of smaller countries, or forge alliances with Russia or even (historically hostile) China.

New Currencies Rivaling the Dollar

In a sense, the Americans (more like the American politicians, as opposed to already global American investors) are right to worry. They have a major potential rival in the increasingly united governments of Europe. During the first few years of its existence, the euro stumbled. At first, the distribution of currency from the central bank depended on each country's growth rate. Thus, each country had an incentive to spur its economy in the short term, and to fudge the statistics. Moreover, the Maastricht Treaty has led to an enormous financial bureaucracy, ostensibly set up for managing the euro. The bureraucracy has micromanaged the economic affairs of the member countries (whose common name, "Euroland," is becoming the standard way to refer to their shared economic region), and has slowed down the economy of Europe as a whole.

Despite all of this, the euro is a huge vehicle for stability. It defuses the massive swings of speculation in European currencies by substituting a regional currency, which (as we saw in Chapter 5) can't be manipulated by speculators as easily.

Gradually, Europe may well evolve into a "United States of Europe," despite the differences of languages and traditional borders. Something similar happened in the early history of the United States, in fact, when it gradually assimilated Spanish-speaking Northern Mexico, French-speaking Louisiana, and Russian-speaking Alaska. Like the U.S. in its initial stages, Euroland is a loosely federated task force. The growing reliance on networked businesses, such as the Irish call centers, requires increasing interdependence and liberalization of restrictions—so that Spanish-speaking citizens, for instance, could easily move to Dublin from Barcelona as needed when the call centers require them.

If the U.S. and Euroland become economic rivals, then they will primarily clash over access to capital. The rest of the nations of the world may be startled to discover capital flowing away from them. One can imagine other regional currencies emerging in response: the sol from an expanded MERCOSUR ("Mercado Comun del Sur") alliance of Argentina, Brazil, Uruguay, Paraguay, Chile, Peru, Colombia, Venezuela, and Bolivia; or the asea from the Association of Southeast Asian Nations (ASEAN), possibly joined by Japan and Korea. If the yen becomes stable as well, that could be on its own, and would lead to four or five globally stable currencies competing as investment platforms for investors' attention.

Central banks around the world would leave behind their exclusive position in the dollar. They would hedge their investments in triadian fashion, holding at least equal amounts of yen (or Asian currencies as they exist) and euros to the dollar. Hong Kong Bank already announced in 1998 that by 2010, its U.S. dollar reserves will be reduced to 40 percent of their foreign reserves, from 56 percent today.[1] As Figure 9 shows, yen and euros will pick up the slack.

The dollar has the most to lose. In the 1990s, 50 percent of the world's private savings was held in dollars. If this falls to 40 percent, it would represent a capital flight of $350 billion away from the U.S. Pension fund sav-

Foreign Reserves-2010
An Example of Hong Kong Bank

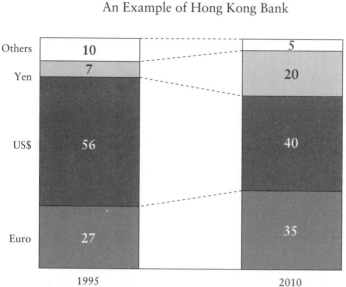

Figure 9. Two profiles of the Hong Kong Bank foreign reserve holdings: in 1995, and projected for 2010. As the diagram shows, the proportion of dollars will decrease by almost one-third, to be replaced by yen and euros. This is one example of the pressure about to be applied to the dollar as a global currency platform, and thus to American economic hegemony. (Source: The Industrial Bank of Japan, "IBJ Report," July 1998.)

ings in particular would probably move from dollar-based investments to euro-based investments. No longer bolstered by the platform of an invincible dollar, the U.S.'s enviable low inflation would finally give way to moderate inflation, or even to strong inflation. American goods, particularly American entertainment and software, would be dumped on the global market. Speculators, as they once arbitraged other currencies, would sell the dollar short. As confidence in the dollar diminishes, creditors from other nations would insist on payment in euros and yen. Americans, including the American government, would now have to pay their debts in other nations' currencies. The American government's national debt, which has contracted since the Clinton administration began, would soar again from the lows of $2.5 trillion of year 2000.

Naturally, American politicians and some American investors would do everything possible to degrade the euro, to keep the dollar from devaluing further. This "Atlantic battle" could be the first skirmish of a new cold war. I imagine both Europe and the U.S. being weakened from their bout, and acting like a pair of weakened boxers, forced to keep sparring with each other but dreading the next blow. They might go into a clinch and merge their currencies into one, the currency of the North Atlantic, the "doro" or "eullar"—a combined dollar and euro.

Currency Speculators as Potential War-Makers

Speculators by nature prefer smaller markets, where they can manipulate government policies, boil up the market, short-sell their way out of it, and escape before the downturn. But this would no longer be feasible with regional currencies like the euro, asea, and doro. So they would descend rapidly on the fragmented currencies of nations without regional unions. That would lead to still more regional currencies, creating even more competition against the dollar. I imagine a doro bloc, an ASEAN asea bloc, a MERCOSUR sol bloc, and a smaller bloc composed of Russia and China together with a currency called "ex-com." Each major bloc would continually do its best to diminish and defeat other blocs' currencies. They would use all the weapons at their disposal: program trading, hedging with multiples, security violations, e-commerce oscillations, spreading disinformation and viruses on the Internet, and various new-continent-style efforts to build up currencies, arbitrage them, and see them fall. Bank after bank would collapse in each of the major nations, unable to resist the gambling fever. The dimension of high multiples would give different "sides" in the battlefield rapidly shifting amounts of firepower. Different groups would try to fight each other with totally different multiples and hedges in the same market. It would be a world of powerful economic aggressors, as unstable and chaotic as our world would be if the U.S. used cruise missiles—as they did in Sudan and Afghanistan—routinely without warning and with no provocation, even though their opponents had only conventional firepower.

In such a world, clever investors would remain calm by diversifying—placing, say, 60 percent of their assets in doro, 30 percent in asea, 10 percent in sol, and nothing in ex-coms. There would be no loyalty whatsoever to the currency of their own government. As asset managers, they would need to be "above it all." Nationalist sentiment would not only seem like a nostalgic affectation, it would be threatening to their affluence and capital.

THE IMPACT OF A NEW COLD WAR

Put all of these factors together without any counterbalancing laws, customs, or social pressures, and you have a world reminiscent of the international relationships in George Orwell's book, *1984*. Orwell's three international blocs—Europa, Eurasia, and Oceania—shifted alliances every ten to fifteen years. But in the post-invisible-continent cold war, economic alliances would shift every day, hundreds of times a day, fighting over $2 trillion that would cross the Atlantic and Pacific every day. Traders would betray their allies, arbitraging their allies' economic positions, and the allies would never know. If an individual trader, feeling pangs of conscience, tried to show restraint, limiting the ill effects of his or her speculation, he or she would simply be outclassed by other traders with fewer scruples.

Most of the damage would probably happen to the less-developed countries. Americans, suffering hyperinflation and depression simultaneously, might think they had it bad—until they saw the plight of the Chinese, Mexicans, Brazilians, Indonesians, and Russians. No matter how compassionate they felt, if Americans thought that their prosperity depended on tightening the screws on these nations, the screws would tighten.

In such a war, every country, every corporation, and even every community would be a potential competitor. In both the tangible old world, and on the new invisible continent, the war would be thoroughly anarchic. The war zone would expand beyond any specific geographic territory to encompass the entire physical world, all of cyberspace, and even the mathematical universe using multiples and derivatives. You could visualize it best by looking under a rock in a field of lush soil; pull back the rock and you can see the insects and grubs swarming and competing for nutrients. Some would dominate and some would not, but all would compete for the same limited resources. They would all be in danger from each other; they would target each other and continually shift sides.

The previous Cold War lasted forty years, because the U.S. and the Soviet Union never directly fought. In this new cold war, that kind of stalemate would be unsustainable. There would be too many players, at too many levels of economic organization: nations, regions, companies, and some individuals. Nor could the United States be written off. As the engine of prosperity for the previous fifty years, the U.S. has made the rest of the world dependent on it. Economic psychology simply couldn't shift that much; people cannot fully see the U.S. as an enemy, even when it behaves as one.

But with this much stress on prosperity, prosperity would diminish even in the wealthiest nations. There could be very little effort to create a prosperous middle class; indeed, much of the world's economic activity would consist of taking any possible measure to impoverish the middle classes and drag them down from their comfortable positions. That (according to conventional wisdom) would make nations more vulnerable and thus more dependent on the doro and the asea. Much of the world would begin to resemble the slums of Calcutta. Kidnappings, terrorism, and other types of crime would dramatically rise.

SHARING A VISION OF WEALTH IN THE NEW ECONOMY

If the United States, or any other country, succeeds in creating a monopoly over the new continent, or even if any countries persist in trying to establish hegemony over the new continent, then a scenario like this—a new cold war—will be the result. The details may vary, but in every conceivable scenario, there is economic aggression: trade wars that take place with an unprecedented ferocity, driving people out of their livelihoods, shutting them away from opportunity for fear of losing dominance over the new world—and thus fostering a faster-growing poverty than the world has ever known before.

The alternative is also possible: a fully interdependent world in which prosperity spreads with Godzilla-like fervor, thereby creating opportunities for wealth everywhere. This would mean, in effect, universalizing the accomplishment of Microsoft. Microsoft's current market capitalization, as I write this, is $550 billion, or equivalent to the Korean national economy. That represents $30 million per employee. It's inconceivable that every Microsoft employee has created that much wealth. The market capitalization should not be taken as a literal measure of the wealth created to date, but of the net present value of the company's potential for creating wealth in the future. Yet, in one sense, the wealth has already been created: any Microsoft employee having stock options can realize this wealth now and then go on to form his or her own company, as Paul Allen has done so visibly already.

In an economy based upon high multiples, the market capitalization is whatever the investors price as the net present value of the company moving forward. That perception has tremendous force in reality. Cisco Systems, with $14 billion annual sales, has a market capitalization of $327 billion, with which it can continue to acquire companies by equity swap. (The range of those investments is shown in Figure 4, in Chapter 4.) That kind of growth is a privilege available only to those who understand the interplay within the new continent, particularly between the cyber-world and the multiples-based economy.

Conversely, any company—or country—that can make a case for potential in the new continent can also generate, or at least redistribute, wealth. The amount of wealth may not add up to billions, but it's also unlikely that Microsoft's or Cisco's market capitalization will remain so disproportionately high. And any country can develop its own strategy for creating wealth in the new continent, as Ireland and Singapore have done.

It can happen, but only if the invisible continent is seen as communal property. Just as the United States forged its identity by welcoming all races, religions, and cultures, the new continent must become a crucible of global contact or an e-hub: a meeting ground of residents from everywhere in the globe. Those who don't physically live in the United States, Europe, or Japan should be able to get the benefits of access—and the United States, Europe, and Japan will benefit from having the broadest possible network. In a way, we need a new group of founding fathers (or mothers) to spell out a new Treaty of Paris and Declaration. This would be equivalent to—or in many ways more important than—the creation of the U.S. It is extremely important to spell out the rules and laws of the new continent, so that it does not become a paradise of the villains.

The leverage, for the moment at least, lies with the same nineteenth-century-oriented politicians, and the same established leaders of corporate titans, who do not fully understand the implications of the invisible continent because they do not know how to live there themselves. Yet, they have control over national policies. They can't create an alternative to the new continent, but they can barricade it from accessibility. They can't rescue their own nations from the effects of the new continent, but they can spoil others' access to it. They can't control the surging tide of new-continent commerce, but they can siphon off significant parts of it.

Or they can foster its growth by opening, rather than closing, themselves to the world. As I write this, the chances for cooperation seem grimmer than they have in years. China, India, Russia, the U.S., and other big nations all have resounded with tones of mistrust and hostility toward other nations. Yet, there are also signs of authentic cooperation. Discussions are under way, for example, toward a multilateral agreement between European Union, NAFTA, and MERCOSUR nations. This alliance, if it takes place, would allow for free trade across the three blocs. Argentina's (then) President Carlos Menem announced in December 1998 that the MERCOSUR nations have already agreed in principle to establish a cross-Atlantic free-trade bloc by the year 2005.

Whether explicitly or intuitively, politicians who opt for this course have found their only source of leverage over Godzilla-style corporations. With its enormously heightened performance, the new-continent company seems like a juggernaut, running roughshod over all opposition, particularly over government opposition. Yet, without consumers, it has no power. The winner on the invisible continent is the consumer who knows how to establish a presence amidst the deregulated, shifting political structures of the new environment. A government that fosters this type of sustainable position by helping its citizens plug in to the new continent, and by offering a higher quality of life in old-world venues, will be able to induce corporations to come to it on much more agreeable terms. While the transition to the new environment seems hopeless at first, and while it requires giving up established habits of thought, there is light at the end of the long tunnel.

We have already seen how certain qualities will be optimal in the political units of the future. These include: A population between 3 and 5 million people. Open borders. Deregulation. Access to the Internet in relatively free and easy fashion. Finally, as we shall see in Chapter 8, high-quality education with effective instruction in everyday English will be critical. But all of these qualities, in themselves, will not guarantee success per se, just as having a good product and a well-trained workforce does not guarantee success for corporations. To succeed, corporations need a strategy: a shared vision of the desired future of the company that helps people determine where to put their resources and how to build their capabilities. Similarly, every successful nation (or, if you prefer, every successful geopolitical unit) will need a strategy to realize that success. Since this strategy will be put into practice by individuals, not by corporations, it will need to be talked about openly. Countries will have to learn how to reach consensus about their shared vision for the future. They need to develop a sense of ownership, shared by their citizenry, of the mission and objectives, the results and rewards, and the problems that await them.

Ireland and Singapore are good examples of countries that have learned how to develop a vision and strategy. Their example also shows how smaller, more coherent countries and city-states have emerged as hubs for the cyber-age and as global financial centers. Not long ago I visited a town of two thousand people near Shannon. Everyone in town has a personal computer; even the kindergarten had PCs. The residents of the town did not seem very wealthy, but they had chosen to invest what money they had in this form of education. They had been involved in discussions around the e-hub concept; they were part of the development of that concept. And they were willing, and capable, of taking their own initiatives to support that concept, even without a mandate from the center. Across Ireland, towns and villages were coming up with other ways to support the e-hub concept and bring it to fruition. They saw that if they could make it work, they would all benefit and prosper as a result.

Japan provides a contrasting example. In the past, shared visions have been the source of strength for us. Forty years ago, for example, the Ministry of Trade and Industry (MITI) said, "The future of Japan is steel." We became, almost overnight, very strong in steel. The same thing happened shortly thereafter with ships, automobiles, and home appliances, all heavy users of steel. In the 1970s, they told us that we were going to be better at semiconductors and chips. We established ourselves as the world leaders in memory chips and in specialized production of semiconductors; that led us to become strong in consumer and office electronic products.

But when the economic crisis of the mid-1990s hit, Japanese leaders stopped talking about the vision of the future. Instead, they started talking about problems: "The biggest problem in Japan is our financial institutions. These bad loans are dragging us down. We have to clean up the mess." It is true, if we clean up the mess, we will have solved a pernicious problem—just as glasnost and perestroika solved some pernicious problems for the Soviets. But solving this problem will not give Japan any sense of a bright future, any more than it did for the Soviets. Nor could we find our way to a bright future with another production-side vision, mandated from the top, let alone a success story in the new continent.

Instead, I would like to hear our leaders say something like this: "We need to find our way to become a great nation, a great people, and a great place to live, by the middle of the next decade. Even though we are your political leaders, we cannot tell you precisely how to get there. No leader can, because we do not know the way. We will have to find the way together."

Before going any further, of course, they would have to establish the government's credibility as a partner with its people. So the prime minister would have to publicly acknowledge the mistakes that were made throughout the 1990s. "When the bubble of the Japanese economy burst," he might say, "we should have let the market take over, not the government. We should have let the weak banks go belly-up, instead of rescuing them with your money. That mismanagement has cost us about $2 trillion. But this is a country with $40 trillion in reserves, including $4 trillion worth of assets, hidden in our national balance sheets, handed down from our ancestors. The people of Japan are sitting on top of a gold mine. We have the largest private savings in the world, of approximately $13 trillion dollars, and most of it is in banks and postal savings, earning just three-tenths of one percent interest. If we commit ourselves to give every one of our urban citizens—the residents of Tokyo and other metropolitan areas—the opportunity to create good lifestyles, then we can build a prosperous, enviable community. We can use some of our money to clear up the impact of the mistakes and pay back the unnecessary debts we have incurred ($2.9 trillion to be precise), and then we could move forward from there."

Implementing this would mean using the law to punish those who have made criminal mistakes with the economy. Many bank leaders would be shown to have complicitly and knowingly compounded the economic problems in Japan. These banks would collapse, but savings would be guaranteed up to 10 million yen (about $100,000) per account. New banks, both foreign and Japanese, would be permitted to replace the old ones. While the banking system might fall apart, Japan's excellent industrial infrastructure would remain. Companies such as Toyota, Sony, Fuji Film, Kyocera, NTT, DoCoMo, Ito-Yokado, and Nintendo would remain strong. Those companies with excellent balance sheets might move into banking, as Mitsubishi (originally a shipping company) and Sumitomo (a copper smelting company) did in the previous century. As noted in Chapter 6, we don't have any good banks left; but we have many good companies, including about fifty that might qualify as financial institutions, just as General Electric Capital Corporation (GECC) emerged as an AAA "bank" out of General Electric.

The reform process would be very painful—an economic equivalent to the Nuremberg war trials. But it could be over in six months. Property-related loans in urban areas would be deregulated; in Tokyo, for instance, the very inefficient "sunshine" laws that prohibit one building from blocking another's light would be changed. In parts of the city, skyscrapers would be permitted. Rent-control laws that hamstring landlords to absurd extents would be removed. (Sometimes a landlord must pay a hundred years' worth of rent to take over an apartment from a tenant.)

After the prime minister sketched out such a future, intensive discussion would begin: What does it mean to have a good lifestyle? What does it mean to be wealthy? In times past, "wealth" was defined as the wealth of nations: the productive capacity of a government and its subjects. Employees who worked patiently could expect that someday they will receive a fair distribution of part of that wealth. But that definition no longer applies, because the arbitrageurs of the invisible continent can simply undermine it. Wealth must now be seen for what it is: the ability of individuals to live according to their choice.

For many people in Japan, I imagine, that would mean better housing, closer to their work, with a more intrinsically rewarding community and more time with one's family (or time to look for a potential life partner). It would mean being able, without the trouble of arbitrage or Internet access, to get the best and cheapest goods and services from anywhere in the world. It would also mean giving people, for the first time in Japanese history, sovereignty over the design of their lives.

It would mean, for instance, giving people a better range of housing choices, out from under government restriction. This would be a win-win solution, helping both the Japanese people and the foreign companies producing housing and other amenities. The Minister of Construction had defended housing regulations in the past on the grounds that "we are a nation of earthquakes and typhoons. That's why we need our complex building codes." Most people in Japan assumed that this provided a good enough reason to pay building costs of two and a half times what someone might pay in Canada or Australia for an equivalent building. Then came the Kobe earthquake in January 1995. Many Japanese-style houses could not withstand a quake of magnitude seven. Many of them collapsed. A handful of sample Australian and American two-by-four-foot frame houses survived better, because they had lighter walls. The traditional way of building houses in Japan was discredited, but the old regulations still linger. The regulations are founded on an illusion that needs to be brought to light so that it can fade away.

Another idea that needs discrediting is that the supply of land in Japan is very limited. This is simply not true. Land shortages in Japan are caused by tariffs on agricultural products from elsewhere and by other short-sighted land-use policies. Within a fifty-kilometer radius of Tokyo, for instance, there are 170,000 hectares of land devoted to agriculture—primarily the growing of rice. In 2007, when many of the bans on food imports are scheduled to be removed in accordance with the WTO agreement, that land will be freed for housing. It represents ten times the amount of real estate currently occupied by housing in the Tokyo area. By importing rice and other grains from abroad, we can also "import the land we need."

In addition to that, an enormous amount of urban land in Japan, particularly along the shores of major cities, was dedicated for industrial use in the postwar era. "Industrial Japan" dedicated the best urban locations to industry while pushing commuters to faraway hillsides, but most of these dedicated docklands and industrial parks fell into disuse when plants consolidated or moved to other Asian countries. This land is now occupied by unused wharves, empty warehouses, and abandoned factories. West of Tokyo, commuters travel for one and a half hours each way by train. In the other direction, toward the Bay of Tokyo, within ten minutes there are thousands of hectares of available land, if only we could push the "Reset" button on real estate policies and reclassify them as residential areas. With the real estate market more open and flexible, Tokyo could develop a very good environment for commuters, because, thanks to the crash, property is actually priced very low. After the reclassification, it will be lower still.

This would also be a good time to create double tracking on the commuter trains and widen the highways. We could do many, many things to improve the quality of life and work in Japanese cities, and to expand the amount of space available to people, taking advantage of low land prices and construction costs. Unlike with other countries, all this is possible with the wealth stored up in $13 trillion of private savings, without borrowing money from abroad.

In this way, without elevating the price of land or borrowing money, Japan could offer a heretofore unattainable quality of life to its people. The result would be a genuine boom, not driven by public works that are paid for by borrowing from the future, but by private-sector quality of life, which, as it grows, helps make the future more prosperous. And coupled with an open-market policy under WTO agreements, this would benefit everyone in the rest of the world. A prosperous Japan would be good news to other nations, who could sell lifestyle-related goods and services to the Japanese consumers. When this kind of reform takes place, capital from all over the world will come in, as the return on such urban rebuilding would be very attractive.

To accelerate this, the government would have to introduce the concept of depreciation into the taxation and accounting system. Currently in Japan (as in most nations), there is little concept of an individual having assets. Individuals have salaries—they are "salary men." They support themselves through cash *flow,* but are not considered to be developers of balance sheets with assets and liabilities. Ironically, of course, the Japanese are the greatest creators of cash stocks in the world, through their savings. But these stocks now need to be converted into fixed assets, particularly high-quality housing. In Japan, where land ownership is practically a religion, banks did not evaluate houses after the fifth year after they were constructed. That's why homes were not reckoned as part of the Japanese sense of wealth.

That could change. The Japanese taxation systems could shift to recognize assets such as homes as wealth, instead of savings and land as wealth. In particular, it could introduce the concept of depreciation, as has been done for companies. Individuals may then choose to invest in expensive tools for building wealth, and receive the tax returns on their depreciation over time. If this were done, the Japanese would increasingly see themselves in an accurate light: as wealthy. They would invest in such tools as computers, and larger homes (with average floor space increasing, say, from 85 square meters today to 120 to 150 square meters in the future) with studies and high-quality furniture that would allow them to work at home. They would tie into the global Internet more assiduously. They would blend their home lives and work lives. They would innovate and build upon their innovations. They would, in thousands of individual ways, accelerate the self-propelled economy into the invisible continent from within Japan. This, in turn, would encourage companies—both foreign and domestic—to assist them on this growth path.

Conversely, if we cannot talk openly about the vision for the future of the country, or if people feel that they can't join in designing and creating that future, then we will be limited to images of the future expressed in conventional journalism, populism, and political discourse over the last hundred years. We will be limited to the conventional wisdom that says, "One country must lose so another can win. One political ideology must be wrong, so that another can be correct." These attitudes will inevitably lead us back into a cold war mode, pitting people of different groups against each other, only now at the speed of cyberspace. Everywhere around the world, as nation-states lose their control over regions, corporations, and people, they still have one critical job remaining: to free up the other institutions so that they can individually explore the new continent. The nation-states' "last job" is to build the stable system on which new-continent economies will prosper, even as the nation-states themselves lose control over their citizens.

Intellectually, I think many government leaders understand this, but they have not got the awareness to act. They continue on the old path. Asking them to change may not yield results, because (as noted in Chapter 5) they are constitutionally incapable of it. Thus, the process will be very bumpy. As in the French Revolution, there is always the danger that any valuable reform could dissolve into tyranny. But that's why it's much better to establish, from the beginning, a charter that gives people reason to talk about the visions and values they wish to see in the forefront of the emerging world. Debating about the new continent is better than letting a purely old-world-oriented system of values decree the worth of the new society.

DON'T SPEAK, FOR FEAR IT MAY HAPPEN

Unfortunately, discussions of any credible shared vision for Japan have faltered in recent years. The reason has to do with an attitude of "shamanism"—the reluctance to speak of difficult things for fear that raising consciousness about them will make them worse. On some deep, primal level, people seem to believe that speech can create reality. Therefore, avoid talking about bad potential futures, even if you need to talk about them to make a noble vision credible. (This is probably the reason why we do not have the subjunctive tense in the Japanese language.)

In 1991–1992, I saw the warning signs of a Japanese economic crash, and began to speak publicly about it. I predicted, for example, the fall of net present value of Tokyo real estate properties by a factor of five. We could only avoid the ill effects, I argued, by preparing for them in advance; and I suggested some approaches as a conversation-opener. But there was no conversation. I presented my analysis to the government, and most of the government officials who heard me said, almost immediately, "It's not as bad as you think." When I persisted, they would typically say, "Maybe it's going to be bad, but we will survive because we have our giant cash reserves." Then I kept pressing, because the magnitude of the crash made it clear that it would dwarf Japan's reserves.

Before too long, one of the ministry officials called me. "You are a respected voice," he said. "Because *you* say this could happen, it will come to pass. Don't talk about it." In other words, simply by raising the possibility of a price collapse, I could make the collapse come true. (You may laugh, but this is a true story. Officials always say, "Because someone like you speaks, everyone believes it, and it will happen. So don't mention it.") In fact, I talk about possible dangers precisely so the government, companies, and individuals can share the facts and relevant information, and thus better prepare for a bad situation.

Shamanism is not unique to Japan. A similar sentiment, I believe, lies behind Alan Greenspan's timid, oracular statements. He is afraid, it is said, of "influencing the markets." If he talks of a potential crash, then he might trigger one. I know that market behavior can react with volatility to a statement, and that there can be a herd effect in which selling begets further selling. But the potential of that herd effect is short-lived—unless there are reasons to sell. In other words, even Greenspan is unlikely to trigger a fall unless one is going to happen anyway. But the pundits hold a shamanistic view that gives Greenspan, and a few other public figures (including Robert Rubin) more power than they actually possess.

The net result of the shamanist attitude is status quo. Questions that should be asked are ignored, and abuses or waste can continue unchecked for decades. For example, there are many unspoken questions that should be asked publicly about the Japanese-American relationship. Why are there large American military bases in the heart of metropolitan Japan— an air base at Yokota, a naval base at Yokosuka, and an army base at Mizuho, all within thirty kilometers of central Tokyo, occupying some of the country's most expensive real estate? These military forces are obviously worth the sacrifice, for they defend Japan against its enemies. But who are Japan's enemies? There is no consensus in the Japanese Diet on that question. We can't even define our enemies, and the one country in the world that has most visibly and vociferously depicted Japan as an enemy is . . . America. If the common enemies were Russia, China, or North Korea, there are cheaper and better locations for military presence at the border of Japan. In effect, these military bases in the metropolitan areas in and around Tokyo represent a continued American occupation of Japan, at the expense of Japanese taxpayers. This has been possible because people do not ask questions—for fear, apparently, of waking up the gods.

Similarly, why doesn't Japan seek its own nuclear arsenal? Why are there no nuclear arms in Yokosuka or Nagasaki? Nobody asks these questions, because it is understood that Japan does not permit nuclear arms within its borders. But then why is so much plutonium piled up in Japan? "Don't ask that question," we are told. According to the Japan-U.S. security treaty, the U.S. cannot bring in nuclear weapons to Japan, and if they do, the Americans must obtain prior permits from the Japanese. Hence the government's official attitude is that American warships in Japanese harbors do not carry nuclear weapons because, "the U.S. has never asked us for the prior permit."

If you are dealing with shamanists, you cannot ask, "What if such and such happens?" You cannot think about even the most basic preparedness. And that means you can't talk effectively about the future for your country.

In this chapter, I described Japan's problems in the '90s, and its hard road ahead in moving into the new continent. I also proposed some possible ways out of the dilemma. I hope the reader will consider his or her own country, and conduct the same exercise. It is extremely important to pause here and think about the fundamental way in which a nation can realign itself to the new continent.

Moreover, in the final chapter, let us eschew shamanism. Let's imagine that a group of people came together and talked, effectively, about building a vision for a particular country—or a region of a country. What sorts of things might we expect to see from the individuals who will create this wealth as producers and as citizens?

8

TAMING THE NEW WILD WEST

Each of the previous chapters has laid out a series of premises for the near future, in light of the emergence of the invisible continent. We have looked at forces that range from attitudes about power and established institutions (the visible dimension), the decline of national boundaries and the emergence of regional strength (the borderless dimension), the knitting together of an unprecedented global communications and commercial infrastructure (the cyber dimension), and the enormous leverage in mathematically driven financial arbitrage (the dimension of high multiples). We have considered all of these forces from the point of view of the two groups of people best positioned to act: the decision-makers in corporations (especially in Chapters 2 through 4) and the politicians and bureaucrats of national and regional governments (especially in Chapters 5 through 8).

As I was putting this book together, some people commented that it is very difficult to address both of these groups together—that corporate leaders and political leaders are not accustomed to thinking of themselves as a single audience, with common concerns and aspirations. But that, too, will change on the invisible continent. If it gets harder and harder to distinguish, say, between General Electric and Singapore, or between Sony and the Los Angeles basin, it will be harder and harder to distinguish between a CEO or managing director, on one hand, and a governor or prime minister on the other. It will similarly be harder and harder to distinguish between the "microeconomics" of corporate decision-making and the "macroeconomics" of government policy. Who knows? Some day Bill Gates, John Chambers, Steve Case, John Reed, Louis Gerstner, Ted Turner, and Scott McNealy may all compete as candidates for U.S. president, or for U.N. secretary general.

Most important of all, it will be harder to distinguish between these types of decisions, and the "super-microeconomics" of personal finance. The kinds of decisions that individuals must make, as they navigate their way across the invisible continent, will not be that different from the decisions made on behalf of nations and corporations. The activities of economic life may vary with scale, but they remain essentially the same: looking for the best price or value through arbitrage; building global and local relationships; establishing "brand names" and identities through which one's price can be set; and honestly seeking the best quality of life and the best places to live and retire.

The invisible continent is an environment of enormous hope. But it is also a lawless, unfettered environment—a place much like the American Wild West during the 1700s and 1800s. Many people are being taken advantage of. Settlements are struggling to survive. There are few established rules, so people are making their own rules, and struggling with the power and responsibility of vigilante justice along the way.

In this chapter, I would like to suggest some of the values and principles that will come to the fore as people settle the invisible continent, creating civilization where none has existed before. This is obviously just one person's view, and it is meant as a starting point for future discussion. No doubt, many points besides these will have to be considered. But each of these issues is critical for all of us, both as individuals and as organizational leaders. Through open debate about all of these issues, the invisible continent can keep and expand its openness, its inclusiveness, its creativity, and its breadth of opportunity. In that way, we could not just tame a new Wild West, but foster the multifaceted evolution of the best of human civilization.

RETHINKING THE VALUE OF WORK

Before people can establish themselves as economic entities, they need to know how to set their price. This means learning how to value their effort and their work. Conventional economics has not helped this process very much. People are aware that their value is created, in the sense of a price, by the mechanism of supply and demand. The more demand there is for them, the higher their price; and the greater the supply, the lower they might have to price their labor. But conventional economics calculates these values in terms of groups of people. On the new continent, with the individual particularity of electronic media, the value of people is determined on a one-by-one basis.

In other words, on the new continent, we are all always on the auction block. The value of our labors is always determined empirically, by arbitrageurs who seek to hire us for more than we can earn elsewhere (if we are special and valuable) or who seek to undercut our wages by hiring someone else, via the Web for example. The measure of our worth is set outside ourselves, without any regard for the cost of production.

I personally experienced this early in my career. As a consultant working for McKinsey, I was billed out at the highest possible rate in Japan. This meant that I had to devote a significant amount of time and effort to making sure that my clients would recoup the cost of the extra money they spent on me. My price—like all invisible-continent labor costs—was based on leverage. The cost of producing services—in terms of either hiring individuals or equipping us with equipment—was not terribly important. As we saw in Chapter 3, anyone who commands a great price does so the same way, not by reducing the cost of production, but by accentuating demand.

That is why I am often tolerant of those who charge me high fees—as long as it remains clear that they are adding value commensurate with the fees they charge. I recognize that I will have to pay extra for the "Michael Jordans" of the world. I recognize that they are making a commitment, in their work, to helping me recoup their cost. Occasionally I realize that I am paying conventional prices for a "Michael Jordan" service. In that case, I am getting a bargain—meaning that I have found a "Michael Jordan" who has not yet learned to arbitrage his or her skills, like Tiger Woods in his Stanford University days.

To be sure, if everyone's value is based on their ability to get a price, that's much more complex to measure. But it's also more evident. People pay a consistently higher price to a firm like McKinsey because the perceived value is greater over time. Phil Knight, founder and CEO of Nike, goes even one step further and refers to his favorite athletes as having the unique quality of "emotional attachment." David Duval, Ernie Els, and Tiger Woods are equally qualified golf champions, but emotional attachment gives Woods a much greater degree of leverage when it's time to negotiate contracts.

Popular wisdom scorns the credibility of leverage-based pricing on the ground that, as often as not, the emperor has no clothes. Just as the emperor in the child's fable was shown to be deluded, so it is assumed that somehow the customer is deluded. The "Michael Jordans" are not worth the price, and as soon as we realize this, the less we will fall for their illusions. But the emperor of the fable existed in a heavily hierarchical establishment. Even in the free markets of the old world, it would be difficult to pull the wool over the public's eyes for very long. And in the fluid environment of the invisible continent, there is no penalty for crying out that the emperor has no clothes. There is only reward, for that is the first step to finding an arbitrage-based solution to a problem. Thus, it's hard to believe that an unworthy provider would continue to rake in Michael Jordan–style fees for very long. Search engines, mining through piles of data, would soon find the "best buy for the price" one way or another.

This type of value is difficult to measure in conventional economic terms because there is no one single metric on which people agree about the value of a product. For instance, what constitutes the value of a car? At the most utilitarian level, the car is helping people to reach point A, from point A to B faster, maybe. But cars are never priced merely for their value as transportation. Nor are they priced for speed, since all roads have speed limits; or for efficiency. The car's price depends on the feeling that the car produces in the driver. In the old world, this feeling depended on the value of materials and craftsmanship, which cost money. Adding value was a matter of balancing the added costs against the added revenues.

I once asked Amar G. Bose, the founder-chairman of Bose Corporation, if he had thought about asking Sony to produce their speakers at a lower cost. He said that the costs would be about the same if Sony used the same materials and components. In other words, Bose earned its price not through perception, but through the quality of its R&D and components. In the old world, that is often the case.

But on the new continent, value is almost independent of cost. The value of Microsoft Windows, just as with the value of a Lexus or a Final Fantasy (a bestselling videogame), depends upon the feeling that the software produces in the user. If it is convenient, reliable, and compatible with other software and computers, it will be worth more. These features are not at all a function of the cost of software development. Nor does the $98 price reflect supply or demand. In the end, Windows is priced according to its status as a platform, and its potential for holding on to that status. Had it sold for $400, the price would have been high enough to encourage competitors to enter the market, and threaten the platform. Had it sold for $20, the price would have been low enough to suggest to competitors that they could produce a higher-margin alternative—and once again, threaten the platform. Bill Gates chose $98 because it was low enough to discourage others from developing competitive products, and high enough to generate margins—and to convince customers that it is worth paying for!

Prices of goods and services alike will henceforth depend on arbitraging competition. If you continue pricing your goods with an old-world measure, based on cost, you will make mistakes on your pricing decisions. In the new continent, you have to set your prices to win. Once you occupy the claimed territory, the value of the "land" goes up, because there will be much more traffic using it as a common platform.

GOVERNING THE NEW FRONTIER

There is no conventional government on the new continent. It is a frontier environment. It has no president—even Bill Gates cannot claim the title of president of the networked society, let alone of the superset—the Internet, the regional activity, and the multiplying mathematics—that constitutes the new continent. This territory will always be somewhat frontier-like, because (since it is composed of shared awareness, and not physical land) there will always be a way to expand it. Yet, just as organizations are limited and constrained by their bylaws, so the boundaries of the new continent will be set by decisions made during the next ten to fifteen years: on cyber-law, regulation of multiples and arbitrage, international financial crime, regulation of cyber-crimes and transactions, and taxation of electronic commerce.

Who should the president of the new continent be? Should he or she be an American? Should he or she be chosen by the strongest, largest, or wealthiest participants? Or by everyone voting? And who is "everyone"? Is it every current resident of the networked society (everyone with a computer or PlayStation 2), every active member of the Internet (everyone with a URL login account), every participant in mediated cyberspace (everyone with an account at a major bank), everyone using the new continent to build equity (every participant in 401K and other pension programs), or every potential resident of the new continent (everyone in the world)? Should this choosing process take place through established institutions—governments, companies, the United Nations, the International Monetary Fund, nongovernmental organizations, or telecommunications providers and banks? Or should it take place through direct, electronically mediated access to an automated voting mechanism? In the Wild West, the best gunman called the shots. But what, on the new continent, constitutes good gunmanship?

All of these questions are yet to be decided. And they cannot be put off for much longer. Too many open-ended concerns are waiting upon them. These include taxation issues, intellectual property protection, freedom of speech and content restriction, regulation of violence and pornography, regulation of privacy violation, fraud, migration of hedge funds, currency speculators with large multiples, willful cyber-terrorism, and more. I do not think any of these matters should be settled quickly, and they all require a form of electoral process to be settled. But they must be settled; they cannot continue to be decided on a case-by-case, anarchical basis.

There is a dangerous reluctance to raise these issues at play, parallel to the way that the American automobile and petroleum industries sabotaged the U.S. railway systems in the mid-1900s, or the way the tobacco industry hid the dangers of long-term smoking. The U.S. government, because of their current supremacy in cyber- and multiples-based economies, is reluctant to talk about regulations and taxations in the new continent. The CEOs of the Godzilla companies similarly have become evangelists for the "low-friction migration" of information, money, and e-commerce. I personally agree with them in principle that less regulation is better than more. But the instability that will characterize the entry path to the new continent cannot be left alone. For example, a military that spends millions of dollars on cyber-terrorism as a potential offensive weapon cannot be tolerated unchecked. We have to agree on the minimum rules and etiquette to navigate our passage through this difficult transition period.

Once we have settled the invisible continent more fully, and the new borders and divisions become clearer, we may change the rules with much better knowledge of the needs of the new society. We need to go through this detour because the technologies of the new continent, while not as visible as traditional warfare technologies, are inherently more penetrating and far-reaching. They may not threaten life as directly, but they create an enormous threat to quality of life, livelihood, assets, and reputations.

For example, in most warlike cultures, such as the old Japanese samurai cultures, the establishment of identity was paramount. If you were confronted by a samurai, you were traditionally always given a minute to describe your name, background, history, and destination—so the warrior could make sure that you were, indeed, the person he wanted to kill. In cyberspace, the most devastating defamations of character can travel rapidly to millions of people, voiced by anonymous accusers, without repercussions to the defamer (who can't be identified), and with very little means of verifying the accusation. Similarly, in traditional warfare, even today, the most difficult part of the battle is getting access to the enemy's inner sanctum; we have seen as much in Iraq and Yugoslavia. But on the new continent, there is no inner sanctum; everything is open to some form of access. A group of speculators can come into a country like Thailand and empty the reserves of the central bank in a few days.

One immediate danger, of course, is the oscillation caused by hedge fund and other high-multiples speculation. While this is a natural fact of life in the new continent, it's far more disruptive than it needs to be. Some businesspeople have an immediate intuitive understanding of the issues; others don't find it natural. Speculation at this new Godzilla level is a taste they must acquire, in an education process that takes time. Some may never acquire the taste. Meanwhile, however, the Julian Robertsons and George Soroses of the world are arbitraging currencies and markets with high multiples, and increasing the oscillation and instability of economies everywhere, including their own net positions. To date, when large investment funds such as Long-Term Capital Management have collapsed, they have mostly been bailed out, thus protecting the system as a whole—at least, so they say. But the costs are very high, because the bailouts often require money-center banks to extend their loans. This means either their depositors get less interest or their shareholders get fewer dividends. It is so difficult to figure out their precise position after a while, they themselves often get poisoned in the process. Furthermore, the damages are not limited to banks and their clients. The damage from a serious multiples-fund collapse could cost countries and companies their lives.

Observers naturally wonder if the fights between speculators and governments (as in the cases of Soros versus the UK or Robertson versus Thailand) are fair games. The speculators are risk takers and not afraid of losing (so long as the losses are temporary). The governments are not, by nature, risk takers; they are, after all, responsible for the well-being of their people. In fact, the speculators are officially endorsed by the investors to take certain levels of risks, and the governments are voted in with a mandate to keep the society peaceful and prosperous. Their constituents do not ask them to create a wildly fluctuating currency or to cause havoc among exports and imports. But the constituents of the speculators, in effect, ask them to do exactly that—which is why many speculators locate their headquarters in places with weak judiciary infrastructures, like the Cayman Islands and the Isle of Man.

Most economic observers tend to side with the "free-market" speculators. But this stance ignores the fact that it takes decades of hard work to build a $5,000-per-capita GNP economy from the poverty of an underdeveloped economy. The more the economy looks promising, the more money comes in from the developed world. The more the government is diligent and reliable, the more money gushes into the country, as such a country is rare, and a rapidly growing economy promises sharper rises in currency and stock prices. The global economy tends to overshoot here. Because everyone in the global financial market finds that a Malaysia is the place to invest, never mind that its capacity to intelligently absorb new capital is limited, every fund manager comes in on a bandwagon named "emerging market." Among them, unfortunately, are some with speculative antitheses. The hedge fund pros come in to seek out faults in the economy and to focus on those points.

For example, the Thai economy was overheated, and the fund-raising engines were Chinese investors from overseas—who were otherwise very nervous investors. At the first signs of problems, such people tend to take the money out to safer havens. Thai officials, being mostly Thai and not Chinese, would not do this. Once Soros and Robertson saw that discrepancy, all they needed to do to exploit it was to sell short, suddenly—in effect, to blast a single gunshot at the height of the speculative party. Everyone ran out of the night club and left the reserves available at bargain-basement prices.

Similarly, in South Korea, the *chaebols* were borrowing excessive amounts of money to finance their overseas expansion. Their governments were passively endorsing it, and not fully preparing for the bad days. Against the size of the (*chaebol*-driven) economy, their central banks had only token reserves. The speculators shot straight at the heart of this weakness. It did not take a Soros. A small speculator, like a third-rate anonymous gunman in a Western movie, was enough. As the Korean currency (the won) dropped sharply, the *chaebols* discovered that they had to return the dollar-based debts in weaker won. This panicked the American money-center banks, along with the Committee of Three, because there was a definite possibility that the Koreans would default on the debt, mostly against the American banks. These banks, meanwhile, have not done a good job of bailing out the Koreans or building economies.

The lessons of the Asian crisis, and the crises in Russia and Latin America, are very clear by now: The speculators do a good job of revealing the weaknesses of economic policies and exploiting them. One might conclude, therefore, that governments should be careful to grow at a stable, steady pace, and give no chance to the speculators. But most developing-country leaders, even the best of the class, are not perfect. And their people are genuinely working hard to join the ranks of the OECD. The governments should not have to operate in an environment where every small mistake can lead to speculative corrections that take the country several years back. Moreover, while the speculators' profits go to wealthy people, the costs of the bailouts are paid by poor taxpayers. The losses that speculators have inflicted on developing countries are borne by average citizens. Ultimately, if nothing is done to correct this abuse of power, then governments and financial institutions will be unnecessarily destroyed.

What's a fair rule, if any, for governing all of this? Until the potential for damage is fully understood, life on the new continent will be as fraught with danger as life in the Wild West was. Conventional government regulations are ineffective at moderating this kind of willful external speculation, because speculators can simply arbitrage themselves to a new location. What's needed, most of all, is an expansion of the understanding, among people playing in the market, of the implications of the currently unregulated, wildly fluctuating marketplace.

In today's financial community, the unspoken rules are created by those who have the guns. Others have been told they must accept it. There is very little talk about finding viable ways to regulate the speculators— except in one place. In the Asian crisis of 1997, Malaysia imposed an unusual set of controls on currency speculation. First, the government effectively removed the value of Malaysian ringgit held offshore, by refusing to accept it back after one month's time. Traders could no longer borrow or sell this currency as a result. The government pegged the exchange rate at 3.80 ringgit to 1 U.S. dollar and abolished "absentee" trading by non-Malaysian speculators who used dummy corporations to buy and sell ringgits.

The active Western world, particularly the Committee of Three, supported the point of view of currency speculators. However, during the ensuing two years, it has become clear that Dr. Mahathir Mohamad, the prime minister of Malaysia, had an important case to make. Without condoning everything that happened in Malaysia, and without endorsing Mahathir's view of the forces that led to speculation, we can recognize the aftermath: The head of Malaysia's government practiced what he preached. The roof did not cave in. The country survived. Ultimately, faced with a coherent set of controls on their activity, the speculators departed.

In a statement published in *Mainichi Shinbun* in August 1999, Dr. Mahathir makes a persuasive case for any country to impose some form of currency controls, as long as these controls are implemented with deliberate criteria and guidelines.[1]

> Currency controls mean different things to different people. To the textbook economists currency control means cutting the country off from every kind of financial links with the rest of the world. The Malaysian control is not a simple turning your back to the world. Malaysia is a trading nation. . . .
>
> And so Malaysian currency control had to be so crafted that it would prevent the currency from being manipulated by foreign currency traders while allowing normal business transactions to be carried out without hindrance. And that is precisely what was formulated and carried out. . . .
>
> Clearly the movement of foreign funds in and out of the country is not affected by our selective currency control. However, short-term investments in the stock market are subject to some tolerable conditions. The capital must stay in the country for at least a year and earlier repatriation would be subjected to an exit tax. Apparently these conditions have not stopped foreign short-term investors from coming in.
>
> Today, Malaysia's economy is growing again. . . . We have said right from the beginning that the present international financial regime exposes newly emerging economies and middle-income countries to very destructive currency trading and manip-

ulation by the hedge funds and other currency traders. The only
way this danger can be eliminated is by curbing the activities of
these traders, by regulating currency trading, by making them
accountable and transparent.

All these things can be done if the powerful economies of the
world agree to do so and assert their authority over their own
nationals. We have seen how a superpower can actually ignore
international norms and arrest the leader of a foreign country to
bring him to trial under the laws of the superpower. If this can be
done I don't see why currency traders who have in fact destroyed
the economies of whole regions of the world, precipitating riots,
looting and killing, cannot be curbed and their activities regulated. Free trade is not a religion that anything done in its name
cannot be modified, regulated or banned altogether.

We are doing nobody any harm by our controls. Indeed we
are doing a lot of good to ourselves and I venture to say, to our
trading partners, investors and even the world's economy. So I
hope we will be left to administer our economy in our own way.
No one should tell us when we should lift the controls.

On September 1, 1999, we will celebrate one year of defying
convention. We would of course make an assessment of the
results. We think it is going to be good. Some will take the money
they have invested in our share market out. That is alright. We
will change their ringgit into whatever currency they wish so they
can take it out. We will not bear any ill feelings toward them.
That is their right and in Malaysia we respect the rights of everyone, including foreigners.

Can other governments follow Malaysia's example? To some degree
they can, but not without a reasonable degree of economic stability and
already existing economic growth. Otherwise, speculators will simply
arbitrage their way around any government regulations. It will be very difficult, even for a Mahathir, to police the invisible continent from the con-
fines of the old world.

Fortunately, the ease of access to information means that the new continent can be self-policing. Investors will learn, fairly quickly, that their
money does better in funds with smaller multiples or even with fixed
income instruments, such as the kind that Bill Gross of the Pacific Investment Management Company (PIMCO) has developed, with good results.[2]
If there is a general view that hedge funds should only be leveraged to
modest multiples of five or six—so that stocks and currencies can be pur-

chased only at margins of five to six times the price—this in itself would prevent the financial industry from threatening economies through over-speculation.

We should also develop guidelines as to what kind of external intrusions should be allowed into what level of economic development. A few simple rules would set this kind of protection into place.

First, there needs to be a mandate for *disclosure* of the degree of speculation in the financial industry—the amount of leverage or multiples in each transaction and overall, for each fund. When the level of disclosure is high, the highest-quality standards become a new "platform" for consumer and investor control that players build upon. Rating agencies, such as Morningstar and Moody's, are inadequate against the hedge funds, which can simply fudge the numbers and create an illusion of safety. We should not expect the speculators to disclose their strategies, but we should certainly demand that they disclose what weapons they use, and how much reserves they have in total. As in the game of poker, this is fair. We all know that the player has only five cards. If there were an open repository of the kinds of information that the rating agencies analyze, then when something happened we could immediately assess if the game was being played fairly and if the players were attending to the rules.

This rule should be established by the rating agencies and brokerages themselves. It is, after all, in the interest of their customers, the investors, to know if they are investing in a group of speculators with honor. As with corporate governance, compliance will be a major factor in shaping the investor relationship. Investors will gravitate toward the exchanges that provide this level of disclosure.

Second, margin speculation should be controlled through international treaty, a kind of equivalent to the Strategic Arms Limitation Treaty (SALT). Any signatory to the treaty would be allowed to extradite any of its citizens who knowingly did speculative damage to the economy of another country. Just as SALT permitted nuclear arms—but only up to the point where they could kill five times the world's population, not twenty times the world's population (a silly distinction, anyway)—these treaties would limit the level of speculation. They would be imperfectly enforced, but they would serve as a legal deterrent. They would also allow us to test the mechanism of international treaties, and see how well they work as deterrents to individual Godzillas who damage the overall economic system.

This treaty would make the global economy into a playing field where any country could potentially prosper—being confident of the protection and policing of the powerful league of developed countries. Later, not only would rules of speculation and etiquette in global markets be written, but also cyber-laws and cyber-courts should be established, and the "playing field" should become a platform in its own right on the invisible continent—a self-governing standard of economic fairness.

Third, by bundling currencies, as discussed in Chapter 5, speculation should be automatically discouraged. In Europe today, eleven countries share one currency. This market is too big for speculators to fool with. They can't make money by artificially pumping up the currency and then short-selling it on the way down—they don't have the resources to pump up a currency that big. If Asian currencies were bundled in a similar fashion, with the yen, the Malaysian ringgit, and the Thai baht all linked to one another, then it would be hard to speculate by arbitraging government policies.

I am certain that eventually there will be three currency groups, each respectively encompassing North America, Europe, and Asia. But I also see a world with one currency—the dollar and euro merging into the doro, and then with the Asian asea to form the "dorea." This will become a reality if the euro succeeds in its transition phase through mid-2002, and if the duel between the dollar and euro becomes a major instability factor, particularly for the U.S.

Fourth, and finally, there needs to be a global ombudsman developed for this new world. Ideally, this would emerge out of the network's own imperatives and needs. This is not a role that elected political leaders can play. They have a vested interest in promoting traditional nineteenth-century-style national sovereignties. It may emerge from Web-based journalism, from nonprofits, from regional institutions, or even from organizations like the annual Davos Conference. But people who are affected by unrestrained speculation need someone to raise their concerns publicly, in a way that reveals the self-indulgence and wanton aspects of the speculators.

As we have seen in the United Nations, the World Trade Organization, and even in the Olympic Committee, so long as we limit discussion of these global issues to representatives of national governments, there will be no quantum jump and breakthrough. We may even have corruption and abuse of power. We have to create the ombudsman first, to provide a channel for individuals to offer points of view on the governance of the new continent, and then have the nations discuss and decide on it.

Above all, we must not let the potential of danger keep us from involving ourselves in the new continent. Nor should we assume that it will remain unstable for long. Even in the most dangerous parts of the Wild West, people settled into families. Households were established. Children were born. Somehow families managed to persist while the rules were being established. There were places like Las Vegas, which were founded as havens for prostitution, gambling, divorce, and organized crime. Today Las Vegas is a worldwide destination for family-oriented tourism and business conventions, with 1 million permanent residents.

AN EVOLVING DESIGN FOR DEMOCRACY

The new continent's economic capabilities have already placed unprecedented pressure on the nation-state and existing economic attitudes. The same will take place in the political realm. As people begin to realize how interconnected they are with people of other nations, they will recognize the fundamental inadequacy of the current democratic model—especially if they believe in the fundamental dignity of human beings.

In current-day democratic models, grounded in the old world, three factors are all-important. First, votes are based on residence; only those who live within a particular community choose the leaders of that community.

Second, the units of governance—the nations and states within nations—are arbitrarily formed. Indonesia, with 189 million people, gets the same number of votes in the United Nations as Belau (of the Caroline Islands), an island nation with only 30,000 people. Conversely, those who live in Quebec, Northern Ireland, Taiwan, East or West Timor, or the Basque region do not have their views heard in any of the international organizations.

Third, votes are based on a type of commitment; only those who actively choose to vote take part in the selection of leaders. Those who live outside the community, or those who don't vote, have no voice. The name of the game, for politicians, is to manipulate these three factors: to keep redesigning the boundaries and voting rules to reinforce their own hold on power.

If you believe that human beings are fundamentally equal in their political status, no matter what their economic and sovereign status might be, then the only kind of political entity that makes sense is one that provides, at every level, for equal representation by population. This means we shift sovereignty from the nations to the individuals. Thus, Indonesia should not have the same number of votes in the U.N. as Belau; and Wyoming, with its 454,000 people (in 1990), should not have the same number of votes in the U.S. Senate as New York, with its nearly 18 million people. In general, probably half of the world's population suffers from this sort of underrepresentation. No one knows what China's billion people really think about their priorities, because they have no legitimate vote nationally, and internationally they are far underrepresented.

One result of the current system is a mentality that assumes that voting doesn't matter, which in turn makes it easy for special interest groups and money brokers to control the lawmaking process. We do not know, when Chinese officials speak at international conventions, if they are speaking on behalf of their people or on their own behalf. For Russia, we almost certainly know that they speak to prolong their own political life.

Another result is a built-in schizophrenia among political people about their local and global accountability. We have already considered the innate contradiction in the behavior of many consumers. They support politicians who preach against free trade while buying as many foreign-made goods as they desire. This means that politicians who represent an antagonistic stance against free trade generally stand a better chance of winning elections. That's why many politicians and politicians-to-be are good actors, sometimes pounding on the tables, like Ross Perot, blaming outsiders for the economic problems of their countries, even though he (and others) are already millionaires and have no reason to be that angry. Perot, criticizing George Bush in 1992, received almost one-fifth of American votes. His single focus on this old-continent protectionist game makes one wonder what he was trying to do; after all, he is a founder of two new-continent companies: EDS and Perot Systems. Perhaps he was merely "on the wings of an eagle"—taking a stance that he assumed (wrongly), represented the sentiments of the voters.

They may come into office as protectionists, but those who are elected soon discover that surviving in office depends on developing a robust economy—which in turn means forming alliances, not antagonisms, with the leading countries and even corporations of the world. The leadership required to win elections is the polar opposite of the kind of leadership required to govern an economy increasingly migrating toward the invisible continent.

This is not an innate characteristic of democracy. It exists because voting has been linked to residence—and that is, as much as anything, an artifact of the state of technology. When votes are counted with paper ballots or using primitive machines, a locally based and group-weighted voting process is the only feasible approach. But the availability of new electronic technologies (for both identification and casting votes) and the interrelationships that are endemic to the new continent make it feasible to fundamentally rethink the concept of "one person, one vote." It is estimated that by 2005, a billion mobile phones will be in use globally. This means, with a proper mechanism, we could have direct voting from 1 billion out of 6 billion residents of the world.

Consider a system, for instance, in which people had votes based upon their relative interest in the political process. For example, suppose that every resident of the United States were given one vote to cast in a presidential election. The president of the United States, in a very real sense, wields extreme power over the rest of the world. For the moment, he is the de facto president of the new continent. Conceivably, every citizen of every other country should get 3 percent of a vote. This figure is based on the fact that the dollar represents 50 percent of the global savings instruments today, while the U.S. GNP accounts for only 30 percent of the world GNP. Thus, the 6 billion people of the world own 40 percent of the U.S. dollar.

Similarly, those who have money invested in Japan, by virtue of being stakeholders there, probably deserve some percentage of a vote for the Japanese Diet. Computer-managed election systems could keep track of all of these percentages, while facilitating some kind of encryption-and-validation process that lets people vote privately from home.

There is a precedent for this in the Maastricht Treaty, which calculates the number of votes each European Union country has in deliberations about the euro, according to the amount of each country's currency in circulation. It is appropriate that for any country with a significant impact on the world, about 10 percent of the vote for national leaders should be allocated to stakeholders who will be deeply affected by decisions that the U.S. makes, but who don't happen to live there or be citizens. That 10 percent would be very important for a vote-seeking presidential or parliamentary candidate. Instead of being completely oriented to domestic concerns, he or she would be more mindful of the relationship between the individual country and the boundary-spanning new continent.

Other countries could now confidently "outsource" national defense to the U.S., with their technological might—knowing that not only does the world bear the cost of this "global policeman's burden," but people throughout the world contribute to the U.S.'s decisions. The cost-bearing aspect already takes place (for example, through the Japan-U.S. Security Treaty). The voting mechanism would compensate for the fact that the U.S. is not known for its high-quality decision-making in deploying its armaments (as we have seen when their missiles cruise through Sudan and Afghanistan).

Nor would such measures be limited to the United States. They would, for example, provide an ingrained mechanism for avoiding ethnic wars or wars based on border disputes. In an ideal world, residents of Pakistan would provide a tenth of the vote for the prime minister of India while residents of India put forth a certain weight of the vote for the prime minister of Pakistan. Kashmir is a problem because of the mismatch between its population realities—inextricably mixed together, half Hindu and half Muslim—and its political realities. Just as a zebra looks gray from a distance, an exchange of voting rights between the hard-edged black and white stripes could allow the political entity to reflect the nature of the state's people. Malaysia and Thailand could exchange similar voting rights in the regions around the border between them (such as Phuket). In a sense, Ireland and the United Kingdom, through their participation in the European Union, already have done this.

This might seem like a Swiftian modest proposal, and also impossible to put into practice—but it simply represents one way to develop an international political situation that accurately captures the interdependence already existing in the world. As the invisible continent expands its influence, the interdependence will increase, in ways that are probably unfathomable today, and immense pressure will be placed on governments to respond. Today that pressure takes the form of transnational lobbying. Chinese and Indonesian lobbyists curry favor with American presidents in vaguely illegitimate fashion precisely because they have no legitimate means for influencing policies that shape their destiny. The same will be true of every leading country in the world: Japan, Germany, the United Kingdom, and ultimately China itself. Is it better to channel that pressure through the clandestine byways of lobbying and influence-peddling, or to bring it into the light by making it a part of the democratic process?

From my vantage point in Japan, which blindly obeys U.S. foreign policies, I feel that much of this proposal is tacitly poised to happen. Since World War II, the Japanese have watched our enemies sequentially change—even though we are raised with the idea of being friends with everyone in the world. As I have mentioned earlier, our postwar "enemies" at various times have included such countries as the USSR, China, Cuba, all Eastern European (COCOM) countries, Guatemala, Panama, Libya, Iran, the PLO, Iraq, Haiti, Myanmar, North Korea, and recently Serbia. Sometimes these enmities are assigned on account of ideology (such as communism) or terrorism, and other times because of human rights violations and ethnic cleansing. Increasingly, such "enemies" of the U.S. seem to be chosen by the U.S. media (most notably CNN). If the initial aggression is "well received," then the U.S. government tends to go all the way. However, if the attack is unpopular, as in the second "Desert Storm" in 1998 against Iraq, Uncle Sam tends to "take it easy." Perhaps the citizens of the world are already voting for or against these wars, through the Nielsen ratings.

However they are chosen, *we the people of Japan never get a say about who our enemies will be,* because they are always chosen as part of our alliance with stronger military partners, such as the U.S. and the U.K. Since we have to pay for it (Japan paid $10 billion for Desert Storm), we might as well have a say in this process.

EDUCATING THE NEW CITIZEN

The most fundamental lever for success in the new continent is education; the best telecommunications system in the world will not help a country thrive if the people are not equipped to use it effectively, or to offer their services in the global marketplace. The role of higher-education institutions, such as Stanford University in Silicon Valley and MIT in Boston, cannot be overemphasized. But the real education of the invisible continent will start at home. Parents need to understand the importance of the revolution taking place simultaneously in the globalization and cybernation of the economy. Children need to understand that tomorrow will be different from today, and that "doing more better" by following their parents' footsteps, will not be good enough. In this world, children may often lead, because their parents will be busy unlearning the heritage of the last century.

And then there are the primary and secondary schools. Not long ago, a foreign correspondent stationed in Japan told me that he and others like him were often astounded at the common Japanese reaction to any crisis: "*Shikata ga nai.*" This common Japanese expression is a statement of resignation. Literally translated as, "There is no other choice," it signifies that something can't be helped. Just get used to it. "This suggests to me," the correspondent continued, "that perhaps Japan really isn't a democracy. Why else would the voting turnouts be so low? Why aren't the Japanese people more angry?" (Voter turnout in Japan averages 60 percent. Ironically, his own country, the United States, has even lower voting turnouts, averaging around 40 percent.)

I replied that the apathy he saw was a victory of the Ministry of Education, which deliberately trained our people to shy away from anger. The Ministry of Education, through its role as the central publisher of textbooks, has trained these people to be obedient: to memorize and repeat what they have been taught by rote. In addition, there is a generational factor. The oldest generations, including my own, have been too complacent to rebel. The system serves them too well to throw it over. These are people who, in the 1960s after the Japan-U.S. Security Treaty was ratified, threw Molotov cocktails at the police. It was fashionable in the years after World War II, around 1960 and again in 1970, to go on the street and be angry. But today it is quite *dasai* (unfashionable) to do the same thing. Older people have no reason to be angry; they expect enormous pensions to usher them into a happy retirement. They hold a heartfelt attitude: Don't rock the boat.

But this complacency and obedience have not carried down to

younger generations. The "Shonen Jump" generation, now in their thirties and early forties, is fundamentally different from any generation before. (*Shonen Jump* is a cartoon magazine that used to circulate 6 million copies every week. That generation is known for its inability to think as logically and sequentially as the generation that preceded it. Their ideas and thoughts warp from one scene to another, without transitions, in a similar way to those of Western youngsters who grew up with MTV.) This generation has been stereotyped as "weaker." It's said that they don't have the resilience of the older generation; they didn't have to pull through the same kinds of difficulties as their parents and grandparents. Nor do they have the imagination and drive of the generation that follows them, the "Nintendo kids." They are a lost generation; one of the reasons behind the current stagnation of the Japanese economy, since they constitute the heart of the working population.

But the generation that will succeed them—the "Nintendo kids," now in their twenties and early thirties—has more hope. The role-playing games (RPGs) they have grown up with form the characteristics of this generation. They try all possibilities. They are flexible and much more creative than any other generation before. They do have one problem. When times get tough, they react as if life were a computer game—by pushing the "Reset" button. They seek a new job, a new location, a new career. "Game over. Start again." They are full of imagination and enthusiasm for "shoot-before-aim"-type action. These seeming inadequacies actually make them much more effective as citizens of the new continent. But while they (and the generations that follow them) are culturally equipped for the new continent, their education has not caught up. One of the most critical challenges for Japan, and for every nation including the United States, is to redesign the educational system to match the resilience and need of the new generation. In Japan, for example, students waste their time studying the rote grammar and vocabulary of English, instead of starting with conversational, spoken English. They are punished for every mistake in grammar and spelling. The result is the famous Japanese style of English-speaking, thoroughly ill-suited for conducting business or colloquy in any English-speaking environment (including the Internet's English-speaking chat rooms).

Seventeen million Japanese people go abroad every year, and nearly all of them have been required to study English for at least six years. Yet, many can't answer the three questions posed to them by American or Australian or English immigration: "How long do you expect to stay? What is the purpose of your visit? What is your address while you are here?" The educational process is so standardized, so machine-like, and so fraught with fear and punishment that it induces people to forget their English almost as fast as the exam is over.

The United States, by contrast to Japan, has opted for a random approach to education, in which each school district has a high degree of sovereignty. This has led to a wide variation in education, and some remarkable pockets of quality—but there are still an enormous number of frustrations. Indeed, I don't know of a country that is happy with its educational system. That is because we have failed to articulate the kinds of citizens who will be needed in a future that bridges the invisible continent and the old world. Most education systems are crafted for the industrial society, and for mass production, with a few elites guiding thousands of workers. In the new continent, the ratio is completely different. Unless you can add intellectual value in the cyber dimension, you can't earn a good living. Unless you understand the mathematics of high multiples, you stand to lose in the fierce 401K game.

Thus, education is the first and foremost priority for any nation (or region). Preparing youngsters to comprehend the invisible continent and compete in its endeavors and explorations is the best investment that a government (or parents, for that matter) can make. This is particularly valuable for developing countries, which have no sophisticated infrastructure and no expertise to build one—but which have the incalculable resource of an energetic population of fifteen- to eighteen-year-olds. All it takes is giving a sufficient number of these people a five-year education in skills in computers and communication, and the ability to act on that education. Education should not just be technical. It should emphasize a "T-shaped" human being, with the horizontal bar representing the knowledge and experience of humanity, global issues, social values, and common sense, while the vertical bar represents special skills, such as information technology, marketing, finance operation, and variations thereof. Furthermore, schools in every country should be naturally multilingual. They should teach science in English, history in Chinese, and literature in Spanish—the three languages most likely to become platforms on the new continent—as well as their mother tongue. Then they should switch, and invite students to talk about science in Spanish, history in English, and literature in Chinese.

Pedagogically, they should emphasize humanity, adventure, entrepreneurship, leadership, teamwork, problem-solving, and experimentation, instead of rote learning. Children should be free at school to explore ideas and inventions of their own design. Computers should be naturally available as tools—not to be taught by rote, with a teacher at the front of the room, but for students to use in simulations, research, and inquiry. Let students teach their classmates; let students teach their teachers; let professionals share their expertise with students, and use the networks to tie everyone together.

Kids who grow up in this kind of situation become very different kinds of people. Instead of being told the answers all their lives—that periodic tables consist of 108 elements and the Pythagorean theorem can be proved in such-and-such a manner—they grow up accustomed to finding their own answers. They acquire an inquisitive mind and the courage of a pathfinder. If you haven't had an education like that yourself, you can appreciate it a bit by playing a computer game such as Maxim's Sim City. In that simulation, the player becomes the mayor of a small town, operating with a limited budget and a series of constraints. Raise the taxes too high and the population goes down, because people move away. Let the taxes fall too low, and crime goes up and garbage piles up. Spend too much on roads and it strains the city's budget; spend too little and traffic overwhelms the citizenry. These trade-offs (and the gain versus risk involved in them) become instilled in the students' minds. There is no set solution. Society is composed of a series of delicate balances. And students internalize this wisdom. Usually taxpayers and voters don't think in this manner. They assume that "less is good" (in taxes) and the "more is better" (in pensions), and do not maintain the overall perspective of a delicate world of trade-offs, a perspective needed for living on the new continent. In other games, such as Final Fantasy, children learn to be proactive in exploring untapped terrain, and adventurous and courageous in undertaking difficult tasks.

We need a kind of education that can help develop and refine this perspective further. To be sure, students will still need to learn the periodic table and Pythagorean theorem, but now they should learn them in context, and they should retain the ability to use them all their lives. We need to develop people who are skilled and confident at both technological issues and human relations; who are conscious of the pressures on society and the ramifications of the tools they use. We need to recognize that some parts of the curriculum are worth dropping (except for very specialized people), while others are worth expanding. I was trained as a nuclear engineer, and I know some very complex forms of math, including diffusion and transportation equations; matrix and tensor. But I have never used any of them since joining McKinsey twenty-seven years ago. Even statistics and logarithms are not used very often. It is enough for me to know how to multiply, divide, add, and subtract. Yet, the ability to understand a financial plan—something I never learned in school—would have served me all through my career.

Education should also include a real-world component where students learn how people work. For example, on Thursday afternoons a student might apprentice himself or herself to a retail shop. They would clear and stock shelves, learn purchasing, practice bookkeeping using Quicken, learn to understand procurement, develop a feel for customers, and begin to understand marketing (especially if they succeed in getting more customers in). Going to a government office, they might learn how things are actually done in society. Working in a park, they might learn how to keep society clean and environment intact; they might learn about service in a retirement home. In all these cases, there must be ample time for discussion, to make sense of these experiences, so they represent more than busywork.

Other times, businesspersons might come to a school from outside and present the choices they have made and the reasons for them. A lawyer might come in and say, "Do you know that in our area we have seven million people who default on their loans annually?"—and help students understand the ramifications of their credit cards. Psychotherapists might come in to talk about cognitive science. All of this would help ameliorate one of the most pernicious problems of affluent societies: the fact that children grow up complacent, not worrying about other people or other countries. Only when that can take place with education will we be ready for a world embedded in a new continent.

THE REVOLUTION AGAINST OURSELVES

Today we are witnessing a sweeping revolution in the fundamental ways we live, work, shop, think, fight, communicate, and create wealth. New systems of production, procurement, and organization have literally spread throughout the world as if the entire globe were a combined factory, laboratory, design space, and marketplace. Our nerves are in full gear around the clock, with both individuals and institutions tuned in, full-time, to colleagues on the network. Our wealth-creation power has been multiplied exponentially as information is shared among investors almost instantaneously throughout the world, and the mathematical equations to calculate the value have been advanced by "rocket scientists" of the new finance. The invisible continent that we have just begun to enter is full of both promises and dangers. Since the migration of the new world is driven by the technological breakthroughs, as in the case of the past industrial revolutions, the shift is essentially irreversible. We just have to make the best of it.

In the past, human revolutions (as opposed to industrial revolutions) had a clear dialectic overtone. In the French, Russian, and even the American revolutions, there were "haves" and "have-nots," powerful and powerless, nobility and peasants, and capitalists and laborers. The target of attack in a revolution was always clear. People fought against the exploitative rulers.

This time, as we move into the invisible continent, the exploiters are more difficult to recognize. The aristocratic "target," the focus of the revolution's enmity, the source of resistance, the bearer of the old wave—is *you*! There is no "they," no enemy who has to change. It is you (and me, and most of us) who need to change. The resistance is inside. It exists in a conservative component to our psyches, a component that wishes tomorrow could be like yesterday. If you could listen to the voice of this component of yourself clearly, you would hear arguments like this: "I have learned much in life already and don't want to learn more. I had hoped that the skills I have acquired with such difficulty, and the degrees I have earned, would feed me well for the remainder of my life. I don't want to change my direction. I wish the world would change instead. I want the economy to recover (or continue to flourish) so I don't have to lose my job."

As I have noted at length in this book, the greed of the 401K-ites is now controlling the fate of the American presidential position, and the stability of the global financial system. The 401K-ites, in other words, are like the aristocrats before the French Revolution, feeling complacent and secure. This is not unique to America. For the first time in the history of mankind, the *majority* of the people in the most developed countries have become the "haves." They have no nobility to attack. They *are* the nobility—the kings and queens. Like nobility everywhere, they are dictating to the politicians and bureaucrats (and the rest of the world) what to do. Such a society is inherently unstable.

Resistance to change and innate conservatism are hallmarks of a good and prosperous society. Even greed can be a signal of resilience and stability in the old world. But on the invisible continent, these qualities may turn out to be dangerous signs of instability, decline, even defeat. We just don't know what it will take to succeed, let alone to sustain success, on the multifactor-driven and inherently volatile invisible continent.

In short, this is a time when not just the fact of hegemony, but the structure of hegemony, has changed—not only from nations to individuals, but also to families, communities, corporations, regions . . . and nations again. Every country, community, company, family, and individual will be subject to brutal reality checks as the nature of the new continent manifests itself. Most innate conservatives will not make the transition smoothly, because the prevailing paradigm has changed. A corporation sitting on yesterday's laurels will lose investors almost instantaneously. Education at all levels has become the weapon for winning the new war. This time, education will not exist to teach knowledge to last for decades, but to impart wisdom to challenge the status quo and learn the paths as you go. Self-denial and self-renewal, as GE's Jack Welch has been stressing, are the only sure passports to the ports of entry into the invisible continent.

A DECLARATION OF INTERDEPENDENCE

One of the most hopeful signs of recent years is the willingness of people, from corporate titans to ordinary citizens (particularly in Europe), to recast themselves as residents of the entire world, not residents of their narrow countries. For example, there has been a quiet sea change in corporate attitudes about their overseas business. Traditionally, Western companies had two ways of doing things. They would act one way at home, and then another way abroad. Overseas, they played a role that was both shyer and more imperious. They offered far fewer services, they got far less involved in the communities there, and they did their best to control every little part of their operations.

Now these businesspeople see themselves increasingly as serving the global customers at once, not just Americans like themselves. Because of the formation of Europe into an attractive market, because of the maturation of the American market and the need to look further for new markets, and because the increasing sphere of influence of American companies has led them to feel more capable abroad, these companies are now willing to take the risks of becoming dominant players (but welcome) in the global marketplace. European, Japanese, Brazilian, Taiwanese, and Korean companies are tracking as well.

The same is true of citizens everywhere. They see the interdependence taking shape around them. They do not need to be convinced that the invisible continent is important. All of us recognize the demands that it places upon us—individually and socially. The problem is, we are only learning how to fulfill those demands. Right now, we are only at the beginning stages.

While the total landscape of the invisible continent is yet to be explored and studied, I hope I have been able to help you develop the feel for its nature, and for the forces that are shaping it. Developing this feel is a difficult task, because nobody has a well-trodden map nor guide. I have done my best to describe what I have seen as an observer of the global economy and the borderless world over the last two decades. As the borders between the real world, the cyber-universe, and mathematical space disappear, the invisible continent will exist beyond our direct sensory perception. Only those who can construct and keep in mind an ongoing conceptual model of it will understand geopolitical and economic events.

The new continent still has no constitution. It only has a declaration—a declaration of interdependence. We hold this truth to be self-evident: All people are created in connection with each other. As the pace of that connection speeds up, we know each other and need each other as we never have before. Let us find a way to reflect that interdependence in our businesses, in our schools, in our governments, and in the quality of our lives.

Epilogue

It is helpful, when looking ahead, to summarize what we have learned so far. And the world has already learned quite a bit about the invisible continent. First, we are moving into a new economy that is characterized by a new set of dimensions—one of cyber connections, economic multiples, and "borderless" cross-national activity. While in the U.S., the productivity gains from the cyber dimension have been the most obvious part of the new economy, its behavior as a whole is much more complex than it seems at first glance. The borderless dimension makes the migration of information, capital, corporation, and consumers across the traditional national boundaries so easy that it can lead anyone to unprecedented gains in prosperity and productivity, but those gains are not guaranteed.

The cyber aspect of the new economy is an enigma. It has the potential to increase productivity for producers who occupy the "commanding heights" of a cyber platform. As traffic increases, more customers will pay for the use of the platform. But another characteristic of any platform is a constant arbitrage by other platforms. When the traffic goes away and the owner of the platform is left with high fixed costs and low marginal contributions, the productivity can easily swing to negative. A company or industry that might have seemed highly productive can, all of a sudden, find itself caught in a vicious cycle: spending a great deal on advertising to get its traffic back, or on capital to fix the platform facilities, often to no avail.

There is no inherent reason why the cyber dimension should yield a higher productivity. The lack of competition, and the ease with which some American companies have claimed the new territory in cyberspace, has produced an illusion of "Eldorado" for the early pioneers. But as we are already witnessing, the building and maintenance of a successful dot.com e-commerce site is often more expensive than building a success-ful shopping mall in the suburbs. The privilege of easy high productivity is available only to the truly innovative early pioneers. And that is no differ-ent from the old world. However, this does not mean that most companies should stay in the old world. The economy itself is rapidly migrating into the global and cyber dimensions, and this means that no matter how diffi-cult the passage might be, every company must explore the new economic dimensions with its eyes wide open.

Finally, the dimension of high multiples makes the new economy inherently unstable when coupled with the borderless and cyber economies. When the financial arbitrage starts to be common across different geogra-phies, in cyberspace, and through a variety of financial instruments with different risk profiles, then even the best mathematician cannot take all the key parameters into account. That is why the best mathematicians can be defeated by speculators who play the game intuitively and sometimes with sheer guts, like high rollers in a casino. The speculators come and go. But the world is buffeted, nonetheless, by the tsunamis that they induce. As we stand at the point of entry into the new economy of the invisible continent, it's natural to feel overwhelmed by the challenges ahead.

In this book, we have learned that institutions and individuals alike must learn the new forces at work in the new continent. But to do so, we have to go through two fundamental steps:

Step one: Freeing ourselves from the legacies of the old world. For a country or region, this means deregulation and a series of transitional policies that can put the system to work with the global economy. Purely national sovereignty must be replaced with consumer and citizen sove-reignty, so that the latter can exercise their choice.

Step two: Preparing for life in the new continent. Like runners prepar-ing to travel around the globe, we have to retrain our minds and muscles. For a country, this means renewed emphasis on education, rewritten laws, and rebuilt, cybercompatible infrastructural and financial systems. For a company, this means developing a networked and Web-like organization. Often, this may require creating a new company, if the modification of the existing institution is too cumbersome. For the individual, this means being prepared to live anywhere in the world with the skills and languages that are becoming increasingly universal throughout the new continent.

Most countries have not yet started step one, let alone step two. That is why they have a long tunnel ahead. Steps one and two must be followed sequentially. While migration along step two is crucial in winning an attractive position in the new continent, it cannot be done without com-pleting step one. The U.S. was an early settler in the new continent precisely because it initiated step one in the 1980s, and pursued step two aggressively in the mid-90s. It has thus occupied a unique and beneficial position in all of the four dimensions of the new economy:

- In the global dimension, American multinationals operate all over the world and American consumers are accustomed to buying the cheapest and best from anywhere in the world.

- In the cyber dimension, the key platforms are currently all American and the key intellectual content is also American, and written in the English language.

- In the dimension of high multiples, excessive liquidity worldwide has found a haven in NASDAQ, U.S. government bonds, and American hedge funds. Since the dollar is the key currency for settlement and savings worldwide, the triple deficits of America (trade, government budget, and balance of trade) represent no problem. And the consumers' balance sheets have expanded to produce additional spending power from the appreciation of their assets and pension reserves.

- In the dimension of the old-world "real economy," the bubble created by the other three dimensions has produced (albeit temporarily) unprecedented wealth and employment. This has enabled old-world companies and industries to conduct more aggressive restructuring in an environment where layoffs are more acceptable. The old world, in short, has also benefited from low unemployment and more consumption in the U.S.

Contrary to the U.S. experience, many countries are still suffering from a loss of their sense of direction. Malaysia has tried to jump into cyber utopia without converting the country into a global economy first. Some regions of India are simply trying to serve the rest of the world as a cyber backyard, without the country becoming part of the global economy as a whole. China wants to join WTO, but does not want the Internet to prevail over its 1 billion people. Japan wishes to promote the cyber and multiples aspects without fully opening up to the global dimension and giving up the old part of its economy.

Figure 10 demonstrates the choices that many countries have made.

Score Card of National Readiness
to Move into the Invisible Continent

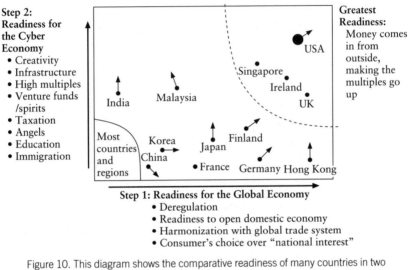

Figure 10. This diagram shows the comparative readiness of many countries in two dimensions in the invisible continent. The x-axis shows the degree of readiness for the "borderless" dimension; the y-axis shows the readiness for the "cyber" dimension. Most countries are still highly unprepared on either dimension.

The passage to prosperity lies clearly toward the right (step one) and toward the top (step two) in order to gain the benefits of capital to flow in from all over the world. In this way, the construction of a new continent economy does not have to rely solely on the money of taxpayers within the country. Many national leaders wish that they could gain the benefit of a cyber economy and NASDAQ multiples without losing their traditional sovereign grip. That will not happen because, first, you have to free individuals and corporations so that they can survive in the global economy before they can migrate into the cyber economy and begin to attract enviable multiples with global investors. The sustaining winners will be those who understand the complexity of the new-world makeup, and who understand how to harness the forces at work, rather than those who simply rely on a one-time "lucky strike" of gold.

Finally, how should we interpret the bubbly multiples we often see in NASDAQ, Mothers (Tokyo), and the various "New Markets" in Europe? As we have learned in this book, the multiples in the stock market are no longer related to the net present value (NPV) of the businesses moving forward. They represent either an expectation, by investors, that the company will occupy some vast range of territory in the invisible continent, or a round of ammunition given by the investors to a particular CEO, for use in conquering some of the territory in the invisible continent. The $20 billion market cap given to Priceline.com on day one is an example of the first case. With its business concept, investors expected the company to take up a central location in the new business of online commercial exchange. The second case is exemplified by AOL's Steve Case and Robert Pittman, who used the ammunition of their $168 billion market cap and fired the right bullet at Time Warner at the right time. If they had sat on their laurels without doing anything, the company's market value would have decayed very rapidly. Some move was necessary because the whole industry of ISPs (internet service providers) was losing it's ability to charge regular fees to its members. Similarly, WorldCom used its multiples effectively to integrate MCI and Sprint, Qwest to overtake U.S. West, and Cisco to absorb dozens of companies with critical technologies. If the management does not use the rich ammunition in a timely fashion, then investors will go away and the high multiples will decline to an ordinary level.

Thus, the high multiples of, say, NASDAQ, are not just bubbles. They represent the stock markets' recognition of the most effective potential "gun men" and "stake holders" on the invisible continent. If these players don't do a good job meeting investors' expectations, then they will disappear rather quickly. Unlike the Tulip Bubble of Holland (1634–1636), South Sea Bubble of the U.K. (ca. 1720), and the Property Bubble of Japan (1980s), the NASDAQ "bubble" has adequate liquidity for investors. History will tell which particular stocks were the bubbles and which were not. But there is no question that the huge expectations of Internet companies do have an overall basis in value. While the entire continent still exists, in part, only in the minds of those who care to see it with a bit of knowledge and imagination, its shape will become clearer and sharper as we move into the labyrinths of the twenty-first-century economy.

ENDNOTES

Chapter 1

1. Kenichi Ohmae, *Triad Power* (New York: The Free Press, 1985); Kenichi Ohmae, *The Borderless World* (New York, HarperCollins, 1990); Kenichi Ohmae, *The End of the Nation-State* (New York: The Free Press, 1995).

2. Marshall McLuhan, *Understanding Media: The Extensions of Man* (New York: McGraw-Hill, 1964); Herman Kahn, *The Next 200 Years: A Scenario for America and the World* (New York: William Morrow, 1976); Alvin Toffler, *Future Shock* (New York: Random House, 1970); Alvin Toffler, *The Third Wave* (New York: William Morrow, 1980); Alvin Toffler, *Powershift* (New York: Bantam Books, 1990); Nicholas Negroponte, *Being Digital* (New York: Knopf, 1995); Peter Drucker, *The New Realities* (New York: Harper and Row, 1989); Peter Drucker, *Post-Capitalist Society* (New York: HarperCollins, 1993); Peter Drucker, *Management Challenges for the 21st Century* (New York: HarperBusiness, 1999).

3. Kenichi Ohmae, "What Moves Exchange Rates? New Dynamics Challenge Traditional Theories," *Japan Times,* July 29, 1987; Revised and reprinted as Appendix A in *The End of the Nation-State* (New York: The Free Press, 1995).

4. Source: ÅFCybercash, (Forrester Research Report 11/98, "Cybercash Report"; Nilson Report 3Q98).

5. Martin Kohr, "Prying Open the South's Government Business," *Third World Resurgence,* October 1997.

6. Stanley J. Modic, "Few Tears over Passing of 1985," (editorial) *Industry Week,* vol. 227, no. 1, December 9, 1985, p. 9.

7. I commented upon this in my own book, *Triad Power,* (New York: The Free Press, 1985). This prediction, grounded in the shifting dynamics of markets that were already visible in 1985, has in fact come to pass.

Chapter 2

1. Source: Report by C. Fred Bergsten for the Institute for International Economics, June 1996.
2. See, for example, Kenichi Ohmae, *The Borderless World* (New York: HarperCollins, 1990).
3. Source: U.S. Merchandise Trade Balance with Japan, 1983–1999, Bureau of the Census, U.S. Department of Commerce, distributed by Dr. Edward Yardeni's Economics Network (www.yardeni.com).
4. See my own analysis of this in *The Mind of the Strategist* (New York: McGraw-Hill, 1982), particularly Chapters 6, 7, and 9.
5. Source: Forrester Research, cited by Maryanne Murray Buechner in "How'd They Do? (E-Companies)," *Time,* January 24, 2000, p. B2.
6. Edward D. Horowitz, Commentary, *Investor's Business Daily,* June 1, 1999.
7. James Sarowieki, "Reality Bites Value America," *Money Box,* December 30, 1999.
8. Source: First Call earning projections for Priceline.com, published in the Investor's Overview of Priceline.com, Corporate Communications Broadcast Network (www.corporate—ir.net), June 27, 1999.

Chapter 3

1. Kenichi Ohmae, *The End of the Nation-State* (New York: Free Press, 1995), p. 2ff.
2. See, for example, Charles Ferguson's book, *High Stakes: No Prisoners* (New York: Times Books, 1999).
3. This advice to American producers, written by Bargain America CEO Tom Sato (the former Microsoft Japan manager) and posted on the company's Web site, delineates the arbitraging territory that Bargain America staked out: "In Japan, it used to be that spending vast sums of money without regard to the true value of products was a macho thing to do. Alas, those bubble days are gone. Now, Japanese are extremely value conscious. This news can be a good thing for American merchants. If products are priced at their fair US market value and lend themselves to easy shipping, chances are, they will be attractive when compared with Tokyo merchants and their legendary high retail

prices. And remember—shipments under about $300 for most items arrive in Japan duty free, and are also exempt from US sales tax."

4. Source: Economic Policy Institute and Center on Budget and Policy Priorities Web site, January 18, 2000 (www.cbpp.org/1-18-oosfp. html).

5. Art Kleiner, *The Age of Heretics* (New York: Doubleday, 1996), p. 316.

Chapter 4

1. See, for example, Alfred Chandler, *The Visible Hand: The Managerial Revolution in American Business* (Cambridge: Harvard University Press, 1977), p. 145ff; and John Steele Gordon, *The Scarlet Woman of Wall Street* (New York: Weidenfeld & Nicolson, 1988).

2. Kenichi Ohmae, *The Mind of the Strategist* (New York: McGraw-Hill, 1982), p. 92.

3. Rob Guth, "Sony, General Instrument in Set-top Deal," *Industry Standard*, December 2, 1998.

4. Mark Anderson, "Our Stuff: The Key to Computer's Future," *Strategic News Services* newsletter, October 13, 1998.

5. Kenichi Ohmae, *Triad Power* (New York: The Free Press, 1985), p. 123.

6. Eden Ross Lipson, "Books' Hero Wins Young Minds: An Apprentice Wizard Rules the World," *New York Times,* July 12, 1999, p. D1.

7. Henry Goldblatt, "The Telecom Tug of War: Qwest and Global Crossing Duked it Out Over US West and Frontier," *Fortune,* July 19, 1999, p. 115ff.

Chapter 5

1. In my work as a consultant to Malaysia in 1994 in designing the concept of Multimedia Super Corridor (MSC), I studied the Financial Services Center in Dublin carefully as a reference. (The other example studied was Electric City in Bangalore, India.)

2. Source: Letter dated August 16, 1999, from Brian Cogan, director, Asia-Pacific office, Industrial Development Agency of Ireland.

3. Niall McKay, "Ireland, the Silicon Isle." Hotwired.com, Oct. 29, 1998.

4. Source: Letter dated August 16, 1999, from Brian Cogan, Director, Asia-Pacific office, Industrial Development Agency of Ireland.

5. Kenichi Ohmae, *The End of the Nation-State* (New York: Free Press, 1995), p. 136.

6. Thomas L. Friedman, *The Lexus and the Olive Tree* (New York: Farrar, Straus and Giroux, 1999), p. 62.

7. Benjamin R. Barber, *Jihad vs. McWorld* (New York: Times Books, 1995), p. 276. Barber identifies Ohmae as one of the chief "detractors" of the nation-state, in favor of global capitalism, misinterpreting Ohmae as "calling on the nation-state to participate in its own liquidation," p. 149.

8. Joel Garreau, *The Nine Nations of North America* (Boston: Houghton Mifflin, 1981).

9. Kenichi Ohmae, *The End of the Nation-State* (New York: Free Press, 1995), p. 89.

Chapter 6

1. Source: Report of the Japanese Ministry of International Trade and Industry (MITI), 1994.

2. Robert Bartley, *The Seven Fat Years* (New York: The Free Press, 1992), pp. 40–42.

3. Daniel Yergin and Joseph Stanislaw, *The Commanding Heights* (New York: Simon & Schuster, 1998), p. 119.

4. Kenichi Ohmae, "1997: Year of Transition—Not So Bad, After All." *Asiaweek*, January 1998, pp 4–11.

5. Kenichi Ohmae, *Triad Power* (New York: The Free Press, 1985), p. 55ff.

6. "If they fall, so will our stock markets—Tokyo's soaring property prices," *New York Times,* October 11, 1987.

7. Source: *Yomiuri Shinbun,* September 3, 1998.

8. Kenichi Ohmae, "How Asia's Misery Made the U.S. Market." *The Australian Financial Review,* May 1, 1999.

9. Akio Morita and Shintaro Ishihara, *The Japan That Can Say No: The New US-Japan Relations Card* (Tokyo: Kobunsha Publishing Ltd, 1989).

10. Kenichi Ohmae, *The Borderless World* (New York: Harper-Collins,1990).

11. Janine R. Wedel, *Collision and Collusion: The Strange Case of Western Aid to Eastern Europe 1989–1998* (New York: St. Martin's, 1998); also, I suggest reading the author's article on the subject in *The Nation,* June 1, 1998.

12. See, for example, William Pfaff, "Scandal? No, Theft of a Nation." *Los Angeles Times,* September 4, 1999.

Chapter 7

1. Source: Report of the Industrial Bank of Japan, July 1998.

Chapter 8

1. Mahathir Mohamad, "Case Study for a Country Under Economic Stress," *Mainichi Shinbun*, August 2, 1999, p. 1.
2. William H. Gross, *Bill Gross on Investing* (New York: John Wiley & Sons, 1988).

INDEX

Afghanistan, 198, 225
AgeCare, 7
Age of Heretics, The (Kleiner), 86
AirTouch, 113, 132
Akabo (Red Cap), 56
Allen, Paul, 90, 200
Altair computer, 90
Amazon.com, 7, 19, 20, 30, 43,
    46, 50, 51, 62–63, 71, 73,
    91, 93–94, 100, 104, 110,
    113, 116, 117
  as platform, 44–45
American Airlines, 47
American Bar Association, 79
American Express, 52, 53
American Medical Association, 79
"American paradox," 141
American Telephone and Tele-
    graph (AT&T), 43, 104,
    142–43, 144
America Online (AOL), 7, 20, 27,
    30, 42, 63, 83, 84, 90, 97,
    100, 102, 103, 104, 239
  Time Warner bought by, 19,
    63, 92, 104, 113, 239
Amoco, 113
AMP, 47

AM/PM, 55
Andersen Consulting, 102
Anderson, Mark, 104
Aperios operating system, 97
Apple, 99
  Macintosh, 32, 44, 50, 55,
    105
arbitrage, 21, 61–87, 235
  Asian financial crisis and, 161
  bureaucracy and, 73–75
  celebrity and, 76
  communications and, 68–69
  consumer power and, 82–84
  credit card purchase as,
    70–71
  defined, 64
  disposable income and, 80–81
  distribution and, 68–69
  of Japanese postal system, 68
  middleman and, 66–68
  national currencies and,
    70–71
  nature of, 63–65
  portal revolution and, 84–85
  price-setting and, 78–82
  productivity gains and, 87
  of professions, 75–78

region-states favored by,
130–31
tax laws and, 71, 73
time limits and, 69–70
trade and tariff restrictions
and, 72–73
traditional value chain and,
65–66
by Value America, 65–66
Argentina, 135, 136, 137, 138,
157, 196, 201
Asahi Shinbun, 81
asea, 137, 198, 200, 222
Ashford.com, 19, 110
Asian financial crisis of 1997,
9–10, 37, 137, 158–62,
164, 178, 184–85
Malaysia in, 174–76, 218–20
Asian Monetary Fund (AMF),
161
"Asian Tigers," 22
Association of Southeast Asian
Nations (ASEAN), 137,
160, 175, 196, 198
Atari, 22
Aucnet, 66
Australia, 5, 14, 29, 33, 130, 136,
205
Autobytel, 46, 50
pointcast marketing by,
109–10
Automated Network Exchange
(ANX), 47
Automobile Industry Action
Group (AIAG), 47–48
AutoVantage, 45–46

BAAN, 91
baht, Thai, 160, 161, 175, 222
Bali, 176–77
Baltimore Technologies, 120
Bankers Trust, 23

banking industry, 144, 147, 204
Japanese, 163–64
regulatory structure of,
190–91
Bank of America, 143
Bank One, 30
Barber, Benjamin, 123
Bargain America, 72
Barnes & Noble, 19, 44, 94, 117
Bartley, Robert, 146
Basic computer language, 90
BayNet, 66
"Bell System," 144
Bennis, Warren, 182
Bergsten, C. Fred, 36
Bezos, Jeff, 19, 20, 45, 53, 93
Blair, Tony, 158
Bluemountain.com, 110
Bodin, Jean, 122
Boesky, Ivan, 64
Bolivia, 196
borderless dimension, defined, 4–6
Borderless World, The (Ohmae), 2,
5
Bose, Amar G., 214
Bose Corporation, 214
Braddock, Richard, 53
Brazil, 17, 37, 40, 135, 137, 138,
156, 161, 179, 191, 196
Bridgestone, 113
British Broadcasting Corporation
(BBC), 147, 185
British Petroleum, 113
British Rail, 147
British Telecom, 147
Broadcast.com, 63
broadcast marketing, 108–11
brokers' funds, 6, 189
Brunei, 137
Buchanan, Patrick, 24
bureaucracy, 196
arbitrage and, 73–75

Japanese mismanagement and, 72–73, 126–27, 132, 135–36, 151–52, 164–65, 202–3, 246
Bush, George, 142, 224
Business Breakthrough, 77–78
business process redesign (BPR), 93

Cable News Network (CNN), 5, 21, 22, 51, 90, 103, 108, 112, 226
California Teachers' Retirement Funds, 9
Canada, 17, 22, 33, 35, 69, 124, 128, 137, 205
Carter, Jimmy, 142, 143
"cartographic illusion," 5
Case, Steve, 211, 239
celebrity, 76
Cendant Corporation, 45–46
Chambers, John, 90, 93, 95, 102, 104, 114, 211
Chile, 135, 196
China, People's Republic of, 16, 34, 122, 129, 130, 158, 160, 164, 188, 195, 198, 201, 208, 223, 226, 237
Japan's economy contrasted with, 82
new market experimentation by, 191–92
unstable economy of, 180–82
Chrysler, 23, 113
Circuit City, 99
Cisco Systems, 10, 21, 23, 27, 39, 63, 90, 93, 95, 103, 104, 108, 239
acquisitions by, 113–14
customer primacy and, 106
market capitalization of, 200–201

supply chain system of, 100–102
Citibank, Citicorp, 30, 93, 143
electronic wallet concept of, 42, 47, 116
Internet services of, 69–70
Reed hired by, 59–60
Civil Aeronautics Board, 143
Clinton, Bill, 51, 142, 158, 169, 170, 172, 192–93
Clinton administration, 15, 168–69, 197
COCOM, 226
Cold War, 176, 183–84, 188, 192, 199
see also new cold war
Colombia, 196
COMDEX, 168
Commerce Department, U.S., 45, 194
Committee of Three, 40–41, 169, 218, 219
common carriers, 43
Communist Party, Soviet, 157
ComputerLand, 100
computer-telephony integration (CTI), 56, 91, 112
Congress, U.S., 23, 144, 172
Conrail, 143–44
consumer, customer, 86, 112
arbitrage and power of, 82–84
contradictory behavior of, 224
corporate strategy and, 99–100, 105–6
inflation and, 85
platforms and decisions of, 31–32
pointcast marketing and, 108–11
portal revolution and, 84–85
retailing and, 99–100

corporate strategy, 89–118
  broadcast marketing and,
    108–11
  clarity of focus and, 103–5
  competition and, 97–99
  core competence and, 100–103
  customer primacy and, 105–6
  customer relationships and,
    99–100
  fast market and, 114–15
  need for, 202
  outsourcing and, 100–103
  pointcast marketing and,
    108–11
  retail, 99–100
  supply chain process and,
    100–103
  web-shaped organizations and,
    111–12, 114
  zero-based organization and,
    106–7
  see also Godzilla-style compa-
    nies
credit authorization terminal
  (CAT), 52
credit cards, 6, 10, 55, 65
  arbitrage and, 70–71
  measuring transactions using,
    10–11
  micropayment system for,
    51–53
  platforms and, 51–53
  taxation and, 71
  Visa and MasterCard as plat-
    forms for, 30
Cuba, 174, 226
customer relationship management (CRM), 91, 120
CyberCash, 11, 30, 42
cyber dimension, defined, 6
cyber-economy, internalized,
  153–54

"Cyberia," 3
Cyberjaya, 57
Cyber Law (Communications and
  Multimedia Act) of 1998,
  Malaysian, 57

Daimler-Benz, 23, 113
"data mining" technology, 110
Davos Conference, 222
D.C.M., 90
DDI, 69
Defense Department, U.S., 143
Della.com, 110
Dell Computers, 21, 23, 27, 83,
  90, 99, 100, 103, 108, 109,
  112, 120, 134
  FedEx and, 41–42, 58
Del Monte, 81
democracy, 223–26
  national sovereignty and, 223
  political process and, 224
  voting system and, 224–25
Deng Xiaoping, 192
deregulation, 202, 236
  charismatic leadership and,
    156–58
  diplomacy and, 155–56
  global economy and, 134–35
  internalized cyber-economy
    and, 153–54
  Japan's need for, 165–68
  mainstream economic values
    and, 154–55
  in New Zealand, 147–48, 157
  open marketplace and, 150–53
  in Reagan era, 141–45
  stable currency and, 149–50
  of telecommunications indus-
    try, 134–35, 142–47, 153,
    154
Deutsche Bank, 23
developing nations, 85

DHL, 56, 116
Diet, Japanese, 208, 225
digital subscriber line (DSL) technology, 20
digital video disk (DVD), 31, 32, 48–49
dimensions of invisible continent, defined, 3–7
direct mail (DM), 109
Disney, Walt, 20, 125, 134
Disney Corporation, 20, 125
DoCoMo, 55, 68, 98, 204
dollar, Hong Kong, 180–81
dollar, U.S., 3, 22, 23, 70, 137, 160, 163, 225, 237
   Chinese currency and, 180–81
   Committee of Three and, 40–41
   debt spiral and, 40
   euro and, 138, 222
   foreign hoarding of, 36
   "homecoming," 36
   new currencies in rivalry with, 195–98
   as platform, 30, 35–40, 149–50, 163, 171, 197
   tradeability of, 36–37
   volatility of, 35–36, 115
   yen and, 8, 11, 35–36, 151
dorea, 222
doro, 198, 200, 222
dot.com companies, 14–15, 63
Douglas, Roger, 147, 157
downsizing, 146
Drucker, Peter, 2, 182
Duskin corporation, 109
Duval, David, 80, 213

East Timor, 176, 223
Easy Permit, 74
eBay, 19, 27, 73, 84, 91

e-commerce, 5, 18, 42, 47, 59, 83–84, 108, 121
   English language and, 35
EDS, 224
education, 202, 227–33
Education Ministry, Japanese, 227
e-hub concept, 119–21, 129, 134, 185, 201, 202
   see also region-state
"electronic signature," 74
electronic wallets, 42, 47, 55, 83, 116
Els, Ernie, 213
End of the Nation-State, The (Ohmae), 2, 62, 122, 123, 128
English language, 32, 119, 163, 202
   on Internet, 33–34
   as universal language, 29–30
enterprise resource planning (ERP), 91
Ericsson, 49
Esperanto, 29
E*Trade, 27, 30, 50, 117, 168
eullar, 198
euro, 70, 120, 123, 137, 150, 155, 195–96, 197, 198, 225
   dollar and, 138, 222
Europe, 22, 23, 37, 49, 69, 120, 148, 169, 170, 195, 221, 233
   as "United States of Europe," 196
   U.S. currency rivalry with, 195–98
   see also specific countries
European Common Market, 137
European Community Commission, 155
European Union, 119, 121, 128, 136–37, 201, 225, 226

Excel, 105
Excite@Home, 110
ex-com, 198

Falun Gong cult, 16
Family Lawyer, 77
Federal Communications Commission, 142
Federal Reserve, 36
FedEx, 24, 30, 32, 51, 66, 83, 102, 116
    Dell and, 41–42, 58
Final Fantasy, 230
Finance Ministry, Japanese, 163
Financial Institutions Recovery Act, Japanese, 164
Financial Services Center of Dublin, 120
Finland, 108, 121, 129, 131, 154, 183, 195
Firestone, 113
First USA Credicard, 30
Ford, 95
401K investors, 39, 147, 169–70, 171, 172, 173, 215, 232
    new cold war and, 193–94
France, 23, 34, 122, 124, 127
free trade, 4–5, 72–73, 83, 193, 201, 219, 224
Friedman, Thomas, 123
Fuji Film, 204
Fujitsu, 102, 131

Gandhi, Mohandas, 176
Garreau, Joel, 124
Gates, Bill, 44, 59, 90, 104, 107, 117, 127, 211, 214, 215
Gateway, 23, 83, 99, 100, 103, 106, 108, 120, 134
    2000 computer, 21, 90, 111–12
    UPS and, 41–42, 111–12

General Electric, 47, 92, 93, 100, 115, 145, 204, 211
General Electric Capital Corporation (GECC), 204
General Motors, 95, 145, 146
GeoCities, 19–20
Gephardt, Richard, 24, 83, 84
German Industrial Code (DIN), 151
Germany, West, 7, 23, 35, 82, 122, 127, 128, 131, 151, 167, 183, 226
Gerstner, Louis, 93, 95, 211
Ghana, 138
Global Crossing, 63, 113
globalization, 22–23, 123, 131, 194
    "sprinkler" model of, 112
Godzilla-style companies, 89–118
    acquisitions through relationships of, 113–14
    age of CEOs of, 92–93
    borderless dimension and, 92
    cyber dimension and, 91
    fundamental features of, 103–17
    greenfield values and, 106–7
    headquarters location and, 103, 107–8, 112
    making transition to, 117
    and mergers across boundaries, 113–14
    people involved in, 118
    profitless notoriety of, 90–91
    retailing and, 93–94
    rule of law and, 107
    traditional corporations and, 92–96
    use of multiples by, 91–92
    and vulnerability to value destruction, 116–17
    see also corporate strategy

Gone With the Wind (film), 81
Gorbachev, Mikhail, 23, 157, 184, 185
Gould, Jay, 94–95
government, 215–22
    speculators and, 216–18
Gramm, Phil, 23, 146
Gramm-Rudman Act of 1985 (U.S.), 146, 165–66, 169
Great Britain, *see* United Kingdom
Great Depression, 6, 189
greenfield values, 106–7
Greenspan, Alan, 15, 39, 40, 169, 170, 172, 208
Gross, Bill, 220
Group of Five, 23
G–7, 40, 41, 136
Guandong International Trust and Investment Corp. (GITIC), 192
Guatemala, 226

Haiti, 193, 226
Hamel, Gary, 96
hedge funds, 12, 161, 189, 219, 220, 237
Heinz, 81
Heisenberg, Werner, 61
Hewlett-Packard, 92, 105
Hikari Tsushin, 25
Hill, James J., 94–95
Honda, 14
Hong Kong, 14, 68, 121, 130, 136, 138, 162
Hong Kong Bank, 196
Horowitz, Edward D., 47
Hussein, Saddam, 193, 195

Iacocca, Lee, 5
IBM, 51, 66, 82, 90, 92, 93, 99, 120
    downsizing by, 95

Ibrahim, Anwar, 57, 174
Iceland, 124
IDO, 69
i-mode, 55, 68
income, disposable, 80–81
India, 33, 35, 82, 108, 121, 129–30, 131, 154, 176, 182, 195, 201, 225, 237
Indonesia, 13, 137, 156, 158, 162, 164, 179, 183, 223
    governance structure of, 176–77
Industrial Development Agency, Irish, 121
Industrial Revolution, 34, 107
Industry Net, 67–68
Industry Week, 22
inflation, 84–85
information technology, productivity from, 87
InfoSys, 130
In Search of Excellence (Waterman and Peters), 22
Institute for International Economics, 36
Intel, 100, 120, 134
International Accounting Standard (IAS), 191
International Monetary Fund (IMF), 40, 135, 149, 169, 177, 178, 215
International Settlement Bank (BIS), 190
International Telecommunications Union, 31
Internet, 5, 6, 20, 29, 30, 32, 47, 49, 55, 65, 77, 90, 94, 95, 98, 102, 112, 131, 143, 198, 202, 206, 215, 227, 237, 239
    cross-border information flow and, 16–17

Internet (*cont*)
English language and, 33–34
IRS filing via, 105
Japanese-language material on, 33
online purchases on, 18, 45, 84, 153–54
PlayStation access to, 97
pointcast marketing and, 110
Smart Valley project and, 56–57
and taxes on purchases, 72–73
telephone calls via, 69
time limits and, 69–70
see also e-commerce
Intuit, 105, 106
invisible continent:
as communal property, 201
cross-border transactions and, 10–12
as cyber-colony of U.S., 26
dimensions of, 4–7
and disparity of scale and speed, 86–87
education and, 227–31
emergence of, 1–3
entry into, 17–20
evolution of democracy and, 223–26
flexibility of, 20
flow of wealth and, 61–63
governing of, 215–22
illusion of Eldorado and, 235
influence of, 11
interdependence and, 233–34
movement of information and, 16–17
national readiness for, 237–38
1985 turning point of, 21–24
as revolution, 231–33
speculators and, 216–21
strategic approach to, 15–21

traditional companies and, 26–27
and world of one currency, 221–22
Iran, 193, 226
Iraq, 174, 193, 216, 226
Ireland, 33, 108, 111, 123, 124, 128, 129, 133, 136, 137, 153, 154, 183, 195, 201, 202, 226
as e-hub, 119–21, 134, 185
Irish Development Agency (IDA), 119
Ishihara, Shintaro, 171
Israel, 159, 195
Italy, 17, 155, 165
Ito-Yokado, 55, 204
IT2000 project, 74

Jackson, Michael, 80
Japan, 2, 5, 7, 12–15, 20, 22, 23, 37, 49, 52–53, 59, 85, 89, 98, 122, 131, 134, 138, 148, 150, 192, 193–94, 225, 226, 237
anti-Americanism in, 171–72
arbitrage of postal system of, 68
Aucnet system in, 66
bureaucratic mismanagement in, 72–73, 126–27, 132, 135–36, 151–52, 164–65, 202–3, 206
China's economy contrasted with, 82
as closed market, 181–83
consumerism in, 13–14
corporate welfare in, 164–65
depreciation concept and, 206
deregulation in, 165–68
education system of, 227–28
GNP of, 158–59, 165

information flow and, 16–17
Internet and language of, 33
investment bubble in, 162–65,
  167, 189, 203, 239
Kobe earthquake of 1995 in,
  205
Meiji Restoration in, 34, 108,
  156
national debt of, 165, 167
1990s financial crisis in,
  12–13
1992 recession in, 132
"Nintendo kids" generation
  of, 228
nuclear weapons and, 209
overseas tourism and, 13–14
planned unemployment and,
  166–67
private savings in, 167,
  243–44
proposed reform plan for,
  203–4
public works in, 104–5, 206
real estate and housing in,
  205–6, 208
7-Eleven chain in, 55–56
shamanism of, 207–9
"Shonen Jump" generation of,
  227–28
tax system of, 206
U.S. as block to economic
  recovery of, 168–73
U.S. military bases in, 208–9
U.S. trade imbalance with, 40
voter turnout in, 227
yen-dollar relationship and,
  35–36
Japanese Diet, 208, 225
Japanese Industrial Standard (JIS),
  151
Japan That Can Say No, The
  (Morita and Ishihara), 171

Japan-U.S. Security Treaty, 225,
  227
Java, 44, 50, 99, 104, 105
Jihad vs. McWorld (Barber), 123
Jini, 44
Jordan, Michael, 76, 80, 213
Justice Department, U.S., 97, 98,
  144
JVC, 31
J. Walter Thompson, 66

Kahn, Herman, 2, 182
KDD, 69
Keyence, 103
Keynes, John Maynard, 62
Khadafi, Muammar al-, 193
Kim Dae Jung, 177–78
Kim Yong Sam, 161
Kleiner, Art, 86
Knight, Phil, 76, 213
Kobe earthquake of 1995, 205
Korea, People's Democratic
  Republic of (North), 17,
  174, 193, 208, 226
Korea, Republic of (South), 13,
  17, 34, 40, 90, 158, 159,
  161, 162, 164
  chaebols of, 160, 178, 218
  developing country mindset of,
  177–79
Kyocera, 69, 204

Labor Party, New Zealand, 157
Latin America, 34, 37, 135, 137,
  163, 164, 170, 175, 218
  see also specific countries
Lawson, 55–56
Lee Kuan Yew, 32, 157, 161
leverage, 6, 18, 48, 78, 201, 213
Lexus and the Olive Tree, The
  (Friedman), 123
Libya, 193, 226

Li Ka Ching, 132
Linux, 44, 99
Longe, David, 147, 156, 157, 158
Long-Term Capital Management
    (LTCM), 6–7, 189–90, 217
"Look East" programs, 174
Lotus 1–2–3, 105
Lucent Technologies, 92

Maastricht Treaty, 196, 225
McKinsey, 2, 213, 230
McLuhan, Marshall, 2
McNealy, Scott, 104, 211
Magaziner, Ira, 120
Mahathir Mohamad, 57, 157,
    174, 219
Mainichi Shinbun, 219
Malaysia, 108, 137, 138, 158,
    161, 162, 179, 192, 217,
    225, 237
  in Asian crisis of 1997,
    174–76, 218–20
  Multimedia Super Corridor
    (MSC) of, 57, 74, 121, 129
  Penang Island of, 129, 131,
    133
Malone, John, 50
Malone, Karl, 80
Mannesmann, 132
Marshall Plan, 39
Maslow, Abraham, 81
MasterCard, 32, 50, 53
  as platform, 30
Matsushita, Konosuke, 107
Matsushita Electric Industrial, 31,
    107
MCI, 239
Meiji Restoration, 34, 108, 156
Menem, Carlos, 201
Mercado Comun del Sur (MER-
    COSUR), 137, 196, 198,
    201

mergers, 113–14
Merrill Lynch, 94, 117
Mexico, 124, 137, 161, 179
Michelin, 113
micropayments, 51–53
Microsoft, 25, 37, 46, 63, 127
  CE operating system of, 100
  Explorer, 105
  Godzilla style of, 90
  Intel and, 100
  of Japan, 117
  market capitalization of,
    200–201
  MSN, 104
  Office, 104
  Sony PlayStation as competi-
    tion for, 97
  U.S. antitrust suit against,
    43–44, 97, 107
  version 1.0 of, 21
  Windows, 24, 31–32, 43, 48,
    50, 55, 90, 214
Milosevic, Slobodan, 193, 195
"mindshare," 19, 51
Ministry of International Trade
    and Industry (MITI),
    Japanese, 72, 127,
    202–3
Mitsubishi, 22, 204
mobile phones, 49, 55, 98–99,
    224
Moody's, 13, 164, 221
Morningstar, 221
Mothers (Tokyo), 238
MSN, 83
multiples, 6–8, 11, 14, 86, 113,
    138, 221, 236–39
  described, 6–7
  Godzillas' use of, 91–92
  leveraged, 189–90
  uncertainty principle and,
    62

Murdoch, Rupert, 90
Myanmar, 34, 137, 226

narrowcast marketing, 108–10
NASDAQ, 7, 89, 130, 132, 170,
    189, 237, 238, 239
National Digital Park, 121
National Party, New Zealand, 158
National Science Foundation, 143
nation-state, 128, 136
    decline of, 122–23
    global investment and, 131–33
NEC, 102
Negroponte, Nicholas, 2
Nehru, Jawaharlal, 176
net present value (NPV), 4, 238
Netscape, 25, 44, 63, 97, 105
new cold war, 187–209
    financial risk in, 189–90
    401K investors and, 193–94
    impact of, 198–200
    invisible continent and, 24–26
    Keynesian economic decisions
        and, 191–92
    new currencies and, 195–98
    reform of Japanese system and,
        202–7
    regulating structure of, 190–91
    rules and laws in, 201
    smaller regions and, 195
    U.S. cash drain and, 192–93
    and U.S. propensity for ene-
        mies, 193
    vision of wealth in, 200–201
New Deal, 165
News Corporation, 90
Newsweek, 22, 82
New York Times, 44, 116, 163
New Zealand, 35, 120, 121, 129,
    134, 135, 153, 154, 159,
    195
    deregulation in, 147–48, 157

Next Level Communications, 49
NHK Symphony Orchestra, 81
Nicklaus, Jack, 52, 53
Nike, 76, 102–3, 213
*Nine Nations of North America,
    The* (Garreau), 124
1984 (Orwell), 198–99
Nintendo, 49, 51, 98, 204
"Nintendo kids," 228
Nissan, 113
Nixon, Richard M., 142
Nokia, 92, 98, 131
Noriega, Manuel, 193
Normann, Richard, 100
North American Free Trade
    Agreement (NAFTA), 129,
    136, 201
North Atlantic Treaty Organiza-
    tion (NATO), 155
NTT, 204

Official Development Assistance
    programs, 39
Omron, 52
O'Neill, Thomas P. "Tip," 123
online shopping, 18, 45, 153–54
OPEC, 132–33
Oracle, 21, 90, 91, 102, 103
Organization for Economic Coop-
    eration and Development
    (OECD), 41, 158, 169,
    177, 180
O'Rourke, Mary, 120
Orwell, George, 198–99
outsourcing, 100–103

Pacific Investment Management
    Company (PIMCO), 220
Pacific Telesis, 144
Pakistan, 156, 174, 225
Palestine Liberation Organization
    (PLO), 226

Panama, 193, 226
Panasonic, 99
Paraguay, 137, 196
Penang Island, 129, 131, 133
Perot, Ross, 24, 224
Perot Systems, 68, 224
Peru, 135, 196
peso, Mexican, 160
Peters, Tom, 22
Philippines, 137, 156
Phillips, 31
Pittman, Robert, 239
platforms, 26–60
    Amazon as, 44–45
    competition as element of,
        42–43
    consumer decisions and,
        31–32
    credibility and, 46
    credit card system and, 51–53
    customer loyalty and, 56
    defined, 30–31
    English language as, 29–30,
        32–33, 35, 40
    information technology and,
        58–60
    infrastructure and, 46–47
    micropayment system and,
        51–53
    and new avenues to commerce,
        44–48
    oligarchy status of, 48–51
    and openness to potential part-
        ners, 43–44
    potential, 51–55
    Priceline's success as, 53–54
    principles of, 41–57
    "sticky," 50–51
    telecommunications and,
        49–50
    U.S. as open trading field and,
        37–38

U.S. dollar as, 30, 35–40,
    149–50, 171, 197
U.S.-Japan trade and, 35–36
    as vehicle for community,
        55–57
    vulnerability of, 44
    "wearable," 55
    Windows as, 90
Playboy, 51
Plaza Accord of 1985, 23
pointcast marketing, 108–11
Porter, Michael, 66, 96
Postal Service, U.S., 43, 68, 143,
    147
Priceline.com, 19, 62–63, 66–67,
    84, 91, 100, 239
    success of, 53–54
price-setting, 78–82, 213–14
Princeton Bond, 190
privacy, 75
Procter & Gamble, 115
Prodi, Romano, 155
productivity, defined, 141
Professional Air Traffic Con-
    trollers Organization
    (PATCO), 143

Qualcomm, 49
Quantum Fund, 21, 90
Quicken, 77, 105, 231
Qwest, 7, 63, 98, 100, 108, 113,
    239

Ramirez, Rafael, 100
Reagan, Ronald, 23, 156–57,
    158
    deregulation under, 142–48
    economic legacy of, 141–42
réal, Brazilian, 40
Realtor.com, 46
Reed, John S., 59, 93, 211
"Reform of Heisei," 167

Regional Bell Operating Companies (RBOCs), 113
region-state, 123, 128–39
    arbitrage and, 130–31
    China as, 182
    deregulation and, 134–35
    domestic economy and, 138–39
    global speculation and, 137–38
    national currency and, 137–38
    national leadership and, 133–36
    rise of, 128–31
    role of government in, 136–39
    Russia as, 184
Renault, 113
retailing, 65–66
    customer relationships and, 99–100
    Godzilla-style companies and, 93–94
    platform leaders in, 99–100
    see also online shopping
Ricoh, 99
ringgit, Malaysian, 131, 174, 175, 219, 222
"robber barons," 94
Robertson, Julian, 7, 175, 216, 217
Romer, Paul, 8
Roosevelt, Franklin D., 165
RosettaNet, 47
Rubin, Robert, 15, 39, 40–41, 169, 208
ruble, Russian, 160, 183
Rudman, Warren, 23, 146
rupiah, Indonesian, 160
Russian Republic, 17, 25, 38, 40, 122, 124, 138, 161, 164, 170, 174, 192, 195, 198, 201, 208, 218, 223–24
    Keynesian economic decisions in, 191
    mafia-dominated economy of, 182–84

Sabre, 45, 47
Sachs, Jeffrey, 182–83
Sagawa, 56
sales force automation (SFA), 58, 91
SAP, 91
Saqqara Systems, 47
satellite systems, 49, 50
SBC, 49, 144
Scholastic books, 113
Schumacher, Michael, 76
Schwartz, Peter, 182
Sears, Roebuck, 19, 45, 81, 93–94, 104
secured networks, 71
Sega, 49, 98
"self-actualization," 81
Serbia, 174, 193, 226
7-Eleven, 55–56, 98
shared application platforms (ASPs), 58
Sherman Anti-Trust Act of 1890 (U.S.), 43
"Shonen Jump" generation, 227–28
ShoppingList, 19
short-selling, 190
Siberia, 183
Siebel, Tom, 91
Siebel Systems, 58, 91
Sim City, 230
Singapore, 14, 32–33, 69, 74, 108, 121, 136, 137, 154, 158, 159, 162, 179, 183, 195, 201, 202, 211
    as emerging region-state, 129
Slate, 51

Slater, Philip, 182
Smart Valley project, 56–57, 74
SoftBank, 14, 25, 131, 168
sol, 196, 198
Solectron, 101
Son, Masayoshi, 168
Sony, 14, 22, 25, 92, 99, 104,
    152–53, 204, 211, 214
  Betamax system of, 31
  competitors and, 97–98
  PlayStations, 13, 48–49, 51,
    55, 97, 215
Soros, George, 7, 21, 108, 175,
    216, 217, 218
Southland, 55, 98
South Sea Bubble, 239
Soviet Union, 16, 23, 156, 176,
    182, 185, 199, 203, 226
Spain, 130
Sprint, 239
Stanford, Leland, 94–95
Stanislaw, Joseph, 147
Starbuck's, 98
Starr, Kenneth, 51
steel industry, 147, 202–3
stock market crash:
  of 1929, 6, 189
  of 1987, 163
Strategic Arms Limitation Treaty
    (SALT), 221
Sudan, 198, 225
Suharto, 161
Sukarno, 176
Sumitomo, 204
Sumitomo-Dunlop-Goodyear,
    113
Summers, Lawrence, 15, 39, 40,
    169, 172
Sun Microsystems, 21, 90, 103,
    105
supply chain management (SCM),
    23–24, 91

supply chain process, 100–103
Sweden, 166, 177

Taiwan, 69, 121, 158, 160, 162,
    179, 182, 223
tariffs, 72–73
Tateishi, Kazuma, 52
Tax-Link, 105
TCI, 90
telecommunications industry, 227
  deregulation of, 134–35,
    142–47, 153, 154
  education and, 75–76
  platforms and, 49–50
Teligent, 49
Texaco, 115
Thailand, 13, 137, 158, 160, 162,
    164, 179, 192, 217–18, 225
Thatcher, Margaret, 23, 156, 157,
    158
  reforms by, 147, 148–49
Tiger Funds, 138, 175
Time, 22, 82
Time Warner, 103, 105
  AOL buyout of, 19, 63, 92,
    104, 113, 239
Titanic (film), 81
Tito (Josip Broz), 176
Toffler, Alvin, 2
Tokyo Mitsubishi Bank, 164
Tomlin, Lily, 142–43
Toshiba, 31, 48–49, 102
Toyota, 14, 69, 134, 204
Trading Process Network (TPN)
    Post, 47
Transportation Ministry, Japanese,
    124
Traveler's Advantage (TA), 45, 46,
    47
Travelocity, 47, 48
Treaty of Paris, 127–28
Treaty of Rome, 137

Triad Power (Ohmae), 2, 112
Trinidad-Tobago, 129
Tulip Bubble, 239
Turkey, 179
Turner, Ted, 211
Tyson, Mike, 80

Ukraine, 136
uncertainty principle, 61–63
Underwriters Laboratory, 151
unemployment, 39, 145–46,
    148–49, 154–55
  planned, 166–67
Uniroyal-Goodrich, 113
United Kingdom, 23, 29, 35, 122,
    123, 127, 154, 157, 177,
    179, 181, 185, 192, 217, 226
  Thatcher era reforms in, 147,
    148–49
United Nations, 40, 215, 223
United Parcel Service (UPS), 24,
    30, 32, 66, 68, 83, 102, 111
  Gateway and, 41–42, 111–12
United States, 5, 14, 16, 29, 85,
    122, 128, 131, 137, 138,
    139, 154, 176, 183, 185,
    188, 199, 200, 216, 224,
    235, 236
  as block to Japan's economic
    recovery, 168–73
  culture of creativity in, 39
  dollar's platform status and,
    30, 35–40, 149–50, 163,
    171, 197
  dollar-yen relationship and,
    35–36
  e-commerce and economy of,
    18
  education system of, 229
  "enemies" of, 193, 226
  English language advantage of,
    33, 35, 163

  401K investors in, 39, 147,
    169–70, 171, 172, 173,
    193–94, 215, 232
  federal deficit of, 22
  Industrial Revolution and, 107
  internalized cyber-economy of,
    153–54
  international cash drain and,
    192–93
  international resentment of,
    26, 39–40
  Japanese military bases of,
    208–9
  Japan's trade imbalance with,
    40
  Microsoft antitrust suit by,
    43–44, 97, 107
  national debt of, 192–93
  as open trading field, 37–38,
    150–51
  and paradox of low inflation
    and high employment, 141
  Reagan era deregulation in,
    141–45
  Savings and Loan crisis in, 144
  stock market boom in,
    170–71, 192
  surpluses of, 166, 192–93
  telephone system of, 68–69
  trade deficit of, 36, 38, 39–40,
    237
  voter turnout in, 228
  zebra economy of, 124–28
United States Trade Representative
  (USTR), 72, 194
Unix, 50, 90, 99, 103, 105
Uruguay, 137, 196
US West, 7, 49, 98, 113, 239

Value America, 19, 51, 73
  arbitrage by, 65–66
value chain, 65–66, 83, 104, 106

value group (*keiretsu*), 100
value of goods, value of stock vs., 62–63
Vanderbilt, Cornelius, 94–95
Venezuela, 196
very high speed digital subscriber line (VDSL), 49
VHS, 31
Vienna Philharmonic, 81
Vietnam, 137
virtual private network (VPT), 47
virtual single company (VSC), 41, 100
Visa, 10, 32, 50, 53
  as platform, 30
visible dimension, defined, 4
"Vision 2020," 174
Vodaphone, 113, 132
voice-over-IP, 32
voice pattern recognition, 74
V2000, 31

Walker, Jay, 53
Wall Street Journal, 146
Wal-Mart, 19, 45, 81, 93–94, 99
Waterman, Bob, 22
wealth, defined, 204
web-shaped organizations, 66, 111–12, 114
Wedding411, 110
Welch, Jack, 93, 95, 233
wide-band CDMA technology, 32

wideband code division multiple access (WCDMA), 49
Wintel operating system, 30
wireless local loops (WLL), 49, 98
won, Korean, 218
Woods, Tiger, 76, 80, 213
work, value of, 212–14
World Bank, 135, 149
WorldCom, 63, 239
World Trade Organization (WTO), 4–5, 16, 41, 205, 206, 237
Wriston, Walter, 59

X-Box, 49

Yahoo, 19–20, 42, 63, 83, 84, 104, 116, 168
  narrowcast marketing by, 110–11
Yamato, 56, 83
Yeltsin, Boris, 183
yen, Japanese, 8, 11, 70, 160, 166, 196, 197, 222
  dollar and, 8, 11, 35–36, 151
  volatile movement of, 115
Yergin, Daniel, 147
yuan, Chinese, 149–50, 180
Yugoslavia, 176, 216

Zamenhof, Ludovik, 29
zero-based organization, 106–7
Ziff-Davis, 168